The Collected Works
of Herman Dooyeweerd

Series B, Volume 16

GENERAL EDITOR: D.F.M. Strauss

The Crisis in Humanist Political Theory

As Seen from a Calvinist Cosmology and Epistemology

Series B, Volume 16

Herman Dooyeweerd

PAIDEIA
PRESS

Library of Congress Cataloging-in-Publication Data
Dooyeweerd, H. (Herman), 1894-1977.
The Crisis in Humanist Political Theory
Herman Dooyeweerd.
p. cm.
Includes bibliographical references and index

ISBN 978-0-88815-331-9

This is Series B in the continuing series
The Collected Works of Herman Dooyeweerd

Edited by D. F. M. Strauss and Harry van Dyke

The Collected Works comprise the following series:
Series A contains multi-volume works by Dooyeweerd,
Series B contains smaller works and collections of essays,
Series C contains reflections on Dooyeweerd's philosophy
designated as: *Dooyeweerd's Living Legacy,* and
Series D contains thematic selections from Series A and B

A CIP catalog record for this book is available from the British Library.

Copyright 2010 © Reprinted 2023
The Dooyeweerd Centre for Christian Philosophy
Redeemer University College, Ancaster, ON, CANADA L9K 1J4

Publisher
PAIDEIA PRESS
Jordan Station, ON. L0R 1S0
www.paideiapress.ca

Editor's Foreword

IN A CONVERSATION Dooyeweerd once made the remark that of all the works he had written this book of 1931 on the *Crisis in the Humanistic Theory of the State* posed the greatest challenge for the reader. It was intended to give a provisional account of his new systematic philosophical insights and he explicitly refers to his forthcoming extensive work *De Wijsbegeerte der Wetsidee* (*The Philosophy of the Law-Idea*). The latter, three-volume work appeared in 1935-36. A comparison between *Crisis* and the 1935-36 *magnum opus* highlights the fact that Dooyeweerd's thought displays an inherent dynamics – both in a terminological sense and in terms of his ripening systematic views. There are therefore a number of considerations to be kept in mind when studying this work:

1) It is the first work in which Dooyeweerd explains the main contours of his new philosophy of time.
2) Throughout this work Dooyeweerd consistently employs the term *function* – but he never speaks about (*modal*) *aspects* or *modalities*. (Yet, for example, in his *Inaugural Address* of 1926[1] he does speak about the jural modality ('rechtsmodaliteit' – p. 69).
3) Initially, in the series of articles on episodes "in the struggle for a Christian politics"[2] as well as in his *Inaugural Address*, Dooyeweerd still frequently used the term 'organic' in order to bring to expression the *coherence* within the cosmic diversity. During the late twenties the general "linguistic turn" – as it later became known – was recognized by Dooyeweerd in his growing preference for the term 'zin' = 'meaning'. *Zin* obtained a qualifying posi-

---

1 *The Significance of the Cosmonomic Idea for the Science of Law and Legal Philosophy. Inaugural Lecture*, Free University, Amsterdam October 15, 1926. [To be published in an English translation in Series B of the *Collected Works of Herman Dooyeweerd*.]

2 H. Dooyeweerd, "In den strijd om een Christelijke Staatkunde. Proeve van een fundeering der Calvinistische levens- en wereldbeschouwing in hare wetsidee," published in the first two years of the monthly journal *Antirevolutionaire Staatkunde* (1924-1926) and concluded in the quarterly by the same name, *Antirevolutionaire Staatkunde* (1927). Eng. transl., *The Struggle for a Christian Politics: An Essay in Grounding the Calvinistic Worldview in Its Law-Idea* (2008).

tion in respect of numerous systematic terms – although the phrase "organic coherence" did not disappear altogether.[1]

4) The almost exceptional emphasis on the "law-idea," found in his earlier writings, entails the distinction between *law* and *subject*. This distinction was employed by both Dooyeweerd and Vollenhoven but it caused an ambiguity, for in connection with what is *subjected* to the law they discerned both *subject*-subject relations and *subject*-object relations – causing the term "subject" to suffer from ambiguity (Vollenhoven side-stepped this ambiguity by using different accents in Dutch).[2] From a systematic perspective the most general approach is to differentiate between *law-side* or *norm-side* and *factual* side – where the latter then comprises *factual* subject-subject and *factual* subject-object relations.

5) Intimately connected to the problem of law-side and factual side is the problem of *universality* and *individuality* – underlying the classical opposition between *realism* and *nominalism*. Although Dooyeweerd is well aware of the fact that the realist tradition accepted a threefold existence for the *universalia*,[3] he overlooks the fact that the difference between the Platonian and Aristotelian views implicitly reflects the distinction between (God's law as) *order for* and the *orderliness of* whatever is subjected to God's law. As a consequence he uses the terms *wet* (law) and *wetmatigheid*

---

[1] The following composite phrases occur in *Crisis*: meaning-analogies; meaning-analysis; meaning-boundaries; meaning-character; meaning-clarity; meaning-coherence; meaning-criterion; meaning-elements; meaning-functions; meaning-individual; meaning-individuality; meaning-substrates; meaning-synthesis; meaning-functional; meaning-individual; meaning many-sidedness; meaning-side; meaning-structure; meaning-systatic. When these phrases are "turned around," for example when the expression *"zin-functioneele"* concept of law" is not translated as the "meaning-functional concept of law" but as "the functional meaning of law," the original intention is lost. Consequently we had to maintain these qualified phrases for the sake of Dooyeweerd's systematic preference, namely to use the term 'meaning' in a *qualifying* way.

[2] Compare D. H. Th. Vollenhoven, 1968:1-2: "Problemen van de tijd in onze kring" [Problems about time in our circles], a presentation to the Amsterdam Chapter, chaired by Dooyeweerd, of the Association for Reformational Philosophy; text based on a tape-recording by J. Kraay, checked and corrected in a few instances by Vollenhoven, who also added a six-point summary. When the factual side is at issue Vollenhoven speaks about "subjèct-zijn" and when it concerns subject-subject and subject-object relations he writes 'subject' as 'súbject'.

[3] Namely *ante rem* as ideas (universal forms) in God's mind (*mente Divina* – the legacy of Plato), *in re* as the universal substantial forms inherent in creaturely entities (the legacy of Aristotle), and *post rem* as subjective concepts within the human mind. Nominalism rejected universalia *ante rem* and *in re*.

(law-conformity) interchangeably. *Conforming* to a *law* is a (*universal*) feature on the *factual side* of reality. (Vollenhoven, by contrast, did acknowledge universality on the factual side of reality.) Dooyeweerd considers the factual side to be strictly *individual*. For that reason in *Crisis* he frequently speaks about "the individual structure of things" and also about what he calls "meaning-individual." In his *magnum opus* he settled for the expression "individualiteitsstructuur" which appears in the English version (*A New Critique of Theoretical Thought*)[1] as "individuality-structure." His primary intention with the phrase "individuality-structure" is to refer to God's *law for* concretely existing entities. A further terminological complication arises from the word 'structure' – which can either mean "law for" or "lawfulness of." The standard practice in the English language is to speak of structures with reference to entities that are *structured* by God's law. Since entities (in their *structuredness*) are not themselves laws, they merely, in their law-conformity, display their *structuredness* (*subjectedness*) to laws.[2] Later on, when Dooyeweerd developed his theory of enkaptic interlacements in more detail, he intended to account for the intertwinement of creaturely subjects, but his terminology, given his denial of the universality on the factual side of reality, creates the misleading impression that his theory is concerned with an interlacement of 'laws' – an interlacement of "individuality-structures."[3]

The above-mentioned points are raised for the sake of providing the broader context and background of this work. They should not, however, detract from the penetrating insights and criticism developed by Dooyeweerd in respect of the foundational problems of the disciplines of sociology, law and political science. His seminal ideas about the nature of the state as a public legal institution delimited by its jural function extend far beyond the modest size of this book. Above all it demonstrates, albeit in a provisional and fallible way, the shortcomings prevalent within modern humanistic theories of the state as well as the direc-

---

1 H. Dooyeweerd, *A New Critique of Theoretical Thought*, 4 vols. (Lewiston, NY: Edwin Mellen Press, 1997). *Collected Works of Herman Dooyeweerd*, Series A, Vols. I-IV.

2 *This* atom (individual side) is *an* atom (universal side). Phrased differently: in its atom-ness every (unique) atom displays in a universal way that it is subjected to (i.e., that it conforms to) the universal order for its existence.

3 Magnus Verbrugge, son-in-law of Dooyeweerd (who made a substantial contribution to the translation of some of Dooyeweerd's works), has been greatly concerned about this ambiguity.

tion in which a Christian theory of the state ought to be articulated – a task to which he made a considerable contribution both in the third volume of his *New Critique* and in his multi-volume *Encyclopedia of the Science of Law*.

In view of the pivotal nature of this work in the Dooyeweerd corpus, we have included more than the usual number of explanatory notes as well as an extensive Index of Subjects in the interest of clarifying the dynamic development of the author's thought since his earlier works.

D. F. M. Strauss, General Editor October 2010
University of the Free State
Bloemfontein, South Africa

Harry Van Dyke, Co-Editor
Director, *Dooyeweerd Centre for Christian Philosophy*
Redeemer University College
Ancaster, Ontario, Canada

Author's Preface

THIS BOOK AROSE out of my rectorial oration on the same topic. Naturally it does not offer a worked-out theory of the state, since its only aim is to put forward the *foundations* of a modern Calvinist view of the state. The preliminary philosophical work required for this purpose is so extensive that it is impossible in this study to commence as well with detailed work in the domain of a general political theory.

For the time being this book may serve the purpose of making public for the first time a more systematic account of the fundamentals of the theory of knowledge and the view of reality that I have worked out at length in my forthcoming work *De Wijsbegeerte der Wetsidee* [The Philosophy of the Cosmonomic Idea]. It is my intention to use these fundamentals as the philosophical basis for my lectures in legal philosophy and the encyclopedia of the science of law. My point of departure for a view of the limits of state sovereignty which I set forth in the closing section of this work is consciously taken from the theory of Johannes Althusius. I invite comments and objections in respect of this theory and will carefully consider them. Regarding my conception of the limits of government interference in industrial life, this invitation applies particularly to the basic ideas that I have explained at the annual meeting held in Groningen of the Association for Christian Employers.

H. Dooyeweerd   Amsterdam, 20 Oct. 1931

Contents

Editor's Foreword v
Author's Preface ix

Part I

The crisis in humanist political theory and modern attempts to resolve it

Introduction. 1
1. Origin and nature of the crisis in humanist political theory 3
2. The humanist view of reality and epistemology behind the crisis of humanist political theory 13
3. Nominalistic individualism and the elimination of meaning-individual structural differences of temporal reality as a result of this view of reality and its epistemology. Its manifestation in modern humanist political theory 19
4. The crisis of the humanist personality ideal beneath the crisis of humanist political theory 30
5. The modern reaction to the crisis in humanist political theory. Attempts to reconstruct it on the basis of a dialectical phenomenology. The Berlin School and the Integration Theory. The new humanist view of reality and epistemology in this theory. . 38

Part II

A Calvinist view of the state versus the crisis in humanist political theory

1. The meaning-structure of cosmic reality in light of the Christian idea of law and subject 71
2. The meaning-individual thing-structure of organized human communities. The refutation of the reasoning of dialectical phenomenology. A critical examination of the theory of organized communities as advanced by Gierke and Preuss 96
3. The relation between political theory, the discipline of consti- . . . 118
tutional law and sociology in the light of our Calvinist cosmology. Political theory as a cosmological theory of the structure of the state. The cosmological principle of sphere-sovereignty as applied to the question of juridical competence. Rejection of pluralist (syndicalist) theories

Appendix A – F 163

Works Cited 181
Index of Names 191
Index of Subjects 195

Part I

The crisis in humanist political theory and modern attempts to resolve it

Introduction

Modern political theory has been in a state of crisis for a considerable length of time. This is a situation that merits attention far beyond the narrow circle of its practitioners who are watching it with grave concern. The crisis can best be described as one of "a theory of the state without a state," or, following Nelson,[1] one may also speak of a "science of law without law." These two descriptions, however, are not quite identical, even though it is readily admitted that they are closely related. The positive science of law can still, with a semblance of justice, maintain that an inquiry into the meaning of law falls outside the scope of its expertise, and it can go on to blame the philosophy of law for the emasculation of the concept of law. But general political theory no longer has a guarantor to whom the creditors can present the bill it failed to pay.

The most disturbing symptom of the crisis in modern political science is that scholars in general no longer see the essential difference between a science of law without law and a political theory without a state. The concept of the state has been completely incorporated into the meaning-functional (*zin-functioneele*) concept of law.

The philosophical theory of the law-spheres which I have developed holds that, in the final analysis, the demarcation of the special sciences does not rest on the technical demands for a rational division of labor. Nor is it founded on the various categories of thought as subjective, albeit necessary, methods for the ordering of the content of our consciousness. Rather, this demarcation rests on the meaning-structure (*zinstructuur*) of the law-spheres, each of which is sovereign in its own sphere

---

[1] Leonard Nelson, *Die Rechtswissenschaft ohne Recht. Kritische Betrachtungen über die Grundlagen des Staats- und Volkerrechts, insbesondere über die Lehre von der Souveränität* (Leipzig, 1917).

and with each of which the logical law-sphere, by divine ordinance, is inseparably intertwined within the cosmic order of time.

Law is indeed enclosed within a meaningful law-sphere and this guarantees that the science of law is possible as a distinct discipline or "*special* science" (*vakwetenschap*). But that also makes it impossible to see anything more in its scientific concepts than abstractions from the fullness of temporal reality. The meaning of law is only *functional* in nature. It is a meaning-side (*zin-zijde*), sovereign in its own sphere, of full temporal reality. And this reality only finds its religious fullness of meaning beyond time.

Temporal reality is never given to us within the structure of a single law-sphere, but only in the individual structure of things which have their meaning-functions equally in all the law-spheres. Within such a structure these meaning-functions are uniquely intertwined into a unity. This means that when a special science (be it the science of law, sociology or history) annexes the general theory of the state to itself, it amounts necessarily to denying the reality of the state and, with that, admitting the bankruptcy of political theory. For states are not subjective thought constructions. They are here, existing as real, individual organized communities *prior to* any theory, and their structure demands scientific elucidation. Any constitutional theory which claims it can ignore what is given in naive experience and which proclaims the state to be a fiction, a personification of the legal system, transgresses its boundaries as surely as would the discipline of physics were it to have us believe that nature consists of nothing but electron waves.

The crisis of political theory is merely a symptom of the underlying crisis in the humanist worldview and as such is of general philosophical significance. For this reason I believe I may be allowed to demand special attention for this phenomenon.

First of all I propose to analyze more closely the nature of the crisis and to examine the causes that have given rise to it. In doing this we shall especially shed light on the view of reality and epistemology that operate behind this crisis. Next, consulting some of the recent important literature, we shall examine a variety of attempts to restore both general political theory and the science of constitutional law on the basis of humanist philosophy. Only after we have demonstrated that the fundamental fallacy of these attempts stem from the crisis in humanism's view of science and its personality ideal, will we attempt to answer the question whether Calvinist philosophy can point a way out of the current crisis, and if so, how we are to tackle the problem of the nature, meaning, and structure of the state in a scientific fashion.

1 Origin and nature of the crisis in humanist political theory

The crisis in general political theory first announced itself in a more acute form in the narrow field of constitutional law. This occurred when Carl Friedrich von Gerber and Paul Laband introduced a so-called *purely juridical method* in this particular branch of the science of law.

From the very beginning Otto Friedrich von Gierke, the great antipode of the school of Gerber and Laband, recognized that a consistent implementation of this method could not but lead to a sweeping purge in all concepts of constitutional law from their specific connection with the structural meaning of the state, and that this would have to lead to the collapse of the discipline of constitutional law itself. In a masterful treatise,[1] which is a model of scientific discourse, Gierke brought to light both the merits and the flaws of this new method.

Its merits: it takes seriously the truth that constitutional law is indeed law and therefore must be treated according to a juridical method; and also that it must be sharply distinguished from the common and nebulous confusion that used to mingle juridical, economic, political, and ethical views of the state.

Its basic flaws, and the dangers it poses: it implicitly attempts to view constitutional law "purely logically," outside of the great meaning-coherence (*zinsamenhang*) of its connection with life, thus leading to an emasculation of the meaning of *constitutional law* as well as of *law as such*.

In addition, Gierke saw that the seeming lack of bias of this formalistic positivism conceals a specific philosophical and political bias. Time and again Laband's individualistic view of the state reveals that it was based on an individualistic metaphysics. This is evident in his conception of the legal subjectivity of the state as an *universitas* in accordance with his conception of coordinational law.[2] It is evident when he referred to the private-law figure of a *negotiorum gestio* and applied it to

---

1 Otto von Gierke, "Labands Staatsrecht und die deutsche Rechtswissenschaft," *Schmoller's Jahrbuch für Gesetzgebung, Verwaltung und Volkswirtschaft* 7 (1883): 1097–1196.
2 *General Editor's note*: The expression coordinational relationships intends to reflect what is meant by the Dutch term 'maatschap'. This term 'maatschap' does not have a suitable English equivalent. The intended kind of relationship does not have a permanent authority structure, nor does it possess a solidary unitary character. It concerns social interaction normally related to phenomena of friendship, partnership, fellowship, mate, pal, peer, and the freedom we have to associate with an accountable freedom of choice. For the lack of a better alternative, we want to apply the proposed designation coordinational with the intention to include those connotations shared by the phenomena referred to in the previous sentence – which are all instances of coordinational relationships.

the position of the emperor within the German empire; it is evident as well when he degraded the concept of state organs by construing them as private-law representatives, when he argued that administrative laws lack all juridical quality, and so on and so forth.[1] By reifying the individual this metaphysics has to deny communities any reality.

This so-called "conceptual jurisprudence" was no more than a logicistic mask for a very primitive *a priori* view of reality. Typical of Laband's view was the idea that the general concepts of private law could be introduced into public law simply by "purging" them of their specific features. But did Laband then already possess insight into the typical meaning-individual[2] difference in structure between internal constitutional law and civil private law? The only thing he said about the structural difference was that the state alone could issue coercive orders. And since he also acknowledged a structure of authority in the family community, the entire structural difference between state and non-state communities dissolved for him into the right of each to execute it as a right reserved for the state.[3]

Owing to his positivism, Laband utterly failed to analyze the concept of rule or dominion. As a result he ultimately reduced the entire constitutional relation between a state and its subjects to a system of absolutistic power relations between individuals. It made for a system that was ameliorated only by a series of (strictly speaking inconsistent) concessions to traditional constitutional doctrine.[4]

Behind this concept of the state lurked a naturalistic, individualistic view of reality which gave its content – "dominion" (*Herrschaft*) – that undeniably absolutistic quality. This absolutistic trait is also evident in Laband's denial on principle of the juridical significance of "fundamental rights." The real meaning of these rights is often completely misunderstood and can only be established by first giving an account of the meaning-individual structural difference between, on the one hand, co-ordinational law and the law of organized communities, and on the

---

1 See Paul Laband, *Das Staatsrecht des deutschen Reiches*, 4th ed. (Tübingen, 1901), 2:9: "For no legal relationship between the governing state and another legal subjectivity juxtaposed to it has thus been arranged."
2 *General Editor's note*: What Dooyeweerd here calls "meaning-individual" (*zin-individueel*) eventually – in particular in *A New Critique of Theoretical Thought*, vol. 3 – was designated by the word "typical."
3 See also in this connection Hugo Preuss, *Gemeinde, Staat, Reich als Gebietskörperschaften. Versuch einer deutschen Staatskonstruktion auf Grundlage der Genossenschaftstheorie* (Berlin, 1889), p. 186.
4 Gierke, "Labands Staatsrecht," p. 1131. A fortunate inconsistency on this point is also present in that Laband's theory of the sources of law maintained, next to positive law, *autonomy* and *customary law* as independent sources of law, without, however, being able to provide a proper systematic connection between these sources.

other, constitutional law and the law of non-state organized communities.

On the Calvinist view of the state, the question of fundamental or basic rights, insofar as these are freedoms, simply means that the general cosmological principle of sphere-sovereignty needs to be applied to the structural differences of the jural law-sphere, a task that will require finding an objective meaning-criterion for the juridical competence of the state vis-à-vis those organized communities and coordinational relationships that are distinct from the state. I shall return to this point in my positive exposition in Part II below, where I deal with the vigorously disputed concept of constitutional sovereignty.

It is an established fact, meanwhile, that whoever denies the essentially juridical significance of fundamental rights, regardless of whether or not they are incorporated in written constitutions, is irretrievably driven to the consequence that the state possesses an unlimited formal juridical competence. This view is at the very core of the foundation which Bodin prescribed for any constitutional system. It is an absolutistic concept of sovereignty, which even Gierke, in spite of his anti-absolutistic tendencies, has not really overcome.[1]

This concept of sovereignty, which by implication does not allow for any inviolable juridical sphere vis-à-vis the state, as we shall demonstrate later, cannot possibly find a foundation in positive law, for it is no more than a political bias based on an essentially individualistic metaphysics. Laband's purely juridical method essentially amounts to abandoning any attempt at understanding the meaning-structure of the state. Taken in his sense, the state shrivels down to a juridical fiction. Beyond individuals as organisms nothing is left. Nation and territory are nothing but substrates of the state, taken to be mere objects of the sovereignty of the state.

Nearly fifty years ago Gierke pointed prophetically at yet another fundamental danger of Gerber's and Laband's so-called strictly juridical method: the undermining of the meaning of law as it comes to light in their very concept of constitutional law, and with that, the destruction of everything that the state with its authority could maintain when confronting the onrushing forces of revolution. Positivistic juridical formal-

---

[1] Gierke explicitly acknowledges the "formal omnipotence" of the state legislator; ibid., p. 1189. Ludwig Waldecker, *Allgemeine Staatslehre* (Berlin, 1927), p. 277, writes without any reservation: "The law of the state, or to be more precise: the law mediating accountability to the state [!], 'breaches' the law of the organized communities in the state if there is to be a state at all." Yet in a footnote he nonetheless calls the power-state conception of Laband a prime example of an alleged theory of constitutional law which in truth is a political doctrine. We shall return to the lack of meaning-analysis of organized communities in the thought of Waldecker himself.

ism found its only complement in a positivistic legal materialism that was increasingly gaining ground. With its overrating of mathematical logic it merely continued the traditions of humanism's rationalistic natural law. In comparison with this natural law, however, it was most definitely at a disadvantage. It no longer believed in an indissoluble natural order, in unbreakable principles of right and morality. Law was debased to a logical, technical form, of which any materialistic interest and physical force could avail itself.

Gierke issued grave warnings against this logicistic "juridical technique without law" when he wrote:

> By sacrificing the ideal content of law, the formalistic science of law weakens its capacity to resist the onslaught of political and ecclesiastic, social and economic forces and interests. Law is never, and least of all in today's public life which is stirred from deep below and fraught with conflicts, relieved of the necessity to uphold and unfold itself every day anew. In the long run only the ideal content gives law the inner strength it requires in order to prevail. Ultimately the "horse and its rider" will not secure it. Nor will its artful technical apparatus guarantee for it the power to rule forever.[1]

Gierke was entirely vindicated by subsequent developments in constitutional science. Laband presented the purely juridical method in the still naive form of "conceptual jurisprudence" based on concepts of Roman private law. For the most part he still kept it within bounds by means of a brilliant juridical intuition as well as political discretion. But since that time, the influential "norm-logical" school of Kelsen has dressed it up in the armor of Marburg transcendental logic and with true fanaticism has eradicated from constitutional science whatever remnants Laband had left intact of a connection with the meaning-structure of the state. The axiom of "methodological purity" has become the shibboleth between the "old and the new theory of the state." With radical consistency the state, first halfheartedly tolerated as "bearer of the legal order," has finally come to be equated with a logically functional system of juridical norms. By means of a rationalistic principle of delegation this juridical system is constructed out of a so-called primal norm as a free hypothesis of scientific thought. All meaningful differences of structure within the juridical sphere are wiped out and the meaning of law, along with the state, is thrown overboard. The state is now identical with Kelsen's rationalist system. Or, as Fritz Sander in his earlier Kelsenian period believed he could characterize the state, it is identical

---

1 Gierke, "Laband's Staatsrecht," p. 1195.

with the Kantian "substance category of judicial procedure." This final, radical step in eliminating the concept of the state at the same time exposed the crisis in general political theory.

A general theory of the state, detached from politics in its broad Aristotelian sense, had only come in for theoretical development since Bluntschli.[1] Remarkably, Bluntschli equated general political theory in this narrower sense with "general constitutional law." And in the first chapter of his *Allgemeines Staatsrecht*, where he introduced his sharp distinction between general constitutional law (in its narrower sense) and politics, we are astonished to read:

> The science of constitutional law looks at the state in its regulated condition, in its proper order. It presents the organization of the state and the enduring conditions of its life, the rules of its existence, the necessity of its relationships. *The state, as it exists, is its constitutional law.*[2]

By contrast, Bluntschli delimited politics as the science which examines the state as it exists and develops, and which investigates the ends and means that "its public action pursues."

We ask in amazement whether the identification of political theory and the discipline of constitutional law was already a fact in Bluntschli. The riddle is solved when we realize that what Bluntschli took "general constitutional law" to mean was indeed a jumble of history, sociology, a baffling naturalistic-organological metaphysics, and the science of law. Nowhere did this become clearer than when Bluntschli ventured to give a definition of the state. He first combined the "historical characteristics" into a general concept of the state and then defined the state as follows:

> ... a collection of people bound together as government and governed on a specific territory into an ethical-organic personality.

This definition already showed little resemblance to a juridical definition of the state if we apply the modern methodological demands for forming a juridical concept. But Bluntschli had not yet finished with his definition. He asked:

> Is the concept of the state as indicated by historical study of various states capable of satisfying the human spirit?

---

1 See Georg Jellinek, *Allgemeine Staatslehre*, 3rd ed. (Berlin, 1919), pp. 61 ff., and Richard Schmidt, *Allgemeine Staatslehre*, vol. 1, *Die gemeinsamen Grundlagen des politischen Lebens* (Leipzig, 1901), pp. 29–30, n. 2, who also refers to the mixture of theoretical and practical politics in the thought of Bluntschli.
2 Johann Kaspar Bluntschli, *Allgemeines Staatsrecht*, 3rd ed. (Munich, 1863), 1:1–2.

His answer was no. The philosophical mind cannot be satisfied with an answer from history. And so he arrived at what he called a "high concept of the state that has never yet been realized":

> The state is organized mankind, but mankind in its male appearance, not in the female form. The state is the man.[1]

This astounding result does indeed sharply point out the level of the general science of constitutional law and of general political theory at the time of the first independent appearance of the latter. Should it surprise us that in this chaotic situation the introduction of a so-called purely juridical method was hailed by many constitutional lawyers as a liberating event?

Scientifically speaking, general political theory was indeed in an extremely precarious position. All kinds of special disciplines attempted to define the essence and structure of the state by means of a peculiar metaphysical striving for absolutizing their particular functional viewpoint. In this respect sociology, in the universalistic synthetic form launched by Auguste Comte, carried the greatest pretensions. By applying the positivist method of natural science its program was to offer a scientific synthesis of the various sides of human society. Was it not the obvious heir to the field of general political theory after the collapse of the metaphysical theories of the state which transcend natural experience? Would sociology not be competent to provide a many-sided causal explanation of the essence and structure of the state *as it is*?

However, against this pretension of natural-scientific sociology, the science of constitutional law, in the interest of self-preservation, once more had to register a sharp protest. The normative meaning of constitutional law cannot be explained with the aid of the natural-scientific method. Norms and natural laws cannot be reduced to one another. If then the juridical meaning-side in the structure of the state cannot be grasped in the pretended synthesis of natural-scientific sociology, how would this sociology be able to grasp the essence of the state in a many-sided synthesis?

Ultimately the basic problem of any general political theory worthy of the name would have to be formulated as follows: *How is a many-sided synthesis of the universal meaning-functions of the state possible in a scientific way?* Given that the metaphysics of the state was increasingly discredited, that sociology as a universal synthetic science of society laid claim to the field of political theory abandoned by philosophy, and given that the science of constitutional law in the spirit of Gerber and Laband increasingly severed any connection with politics

---

[1] Ibid., 1:50.

and sociology, general political theory, insofar as it refused to resolve itself into a natural-scientific sociology, automatically ended up in a dualistic position. On the one hand, ever since the introduction in constitutional law of the so-called purely juridical method, political theory could no longer brandish the misleading flag of a syncretistic general political science, as Bluntschli had done. On the other hand, it could no longer ignore the real contrast with the complex of problems that sociology and modern political science had chosen as their object of study. Consequently, the only way out for political theory seemed to be to operate with a dual concept of the state, the one oriented to a natural-scientific sociology, and the other oriented to a science of juridical norms.

It was especially the methodological and epistemological insights as revived under the auspices of Kant that forced this partition of political theory. Jellinek in his *Allgemeine Staatslehre* brought this about by means of an introduction to methodology that gave currency to the *two-sides theory* of the state. Let us see how this partition was accomplished. Jellinek writes:

> Political science must investigate all sides of the state. It has two principal areas, which correspond with the two viewpoints from which it can be studied. The state is first a communal product, then a juridical institution. Accordingly, political science divides into two doctrines: social political theory, and the science of constitutional law.[1]

Jellinek calls it a gross error to equate political theory with the science of constitutional law, an error that historically harks back to natural law which searched for the jural ground of the state. This natural-law view often confused a state's jural ground with its historical origin, with the result that a state was viewed exclusively as a juridical institution. The science of constitutional law acknowledged politics as a separate science only in the sense of a practical theory of statecraft. Political literature from Machiavelli to Montesquieu, says Jellinek, contained many theoretical investigations which today are counted as belonging to the domain of a sociological theory of the state.

According to Jellinek, the separation of the sociological and juridical view of the state is based upon the different methods operative in these two areas: the first as causal and the other as normative. Political theory therefore, as a many-sided theory of the state, must vigorously reject any one-sided monopoly claimed by either subdivision. Rather, it must demonstrate the internal coherence of the two.

However, as Jellinek sets forth the methodology used by the sociological theory of the state, he forcefully rejects, on the basis of the unique historical character of states, the claims of a natural-causal sociology aimed at the discovery of general natural laws for political life. As the

---

1 Jellinek, *Allgemeine Staatslehre*, pp. 10–11.

proper method for the sociological theory of the state Jellinek designates the drawing up of empirical descriptions of genotypes and existing types in order to provide the interpretation (and thus causal explanation) of political phenomena, a method buttressed with a more precise epistemological foundation by Max Weber, who perfected it.[1]

Anyone can see that the Achilles' heel of this dualistic political theory was located in the way it conceived of the mutual relation and coherence of its two components. For the state to remain an undivided object for scientific investigation, the dualism between a social and a juridical concept could not remain definitive. Epistemology would have to demonstrate the possibility of an ultimate synthesis of the two components. Should general political theory remain wanting on this point, it would self-destruct. Meanwhile, if the mere possibility of a sociological concept that does not make reference to the juridical concept were ever admitted, that itself would result in a hopeless disruption of unity in the concept of the state. Nor could it be repaired again after the fact by conversely letting the juridical concept make reference to the sociological one. It is one or the other. Either the juridical side is essential to the state as an organized community, and in that case a purely sociological concept in the sense of Jellinek is not a concept of the state. Or else the juridical side is not essential, and then the two-sides theory collapses.

Jellinek's entire chapter on the essence of the state proves that he did not even notice this. It again draws a contrast between the two methods used in general political science. This time they are differentiated in an objective and a subjective method. The objective method views the reality of the state as a physical reality, but it can only give an extremely inadequate and scientifically useless picture of it: social phenomena are said to be determined by psychic actions which can only be interpreted by our inner experience, and the physical aspect of political reality depends on this human psychic activity. Only the subjective method of viewing penetrates to the essence of the state by defining the state not just as a physical but as a predominantly psychic reality.

The subjective method can in turn adopt two sharply distinguished approaches. The first approach examines the state as a social phenomenon and focuses on the real subjective and objective processes that make up the concrete life of states. This way of viewing the state is usually designated as the historico-political approach. By means of this approach we get to know the essence and functioning of the state according to its physical and psychical aspects. This investigation is assigned to a combination of disciplines.

The second approach focuses on the juridical aspect of the state. At this juncture we hear from Jellinek that law leads a double life. On the

---

[1] See esp. Weber's treatises "Über einige Kategorien der verstehenden Soziologie" (1913), and "Methodische Grundlagen der Soziologie" (1920), in *Gesammelte Aufsätze zur Wissenschaftslehre* (Tübingen, 1922), pp. 403–50 and 503–23.

one hand it carries out a "factual practice of law," in which capacity it is supposed to be one of the social forces that shape the concrete cultural life of a nation. In this sense the jural belongs to reality and is of course the object of the sociology of law. Conversely, law is a body of norms, destined to be converted into actions. In this particular sense the jural does not belong to the area of what *is* but to the area of what *ought to be*; it is the specific object of a normative juridical method of investigation.

Notice that these distinctions imply not only a dual theory for the state but also a dual approach to law.

Next, Jellinek addresses the task (which has already become impossible because of his entire approach) of determining the essence of the state in a purely sociological fashion. Here he proves to be an adherent of the view of the state as an integrated organized community. Yet he immediately turns on Gierke's realistic theory of organized communities with the weapon of epistemology. To be sure, he grants that as a social reality the state must be seen as an entity. But the concept of an organized community by which we grasp the real, empirical societal state is no more than a subjective, albeit a necessary, category of our thinking by which we combine the empirical phenomena into a synthetic unity. In this sense the unity of the state is a teleologically organized unity. A multitude of human beings is united to our consciousness when they are united for constant, internally coherent aims. The state is a *Zweckverband*, a "purposeful community." And so, after a closer examination of the elements of the reality that is the state, our author arrives at his sociological definition: "The state is an organized communal unit, equipped with original power to rule its inhabitants."[1]

Jellinek expressly declares that our consciousness necessarily "imputes" to the organized communal unit the actions of the organs that exercise the ruling will. The teleological unity of the organized community stands or falls with this imputation concept. Jellinek does not explain how this imputation is feasible when the normative-juridical aspect of the state is eliminated. It is altogether impossible on the basis of purely psychological rules of interpretation or by a methodology of causal explanation. This means, however, that the sociological concept of the state collapses.

Meanwhile it becomes clear that Jellinek wishes to let the communal unity of the state be a mere thought category, a "necessary form of synthesis for our consciousness."[2] To him, the reality of the state is exhausted in its a-normative functions. The state is merely a function of human society, a multitude of objective and subjective natural processes

---

1 Jellinek, *Allgemeine Staatslehre*, pp. 180 f.
2 Ibid., p. 170. Jellinek betrays his orientation to the psychologistic, criticistic position of Christoph Sigwart when he writes that the intended synthesis is just as subjectively psychical as colors, tones, and so on! Ibid., p. 161.

which are combined by our synthetic thought into a unity but which are in no way systatically[1] given as a unity:

> It therefore is definitely not a substance, but exclusively a function. The substance underlying this function are and remain the human beings.[2]

It is extremely important to pay close attention to this view of Jellinek's. The unity of his sociological concept of the state, its unity as a governing community, is for him merely a psychic function of consciousness:

> This function, however, is exclusively of a psychical nature, and even when it calls forth physical activities these are always mediated in a psychic way. In this fashion the state function takes its place among the phenomena of mass psychology.

In this connection Jellinek expressly places the function of the state on a par with a meaning-function (*zinfunctie*) such as language, which he similarly describes as a "mediated psychic function" accomplished by means of vocal and written symbols.[3]

But the most critical point of Jellinek's general political theory is the transition [from the sociological] to the juridical concept of the state. He knows no other way to make this transition acceptable than by the apodictic declaration that juridical knowledge has to link up with the sociological concept of the state. In its juridical aspect the state can only be understood as a juridical subject, more precisely as "a legal entity" (*Körperschaft*), which presumably is a purely juridical concept. Accordingly, he defines the juridical concept of the state as "the legal entity of a settled nation equipped with original ruling power" or as "a territorial entity endowed with original ruling power."

It is clear that on Jellinek's own standpoint this concept cannot but conceal an inner contradiction. He is weaving together two entirely different concepts of the state while he has started out by warning against a methodological mixing of the two.

It has to be one or the other. Either the juridical concept itself is the full concept of the state, which Jellinek categorically denies. Or it encompasses only the normative side of the full-blown state, but then, on his own epistemological standpoint, a juridical concept cannot possibly accommodate such natural sociological concepts as "original ruling power."

---

1 *General Editor's note*: The term *systatic* stems from Dooyeweerd's epistemology, where it is used to refer to the integral coherence of what is given in our non-theoretical experience; cf. *A New Critique*, 3:36 n: "The reader is reminded that this obsolete word is meant to indicate the factual immediacy of our integral experience of reality."
2 Jellinek, *Allgemeine Staatslehre*, p. 174.
3 Ibid., pp. 176–77.

Kelsen therefore dealt this school of political science a mortal blow when he remarked, from a criticistic standpoint, that the two-sides theory must of necessity collapse under the epistemological insight that unity in the "object" can only be determined when there is identity of epistemic orientation.[1]

Indeed, for when Jellinek would have us believe that juridical concepts are nothing but synthetic thought forms by which we grasp natural reality, he overlooks the fact that according to the Kantian conception of experience and reality (to which he fully subscribes) it is impossible to apply normative concepts as forms of knowledge to natural experience.[2]

It should be evident by now how a specifically humanist view of reality and epistemology plays an important role in the crisis of humanist political theory. Apparent in the background of the humanist view of reality and knowledge are the tensions and internal contradictions between the two basic factors in the humanist worldview, namely the Faustian science ideal, and the apostate personality ideal which rejects divine sovereignty. Before we investigate the crisis of humanist political theory in its further development and the attempts to overcome it, we shall first try to shed more light on this background.

2. The humanist view of reality and epistemology behind the crisis of humanist political theory

The pursuit of a "purely juridical" method in constitutional law did not come to an end until Kelsen came on the scene with his doctrine of the state. Behind Kelsen's doctrine, as well as behind the naturalistic concept of the state held by universalist, positivist sociology and Jellinek's dualistic view of the state, there lies concealed a view of reality and epistemology that is peculiarly related to the structure of certain types of the humanist ideas regarding law[3] and subject.

This view of reality goes back in history to attempts at taking reality as it is organically given in the cosmic order of time and tearing it apart into a temporal *phenomenon* and a *noumenon* that is elevated beyond time and is therefore in this sense a transcendent *noumenon*.

In all its countless variations, humanist philosophy is in the first place *immanence philosophy*. That is to say, it chooses the absolute, Archimedean point from which it wishes to understand our reality as a unity and

---

[1] Kelsen, *Allgemeine Staatslehre*, p. 7.
[2] This also topples Jellinek's thesis that "juridical knowledge has to link up with the results of knowledge of the state as a real phenomenon." *Allgemeine Staatslehre*, p. 170.
[3] *General Editor's note*: "law" is here meant in its encompassing ontic sense and not in its *jural* meaning.

coherence *within time itself,* namely in the law-side and subject-side of reality.

The humanist worldview began its triumphal march at the time of the Renaissance by proclaiming the sovereignty of reason over the belief in revelation. This signified a relapse into paganism insofar as it began to look for what is beyond time within time itself.

Human reason is nothing but a complex of spiritual meaning-functions, which are interwoven with all other meaning-functions of cosmic reality in time. When one or more of these meaning-functions, for example, the logical or the moral, are absolutized, that is to say, are declared to subsist "in and of themselves," independent and sovereign, then these functions can themselves no longer be seen as temporal. They must then transcend time. With this, the problem of reality and the problem of time together become the crux of all immanence philosophy.

Already in ancient Greek philosophy the absolutization of reason (*nous*) was of necessity accompanied by a tearing apart of full temporal reality into a timeless *noumenon*, which was said to constitute the true being of temporal reality, and a merely subjective temporal *phenomenon*, based upon the psychic nature of sensory appearances.

The *noumenon*, as the absolute, true reality, was taken to be a substantial thing, according to the definition of Descartes: "*quae nulla re indiget ad existendum.*"[1] Thus, in Plato's objective idealism the ideas, the rational concepts, the *noumena*, are reified into supra-temporal substances. The noumena are assigned to the rational functions of our consciousness; the phenomena on the other hand are correlated to the sensory-psychic function, which cannot discover true reality.

In the humanist view of reality and epistemology this concept of substance acquires an entirely new meaning of its own. This time, the proclamation of the sovereignty of reason issues from the modern humanist ideal of the personality, which in a Faustian desire for power wishes to subject all of reality to itself. After the birth of modern mathematical natural science, this personality ideal was initially concentrated entirely within the typical humanist science ideal, which acknowledged as true reality only that which mathematical, natural-scientific thought had produced on its own in a seemingly free construction. In this fashion the concept of substance became the primary metaphysical basis of this science ideal. Thus Descartes grasped the function of matter in mathematical fashion, essentially reducing it to static space and reifying it as *res extensiva*, a timeless substance behind the temporal sensory functions of

---

1 *General Editor's note*: Descartes writes in his *Principles of Philosophy* 1.51: "By substance we can conceive nothing other than a thing that exists in such a way as to stand in need of nothing beyond itself in order to exist."

nature. Similarly, Hobbes reified as timeless substance the mathematically comprehended kinematic function: *the body in motion*.

The choice of meaning-functions of temporal reality that this new humanist metaphysics was to elevate to *noumenon*, to substance, depended primarily on the scope it wished to assign to its science ideal. Since I have already explained this point repeatedly in another context,[1] it will suffice here to note the basic antinomy between the science and personality ideals, which consists in this, that when consistently elaborated they must cancel each other out.

Intrinsic to both ideals is the peculiar *postulate of continuity* which seeks to apply the sovereignty of reason alike to the boundless self-sufficiency of the personality and to mathematical thought whose power ignores all boundaries between the meaning-functions. As a result, the continuity postulate cannot but reduce all the meaning-functions of temporal reality to a single cosmological basic denominator, so that nothing in that reality should escape the sovereignty of reason.

As a substance, this basic denominator is nothing but a meaning-synthetic abstraction which our deepened antithetic [opposing] thinking lifts out of the fullness of reality. According to the science ideal, a substance can be nothing but what mathematical thought can grasp of the functions of nature. When, as with Hobbes, this science ideal dominates, only one basic denominator, one mathematical substance of nature, is assumed, which is then posited as the basis of all of temporal reality, including spiritual meaning-functions.

The personality ideal, by contrast, arose as the idea of self-sufficiency, of sovereign freedom for the human personality. When in order to confirm its sovereignty the personality ideal called forth the science ideal, it was doomed to perish under the natural necessity of all reality as demonstrated by this very science ideal.

In order to avoid exposing the rational function to dissolution by the science ideal, the personality ideal initially had no alternative but to adopt a second substance next to the first. This second substance (in fact the substance of the personality ideal) could, in the period preceding Kant, only be found in thought itself. And so Descartes presented his *res cogitans* as a spiritual substance next to the *res extensiva* as the natural substance and separated the two basic denominators by an un-

---

1 *General Editor's note*: Cf. H. Dooyeweerd, "In den Strijd om een Christelijke Staatkunde, XV," *Antirevolutionaire Staatkunde* (quarterly) 1 (1927): 159–61; Eng. trans. *The Struggle for a Christian Politics*, pp. 249–51; Dooyeweerd explained the point further in *De Wijsbegeerte der Wetsidee*, 1:323–52; cf. *A New Critique of Theoretical Thought*, 1:357–88.

bridgeable chasm. Hence "to view nature as if no spirit exists, and spirit as if there is no nature" became the self-contradictory task.

A poignant antinomy indeed! For as an abstraction from full temporal reality, nature as a substance existed only by the grace of synthetic thought. The Cartesian and Leibniz-Wolffian metaphysical schools labored without success at resolving this antinomy.

In the meantime the razor-sharp intellect of David Hume unraveled the concept of substance epistemologically. Following John Locke, he chose the synthetically conceived psychical function as the basic denominator for empirical reality and demonstrated that a natural substance independent of our consciousness, assuming it exists, in any case transcends our ability to know it.

In keeping with association psychology (which, by the way, is no less grounded in the science ideal) the concept of substance as the embodiment of all reification was rent asunder into a copy of a bundle of psychic impressions. In accordance with the laws of association psychology Hume explained the whole concept of substance in terms of a synthesis that may be psychologically necessary yet for all that is an untenable illusion insofar as it refers to the things-in-themselves. *Ideas*, after all, are mere copies of original *impressions*; the criterion of truth is to be found simply in the correct connection of the ideas with the corresponding impressions. Now the impression on which the idea of substance rests is that of a constant connection between sensory impressions, of a constant uniformity therefore in the impressing activity itself. And whenever one fails to relate the idea of substance to this constant connection between impressions and relates it instead to some metaphysical identity of the contents of these impressions, the idea becomes false.

By means of a psychologistically distorted science ideal, Hume's psychologistic critique of knowledge undermined the metaphysical foundations not only of the science ideal but also of the personality ideal. For Hume's critique also struck the Cartesian concept of substance in the personality ideal, that is, the absolute reality of the *res cogitans*. In the light of Hume's critique of knowledge the "I" is merely a collective term for a series of impressions that are constantly being ordered according to the laws of association.

It is obvious that this entire critique rested on a simple transfer of immanence philosophy's Archimedean point from physical thought to psychological thought. In point of fact, Hume was no less guilty of reification than the rationalists he attacked; only, in his case it was the psychical function of temporal reality that was reified. All thinking that posits things "in themselves," all reification, regardless of whether one dresses it up as the concept of a thing or as the concept of a function, is based on [inter-functional] synthetic thought. It is a meaning-synthesis on the one hand of the deepened analytical (logical) thought-function and on the other of the a-logical functions of reality abstracted from full reality.[1] With that, the reification of the psychic function collapses, since it only exists by the grace of the logical function. In Hume's so-called empiricism, the whole of empirical reality turns into phenomena in the sense of the reified objective-psychic meaning-function of temporal reality.

We know that Kant, impressed by Hume's critique of knowledge which ended up in skepticism, tried to emancipate the personality ideal from the science ideal. By a "Copernican revolution" he reduced empirical reality (as reality of nature) to a *phenomenon* possessing merely transcendental objectivity. Kant forcefully maintained the science ideal against Hume but limited it to psychic sensibility and detached it from the metaphysical concept of substance. The *noumenon* was transferred wholesale to the supra-sensory realm of normative ideas of reason, a realm in which the personality ideal revealed its deepest tendencies by proclaiming the absolute sovereignty of moral freedom.

As soon as the personality ideal began to emancipate itself from the science ideal and, as with Kant, claimed primacy, it could no longer recognize a substance peculiar to nature. For such a natural substance would contradict the continuity postulate of freedom. Eventually it would have to ground nature itself in the rational idea of the free personality, and in turn liberate this personality in its reified function from the materialization into a substance (to which Kant still clung) by conceiving it as absolute *subjective actuality*. The post-Kantian ethical idealism of Fichte in his first period had already drawn this consequence from Kant's moralistic personality ideal. Kant himself halted at the analytical separation of the two realms of the *phenomenal* reality of nature and the normative freedom that is *noumenal* and therefore only realized by an *a priori* rational faith. Not even his *Critique of Judgment* really succeeded in bridging the divide.

Kant's entire view of reality and critique of knowledge was grounded in a typically dualistic cosmonomic idea [law-idea] which allowed the antagonistic continuity postulates of the science ideal and the personality ideal to balance each other out. Ideally, though, primacy was assigned to the personality ideal. Criticistic epistemology shared this functionalist position with all its humanist predecessors.

The historical direction indicated by the mathematical rationalism of natural science and by psychologistic empiricism allowed our cognitive ability to resolve into two functions of consciousness: the psychic and

---

[1] More about this in Part II, § 1 below.

the logical. Behind this functionalist duality lay hidden the dogmatic prejudice of immanence philosophy's metaphysics: the rending asunder of full temporal reality into a *noumenon* and a *phenomenon*. The *noumenon* was assigned to the analytical function of thought, the *phenomenon* to the psychic function of observation or representation.

This dogmatic position also governed Kant's epistemology. His Copernican deed, however, consisted of [a] withdrawing the *noumenon* from the reach of mathematical thought and limiting the latter to psychic phenomena; [b] distinguishing an *a priori* element of form which makes all experience possible, thus guaranteeing its transcendental objectivity but limiting it to the sensory-psychic matter of all knowledge; and [c] maintaining the transcendental idealist view that no experience is possible except as a constitutive, synthetic connecting of the forms of our knowing consciousness (that is, the transcendental logical categories and the psychic forms of intuition of space and time) with what is solely given in the *Gegenstand*, the matter of sensations. In this fashion our experience of nature, and with that of empirical reality, becomes, in a transcendental idealist sense, a synthesis of our logical-psychical functions of consciousness. The *noumenon* is declared to be transcendent to this reality, and the concept of substance found in nature metaphysics is degraded to a functional category of relation, which can only be applied to temporal sensibility.

The transfer of primacy to the personality ideal is also evident in the repudiation of the Cartesian *res cogitans* as a substance of the knowing person. In light of Kant's critique of knowledge it is replaced with the functionalist transcendental "unity of apperception," which in relating all synthetic epistemic activity to the transcendental form of the "I" is supposed to lie at the base of every synthesis involved in the acquisition of knowledge.

Even pre-theoretic, naive experience is construed according to this epistemological, and in fact *dogmatic*, bias. Whatever in our experience of things transcends the still un-ordered sensory impressions rests on a synthetic formation through our cognitive apparatus. In this manner, the naive concept of a thing, which is often mistakenly confused with the metaphysical concept of substance, dissolves into a concept of function. To our knowing consciousness the normative, supra-sensory and supra-temporal realm of *noumenal* ideas, to which Kant also assigned law and the normative idea of the state, remained separated from empirical reality by an unbridgeable chasm. On this standpoint, a synthesis between *noumenal* and *phenomenal* reality was fundamentally excluded.

One senses immediately that this entire view of reality and of the possibility of knowledge, once it was introduced into political science, could not but create an impasse from which no escape was possible. Right from the start, the decision to restrict all knowledge to the *phenomenal* experience of nature, to dissolve the concept of a thing into a concept of function, and to posit a strict dualism between a so-called empirical reality of nature and a supra-sensory world of norms could not but render impossible any consistent theoretical concept of the state in its many-sided meaning-structure.

In deviation from what Kant taught and for the sake of extending the boundaries of the mathematical science ideal, the Neokantian doctrine of law and the state applied the criticistic form-matter scheme as epistemic scheme to the world of norms by conceiving law as a thought category. Yet even then, the total disparity of norms and natural laws had to be maintained if a relapse into the naturalism of the pre-Kantian empiricism was be to avoided, since the latter would once again completely dissolve the personality ideal. What resulted was fundamentally a trilemma: the naturalistic-monistic view of the state of natural-scientific sociology, the dualistic political theory of the two-sides theory, and the logicistic-monistic theory of pure norm-logic (*reine-Normlogik*).

Given that pure norm-logic cogently demonstrated the impossibility of understanding the state apart from its connection to law, and given that the two-sides theory could not demonstrate the possibility of achieving a meaning-synthesis of the "social" and the "juridical" sides of the state, the Kelsen school scored a formal victory across the board, even though every political theorist had to realize at the same time that Kelsen's methodological triumph spelled the death of political theory. Only the dialectical method of post-Kantian idealism and modern phenomenology could open new possibilities for political science. But to these potential escape routes for humanist political science I shall return later.

3. Nominalistic individualism and the elimination of meaning-individual structural differences of temporal reality as a result of this view of reality and its epistemology. Its manifestation in modern humanist political theory

Up to this point we have outlined the humanist view of reality and knowledge. As we have seen, it is one of the most important factors behind the crisis of modern political science. But our outline will remain incomplete unless we point out an important consequence for its view of individuality.

Theoretically, individuality is the central problem of temporal reality. As given in pre-theoretical experience, individuality is the ultimate refutation of all rationalism. It is the proof that it is simply not possible to dissolve the subject-side of our temporal cosmos into its law-side and at the same time to detach the subject-side from the law-side. Temporal reality, as we shall see later, reveals that this individuality is inseparably connected with the structure of things. And in the Christian view it finds its supra-temporal, transcendent foundation in the religious root of our cosmos.

On the functionalist viewpoint of immanence philosophy, the problem of individuality becomes a hopeless crux.

Rationalism has really only a law-idea, but no subject-idea. Hence it must try to eliminate individuality as a relative being, as a *mè on*, which is done by assigning it a place in the phenomenal world. Conversely, irrationalism really possesses only a subject-idea and no law-idea. Hence it must absolutize individuality into that which is lawless, and debase the law to a phenomenon of a rigidifying conceptual construction (compare in modern times Henri Bergson and Oswald Spengler).

Given their functionalist attitude, both rationalism and irrationalism cannot but thoroughly falsify the problem of individuality. This attitude had already surfaced in the idealist philosophy of Antiquity, with its quest for the *principium individuationis*, which it began to look for in certain meaning-functions of reality.

During the famous controversy about the *universalia* in the Middle Ages, Christian realism revealed its infection by pagan philosophy when it simply took over this manner of posing the question from immanence philosophy and somehow or other reconciled it with a view of individuality that differed at bottom and in essence from the Christian view.

Thomas Aquinas, following Aristotle, looked for the principle of individuation in the *materia quantitate signata*. By this means he managed to salvage individual immortality and the individuality of angels, but only at the price of acute antinomies. Medieval nominalism, it is true, rejected the search for a *principium individuationis*, since it called everything essentially individual and argued against the reality of general concepts. Yet its empiricist epistemology demonstrated the functionalist attitude even more sharply, if that were possible, by limiting reality to its pre-logical functions and categorically denying that spiritual functions partake in the structure of temporal reality. And so its view of individuality remained in the final analysis merely *individual*-istic, a view that is as far removed from comprehending the meaning of individuality as is the view of individuality in realism.

In its science ideal, which makes a clean sweep of the Aristotelian concept of entelechy, humanism's orientation is thoroughly nominalistic and individualistic. By reifying specific natural or spiritual functions it can no longer do justice to naive experience of individual things. No sooner had the science ideal come on the scene, than the aesthetically colored and qualitative individualism of the Early Renaissance was forced to make room for a quantitative, mathematical individualism. In this way a type of mathematical functionalism interfered with any genuine sense of individuality.

From Hobbes to Leibniz this tendency can be demonstrated with increasing clarity. In the nominalist monadological metaphysics of Leibniz all qualitative individual differences in the monads are ultimately quantified by the *lex continui* of his rationalistic law-idea into degrees of greater or lesser clarity in the representational processes within the monads. Once the mathematical principle of infinity in Nicolaus of Cusa's doctrine of the monads had leveled the differences in individuality to quantitative differences of degree, the individuality of an individual entity lay open to logico-mathematical penetration. With this, it ceased to be a bare *mè on* in the Platonic sense. Individuality was basically quantified. Hence this nominalist metaphysics could assent without objection to assigning primacy *to the intellect*. This was in contrast with medieval nominalism, which needed the metaphysical theory regarding the primacy *of the will* in order to found the exclusive reality of the individual.

To the humanist science ideal, the absolutized individual is the isomorphic exemplar of conformity to a mathematical law of nature. This individualism-devoid-of-individuality carried the day in the natural-law constructions of humanism. Not until the Age of *Sturm und Drang* did the humanist view of individuality begin to align itself with humanism's personality ideal. But in that move it quite easily reverted to an irrationalist philosophy of life which reified individuality at the expense of conformity to the law.

Although Kant was the great regenerator of the personality ideal, he himself still placed, in rationalist fashion, the *principium individuationis* in the sensory experience of nature. His *homo noumenon* was no more than the reification of the meaning-functional moral law, the "categorical imperative." In this way Kant's practical philosophy had no room for meaning-individuality. At the same time, however, his moral and legal philosophy was again thoroughly individualistic. Only in his *Critique of Aesthetic Judgment* did individuality acquire a positive accent in his theory of the "creative genius."

As a result of its mathematical, functionalist orientation, the humanist natural-law doctrine lacked any insight into, and appreciation for, the meaning-individuality of things, and it already began to display that unmistakable tendency to eliminate the meaning-individual structural differences as these come to expression within the jural sphere. Only the imperial idea, borrowed from Roman law and welcomed by national monarchies in their pursuit of absolute rule, saved these natural-law theories from a political theory based on the construction of the social contract purely in terms of coordinational law. Hobbes' clever construction of the legal personality of the state perfected Bodin's doctrine of absolute sovereignty, which then became, following the criterion of general and particular interest, the basis for the natural-law distinction between public and private law. On the one hand it introduced a functionalist, logical unity into the doctrine concerning the sources of law by proclaiming the will of the state, via the principle of contract, as the sole source of validity for all positive law. On the other hand, via the well-known Romanist theory of legal personality, it simply equated the infinite variety of non-state internal law of organized communities with functional coordinational law.

Meanwhile the distinction between public and private law, based as it was on the absolutistic doctrine of sovereignty and still upheld by the rationalist theories of natural law, could not stand up to the modern individualistic theory of constitutional law which carried on the natural-law tradition in a positivistic sense only. Its fate was similar to that of Hobbes' doctrine of natural law and Gerber's modern German construction of political theory which regards the state as a legal subject, as an *universitas*. This too could only become problematic as the functionalist, nominalist tendencies continued to erode the entire subject-side of the law to a function of the impersonal norm-side, thus depriving it of all meaning-individuality. Naturalistic sociology collaborated closely toward this end with criticistic positivism, which started out from an entirely different standpoint.

As for the first tendency, Auguste Comte had already announced the program of eliminating all subjective rights, both in public and in private law. To this prime spokesman of the naturalistic science ideal which recognizes no meaning-boundaries, the concept of subjective rights was of the same metaphysical caliber as that of causality in philosophy.

The French constitutional law professor Léon Duguit, heavily influenced by syndicalist ideas, followed Comte and attacked the concept of sovereignty from a "realist" positivist standpoint. He combated the concept of subjective rights in general as well as the view of the state as a real supra-individual community and legal personality. On principle he rejected every attempt at maintaining meaning-individual structural differences between public law and private civil law. That this author, given his nominalistic, thoroughly empirical and individualistic standpoint,[1] failed to draw the only possible negative conclusion about the distinction between public and private law was merely the consequence of one of the many antinomies inherent in this "realist" political theory. Echoing the syndicalist Edouard Berth, Duguit writes, "The state is dead." And he cautiously adds, "or at least the Roman, regal, Jacobin, Napoleonic, or collectivist form is in the process of dying, since under its diverse aspects it is merely one and the same form of the state."[2]

But what remains of the state in this positivist theory of Duguit? Nothing! The state for him is simply a fact of nature, "constituted because a given group had one or several individuals who were capable of forcibly imposing their will on the other members of the group." Guided by this discovery, the author with charming simplicity solves every problem regarding the structure of the state:

> Sovereign rights are gone, as are the controversial questions about the title holder of that sovereignty and about the subject of law in general, as we saw. One rule which addresses everyone, one rule which imposes respect for every voluntary manifestation of the will conforming to objective law – this is all we see, this is all that remains. In truth, why look for anything else? Why invent all those imaginary entities: subjective rights, sovereignty, legal subjects? They all vanish upon a simple observation of the facts.[3]

Thus the state is nothing more than the fact that an individual or a group of individuals is more powerful than all the others and by dint of that superior power can impose its will upon the others. In this sense the state consists of the individual "governors," regardless of whether the groups upon whom they impose their will are united in a certain territory, and regardless of whether their "power" is of a purely physical, moral, religious, intellectual, or (as is often the case) economic nature.[4] These powerful individuals have no rights, only *duties*, duties that flow from the rules of "social solidarity" which hold for all individuals and which are based on the awareness of that solidarity that people share at

---

1   It is rather amusing to see Duguit combating individualism, which he believes originated in the Stoic tradition of Roman law and was stimulated more powerfully than ever by the Reformation, which he calls "an essentially individualistic movement"; Duguit, *Traité de droit constitutionnel*, 3rd ed. (Paris, 1927), 1:201 ff. It is no less amusing to hear him characterize Gierke as an adherent of the "individualistic doctrine"; ibid., p. 646. But a certain degree of philosophical naiveté is part of the more characteristic and in a certain sense even charming traits of Duguit's "realist" legal and political theory!
2   Duguit, *Le droit social, le droit individuel et la transformation de l'état* (Paris, 1908), pp. 38–39.
3   Duguit, *Traité de droit constitutionnel*, 1:674.
4   Ibid., 655.

any given time.¹ They can never be regarded as organs in a collective, public legal organized community, which on the "realist" view does not exist. They merely express their individual, personal, private will, which can only claim compliance to the extent that it derives from objective rules of law that hold for all individuals.

> There is therefore no difference to speak of. Whether the act of a public agent be unilateral or contractual, it has the same character as that of a private individual: it produces the same effects of law and under the same conditions.²

The old distinction between authoritative acts (*actions d'autorité*) and administrative acts (*actions de gestion*) is robbed of all meaning. There is no structural difference for Duguit between public law and private law. In vain do we wrack our brains to understand how Duguit can nevertheless maintain boundaries between public and private law. The solution surfaces as a veritable *deus ex machina*. The difference, he says, lies in "sanctions." Since the state is nothing but the facticity of the greatest physical power, the legal obligations of those who govern cannot directly be enforced by coercion, "since the state, master of coercion, cannot exercise this against itself."³

All this is said by the same Duguit who began by assuring us that it is foolishness to question the justice of executions, since the deed is "purely physical":

> It is simply one force crushing another. In no way is it a case of one will claiming the right to impose itself upon another will by virtue of any juridical power it might possess.⁴

---

1 Ibid., 685.
2 Duguit, *Le droit social*, p. 79.
3 Duguit, *Traité*, 1:710. The true reason why Duguit recoils from identifying law and state is revealed in *Le droit social,* pp. 64–65, where he remarks in reaction to Kelsen's "juridical pantheism" (the term is Duguit's) that an identification in the spirit of Kelsen would render it "very difficult to establish legal limits for the state." For his part, Kelsen would be right in countering that Duguit here employs an "ethical-political" postulate against him which lies outside the competence of positive legal theory. Patently evident in Duguit's thought at this point, so common in humanist positivism, is a reaction of the repressed personality ideal.
4 Duguit, *Le droit social*, p. 78. Even less comprehensible, for that matter, is the standpoint of Henri Berthélemy, *Traité élémentaire de droit administratif*, 5ᵗʰ ed. (Paris, 1908), p. 42, who maintains, over against Duguit, that there is a fundamental difference between "authoritative acts" and "administrative acts" yet who at the same time, in an extremely nominalistic denial of the state as a legal person and an individualistic conception of state action, completely shares Duguit's "realist" standpoint. See also Joseph Barthélemy and Paul Duez, *Traité élémentaire de droit*

And yet this fact of brute force, while juridically purely irrelevant, is said to provide grounds for a juridical distinction between the two kinds of law!

Far more consistent than Duguit are Krabbe and Kelsen, both of whom, when dissolving the concept of the state into respectively a psychologically or logico-mathematically misconstrued function of law, deny any fundamental distinction between public and private law. The Dutch scholar Krabbe, who is a kindred spirit of Duguit, dresses the theory of juridical sovereignty, which Duguit shares, in a psychologistic or psychologistic-sociological garb, while Kelsen gives it a logicistic-mathematical dress. But all three, in consequence, have to reject the dualistic view of the state and are forced to try and reduce the entire concept of the state to a system of legal functions.

According to Krabbe, political theory, as it investigates all sources of obedience and hence of power and authority, is in search of the one source that produces an *obligation* to obey. For this it finds no other source than the law, whose coercive force is rooted in an individual's sense of what is right. This psychological law prompts Krabbe at the same time to derive the postulate of the *unity of the norm*, which then is supposed to explain the majority principle (!).

> Whence it follows that state authority is no more than legal authority, and that the entire concept of the state dissolves into the specific legal practice found among a people.[1]

Meanwhile Krabbe's doctrine of the sovereignty of law is borne up by "the last remnant of moral pathos" that was part of "rationalist natural law from the time of the Enlightenment,"[2] rather than by the methodological consequences that flow from acknowledging the impossibility of a many-sided theory of the state once a dualistic relation is accepted between reality (that is, the "natural functions of reality") and the "realm of norms." Ultimately the state as a monistic jural construction remains a political postulate for Krabbe, something that was scarcely found in the days of absolute government and only realized in the relationships of the modern constitutional state.

---

constitutionnel (Paris, 1926), pp. 77 ff. Duguit is justified in his reaction to this strange inconsistency (Duguit, *Le droit social,* pp. 74–75).

1 See Hugo Krabbe, *Het rechtsgezag; verdediging en toelichting* (The Hague, 1917), p. 39; see also his well-known works, *Die Lehre der Rechtssouveränität. Beitrag zur Staatslehre* (Groningen, 1906) and *De moderne staatsidee* (The Hague, 1915), *passim.*

2 Thus, correctly, Hermann Heller, *Die Souveränität. Ein Beitrag zur Theorie des Staats- und Völkerrechts* (Berlin, 1927), pp. 20 f.

For this reason, Kelsen's *Allgemeine Staatslehre* is a more glaring illustration of the view of reality and epistemology suggesting that beneath the crisis in humanist political theory there is a crisis in the humanist science ideal. In Kelsen, the humanist personality ideal only surfaces in his dualistic distinction between *Sein und Sollen*.[1] As it is, in his hands the mathematical science ideal has banished from the concept of legal norms the last remnant of its sovereign meaning, so that it has become a thought category without content, one which even labels brute force and the rankest tyranny as positive law. And with this the humanist concept of the constitutional state, which in its second phase of development had already been considerably weakened through its concept of the state governed by laws, is as good as dead!

Never before has the connection between the functionalist, rationalist view of reality and the drastic banishment of any meaning-individuality from scientific thought been revealed in a more consistent and at the same time more grotesque form than in this mathematical "norm logic." Here the constitutional concept of sovereignty is debased to that of a legal order that cannot be deduced logically from any higher order. Here the contractual parties of free coordinational interaction are promoted to "state organs" on an equal footing with delinquents. The proper meaning-individuality of "state territory" is banished by characterizing it in logicistic fashion as the formal "range of validity" of a system of norms, a type of system that is equally present in other organized communities as "partial *forms of law*."[2] The entire problem of constitutional forms is reduced to that of "genetic forms of law."[3]

Following the Marburg "logic of origin" with its "category dynamics," the entire individual subject-side of the jural sphere has, in a radically functionalist manner, been transformed into a logical norm function.[4] As a result, all meaning-individuality within the jural sphere has

---

1 Between what *is* and what *ought to be*. See in this connection, and also for a more extensive criticism of the school of Kelsen from the theory of the law-idea, my oration *De Beteekenis der Wetsidee*, pp. 22 ff.
2 Hans Kelsen, *Allgemeine Staatslehre* (Berlin, 1925), p. 143.
3 Ibid., pp. 320 ff.
4 In his polemics with Smend – cf. Kelsen's *Der Staat als Integration* (Vienna, 1930), pp. 12 ff. – Kelsen complains that he is constantly being accused of denying the "reality" of the state whereas in fact he has only attacked the "natural reality" of the state, pointing out that already in his article "Zur Theorie der juristischen Fiktionen," *Annalen der Philosophie* 1 (1919): 630 ff., he characterized the existence of positive law as "a special kind of reality." But Kelsen does not understand the *significance* of the accusation leveled against him. The objection is precisely that he allows the "spiritual reality" of the state to be exhausted by his logicistic system of norms. And when he protests that he has never ignored the relation between this sys-

been hollowed to a mere logical "starting-point for relations," to a mere function in the system of logical norms.

When meaning-individuality is functionalized in a mathematical sense it is essentially eliminated. The juridical system as a logicistic and functional system, epistemologically created from a genetic norm, must completely wipe out all structural differences between internal constitutional law, law of non-political organized communities, and coordinational law. Once the juridical concepts are consistently detached from their meaning-substrates, not a trace remains of either the general or the individual meaning-structure of the jural sphere. Curiously, the only element left in Kelsen's concept of law that reminds us that we are not dealing with a completely senseless "pure logic" is the element of *constraint*. But that is exactly an element of *content*, not of *form*, and therefore does not, according to this whole epistemological standpoint, belong in the concept of law.

On the basis of Kant's dualistic worldview, Kelsen justifies the methodological demand to purge legal concepts of all meaningful connections with natural functions, which alone are seen as reality. This demand, made in order to arrive in this manner at a pure "norm-logic," is characteristic of the reification of logic that hides behind this whole postulate of "purity of method."

Kant could still impart a semblance of meaning to his concept of norm by assigning it the content of the humanist personality ideal, the autonomy principle. But to Kelsen, who has debased the norm into a mathematical category of knowledge and who wants to banish all ethical postulates from his "pure theory of law," this escape route is blocked. For him, the entire meaning of the "ought" has shriveled to formally imputing a relation between two facts, and this assigning in turn is no more than formally arranging logical functions into a logical system. Hence, in the end, the distinction between natural-scientific and norm-logical thinking collapses utterly. After all, natural-scientific positivism, too, wants to reduce the category of causality to a mathematical-logical assignment of functions of thought. As we know, Kelsen's pupil Sander in his second period indeed took the step of banishing the "ethical political bias" from the normative character of law and of transferring, without any hesitation, Kant's table of natural-scientific categories to legal

---

tem of norms and the *natural* human activity that supports the realization of these norms, then it should be pointed out to him that, apart from the fatal antinomy which that very *relation* between the "is" and the "ought" poses for his logicistic monism, the spiritual "reality" of the state can never be found in the abstracted norm – that is, in the law-side – of reality. In typical rationalist fashion Kelsen dissolves the subject-side of the jural into the norm-side and in so doing denatures the state into a mere "system of norms."

experience. Meanwhile, Schreier proposed to replace the term "ought" with the neutral term used in mathematics: "mapping."[1]

The political theories of authors like Duguit, Krabbe, and Kelsen differ markedly in methodology, yet they arrive at remarkably similar results. This can be explained primarily from the fact that at bottom they share a common view of reality based upon a naturalistic humanist standpoint. It is a view that dominates all of current political theory, which considers the state simply an abstraction, a synthesis of thought. Our authors merely push this view of reality to its ultimate conclusions, and so to absurd dimensions. Heller correctly remarks:

> Duguit only lays bare the ontology of current political theory when he argues against the reality of the state by observing that "if I put myself in the physical world I see only one thing: the individual wishes of those in government."[2]

This view of reality is crude and indeed destructive for the personality ideal. This becomes apparent in the fact that Kelsen, who as an anti-metaphysical, functionalist Neokantian can of course salvage nothing of Kant's practical metaphysics, views the real human being as identical with the psycho-physical individual of nature – as nothing but an object for natural science![3]

However, the crux of the critical formalist theory of law and the state, which perfectly exposes the inner antinomy of this entire view of reality, remains the transfer of the Kantian scheme of form and content to the "normative areas of knowledge." This scheme is internally contradictory in Kant himself, as we shall see below in Part 2, §1. But the *identity theory* of law and state, which starts out from a strict dualism between *is* and *ought*, collapses utterly the moment Kelsen, in discussing the problem of positivity, feels compelled to make a logical connection between the two "realms." In my inaugural address[4] I have further analyzed this antinomy, so deadly for "norm-logic."

As we have seen, one of the main factors causing the crisis in humanist political theory is the fundamentally hostile, functionalist attitude of the humanist view of reality with respect to the meaning-individuality of the structure of the state.

---

1 For this unmasking of "norm-logic" see my *De Beteekenis der Wetsidee*, pp. 30 ff., 97.
2 Hermann Heller, "Bemerkungen zur staats- und rechtstheoretische Problematik der Gegenwart," *Archiv des öffentlichen Rechts*, n.s. 16 (1929): 334. I am pleased to see that Heller, too, has begun to speak of a "logical-mathematical science ideal" (ibid., p. 332).
3 Kelsen, *Allgemeine Staatslehre*, p. 7.
4 H. Dooyeweerd, *De Beteekenis der Wetsidee*, pp. 32 ff.

Epistemologically, this functionalist attitude is expressed in the absolutization of meaning-synthetical thought, that is to say, in its internally antinomic separation from meaning-systatic thought[1] about our non-scientific experience of entities.[2] This in turn, as we shall see, results in a total falsification of the meaning of what is given in experience and an utter misinterpretation of so-called *naive realism*. We find the same attitude in the voluminous *Allgemeine Staatslehre* of Professor Ludwig Waldecker of Königsberg, a work that appeared two years after Kelsen's book of the same title.

Waldecker, however, starts out from a historico-sociological standpoint, altogether different from that of Kelsen's theory. For him, an organized community is not a systatically real meaning-unity, no more than it was for Jellinek. Rather, it is nothing but a critical direction of our thinking,

> a logically conditioning and socially generated kind or manner of ordering interconnected events that we encounter and which point to the causally interrelated wills of its participants. We make the observed events comprehensible in their totality by grasping them as a totality.[3]

Waldecker similarly characterizes the essence of the state, which he wants to grasp in a sociological concept – he defines the state as "land and people in their total organization" – as a mere synthesis of thought. The concept "state" thus captures no given systatic unity, for a "state" is nothing but a multitude of psychic, territorially bounded and empirically encountered, functional interactions that we simply *conceive of* as a totality.[4]

Given the view that the state is merely a thought-form, any talk of the "goals" or "ends" of a state is also rejected. The fact that in his theory of organized communities Johannes Althusius was among the first to replace the teleological view with that of symbiotic functions is interpreted by Waldecker – without any scruples, in the spirit of humanism's

---

[1] *General Editor's note*: The Dutch expression is *zin-systatisch denken*. The term "systasis" is intended to designate the integral coherence of reality as it is given in non-scientific experience. As explained in our Foreword, the qualification found in the word *"zin"* is motivated by Dooyeweerd's general characterization of reality as being dependent on God, as existing in, through and to God as the *origin* and *eschaton* of the universe. See Dooyeweerd, *A New Critique of Theoretical Thought*, 2:390 ff.
[2] See below, Part 2, § 1.
[3] Waldecker, *Allgemeine Staatslehre*, pp. 81–82.
[4] Ibid., pp. 214, 215.

immanence philosophy – in terms of humanism's absolutization of synthetic thought.[1]

Is it any wonder that on this functionalist standpoint Waldecker cannot discover any meaning-individual, essential difference between the state and non-state organized communities, and that he also does not find anything wrong in speaking of territorial evangelical churches as "states"? After all, he writes, the fact that today we connect "church" with the image of spiritual interactions is but historically conditioned.

> Neither organizations for certain purposes, say a commercial corporation, nor communal bonds (a municipality, region or province), distinguish themselves qualitatively but always only quantitatively and functionally from the state.[2]

It is obvious that such a functionalist attitude must necessarily obliterate the structural difference between public and private law. According to our author, the category of public law had only historical significance in the antithesis between jurisprudence and political administration (!) and as such is "just as confusing and objectionable as its corresponding category of substantial state violence and its representation of the state as a so-called self-sufficient 'organism' à la Schelling." And our author advises us to "assign this official category of the police state, like so many other things that belong there, to the official scrap heap."[3]

4 The crisis of the humanist personality ideal beneath the crisis of humanist political theory

The crisis of humanist political theory reveals not just a crisis of the humanist science ideal. Its deepest cause is to be found in the immense crisis at the root of the humanist worldview: its personality ideal.

So long as the personality ideal was still concentrated in the mathematical science ideal itself, humanist legal and political theory were borne up by a rock-solid faith in the eternal practical truths of reason, which for natural-law theory were embodied in a natural order. The state and its authority were accounted for in terms of mathematical thought and men had an optimistic view of the possibility to shape all of life in conformity with the eternal truths of reason. Even Rousseau, although already affected by a bitter skepticism about the value of the science ideal for a genuine development of the personality, proclaimed his rationalist theory of popular sovereignty and its *volonté générale* (general will) with the old optimism about the sovereignty of mathematical thought.

1 Ibid., pp. 454–56.
2 Ibid., pp. 217, 224.
3 Ibid., p. 367.

With his epistemology Kant rejected once for all the claims of the science ideal as applied to the domain of practical normativity. The logical mathematical function of reason (the intellect) he declared to be incompetent for proving the scientific truth of normative ideas. And yet in his *Critique of Practical Reason* he started out by allowing an *a priori* and universally valid rational faith to take the place of the mathematical science ideal. And proceeding from the starting point of this rational faith he erected a complete political and legal theory, proclaiming the infallibility of its constructions and conclusions – proclaiming it with even greater assurance, if possible, than his predecessors.

This rationalist faith in eternal truths of reason, on which both state and law were supposed to be founded, has been drastically upset since the nineteenth century by the tidal wave of historicism and positivism. Neokantianism could not turn back this wave with its logicistic world of "forms." To be sure, the idea of the people's sovereignty as the basis for state authority has been solemnly confirmed in many constitutions that have come into being since the [First] World War. Yet, both science and practice have lost faith in this idea, along with faith in the reality of the state as an organized community. Modern political and legal theory vie with each other in ridiculing the idea of an eternal law of reason with constant material standards of justice. After faith in the divine foundations for the state had been undermined, so now faith in its immanent rational foundations was also shaken.

The idea of modern democracy itself is no more than the idea of a skeptical relativism which no longer dares to stand fully committed behind absolute truths. Consequently one is content to demand equal rights for all political viewpoints.[1] It is nearly impossible to survey the growing body of literature today that deals with "the crisis of democracy," "the crisis of parliamentarianism," and so on.[2] The rationalization of authority in modern constitutions, to which especially Mirkine-Guetzévitch has drawn attention,[3] is right in step with the spiritual uprooting of the concept of authority. All personal authority falters, espe-

---

1 See Hans Kelsen, *Vom Wesen und Wert der Demokratie* (Tübingen, 1920), p. 36: "Relativism is therefore a worldview presupposing the idea of democracy." See also the interesting § 50 of his *Allgemeine Staatslehre* where he discusses "Forms of Government and Worldview."
2 For German literature, see Carl Schmitt, *Die geistesgeschichtliche Lage des heutigen Parlamentarismus*, 2nd ed. (Munich, 1926), p. 29. For an important French contribution to this problem, see Joseph Barthélemy, *La Crise de la démocratie contemporaine* (Paris, 1931).
3 See Boris Mirkine-Guetzévitch, *Les nouvelles tendances du droit constitutionnel* (Paris, 1931) and his article, "Die Rationalisierung der Macht im neuen Verfassungsrecht," *Zeitschrift für öffentliches Recht* 8.2 (1929): 259 ff.

cially in Kelsen's "norm-logic," and the theory of the impersonal sovereignty of law bears on its forehead the Mephistophelian sign of the "spirit that forever denies."

Gierke's prediction that the positivist method in political and legal science would undermine the idealistic foundation of both law and state has indeed been confirmed in alarming fashion. The humanist science ideal has cut off its own rootedness in the personality ideal by using the philosophically hollow phrase of *reine Rechtslehre* (pure theory of law), and it does not notice that with its positivistic battle against all so-called "ethical-political postulates" in political theory it cuts into its own flesh since it derives its own foundation, the dualistic separation of natural reality and the realm of norms, from the very moralistic personality ideal against which it thinks it has to wage such a bitter fight.

One cannot illuminate the development of the crisis in the humanist personality ideal within modern political science more acutely than by pointing out the three phases undergone by one of the basic ideas in constitutional humanist political theory:[1] the idea of the constitutional state (*rechtsstaat*).[2] We can draw a parallel between these three phases and three phases in the attitude of the state toward economic life. They are:

1) abstinence by the state: a formal legal standpoint vis-à-vis the economy;
2) social legislation: a substantive legal standpoint vis-à-vis business and industry;
3) direct interference in the internal life of business and industry: a gradual absorption of free organized economic communities into the structure of the power-state and welfare state.

This parallel as well provides a keen overview of the gradual undermining of the humanist idea of the just state.[3]

1) In its classical natural-law phase (Immanuel Kant and Alexander von Humboldt), the theory of the just state champions the inviolable subjective rights of the individual against interference by the state and seeks the purpose of all governmental activities in maintaining and enshrining these rights in law.
2) In its second phase (Friedrich Julius Stahl, Otto Bähr, Rudolf von Gneist), this individualistic natural-law content of the idea of the

---
1 Cf. e.g. Paul Laband, *Das Staatsrecht des deutschen Reiches*, 2:173.
2 *General Editor's note*: The Dutch term "rechtsstaat" and the German term "Rechtsstaat" is here translated as "constitutional state," although it can also be rendered as "a constitutional state under the rule of law" or simply as "a just state."
3 See in this regard the important work, written from a liberal standpoint, by Friedrich Darmstaedter, *Die Grenzen der Wirksamkeit des Rechtsstaates. Eine Untersuchung zur gegenwärtigen Krise des liberalen Staatsgedenkens* (Heidelberg, 1930).

just state is replaced by the idea of the formal legitimacy of state activity for the sake of the legal security of its citizens. This takes place under the influence of the historical view of law and the trans-personalist conceptions of the state in Schelling and Hegel. The formal theory of the just state views law as the sole limit to activity by the state which of its own accord may pursue all possible extra-legal aims. The watchword of this theory of the just state is to subordinate the executive power to the legislative and judicial powers. In this situation the legitimacy of state activity is derived from the essence of the state itself.

3) In its third phase (the positivist doctrine of identity in Kelsen and his school, and in a sense already in Stammler), state and positive law are declared to be identical, causing the last material tie with the personality ideal to vanish by eliminating all "ethical-political postulates" which hitherto had given the idea of the just state its strength and meaning.

Since Kelsen holds that law is "only the form for whatever content" and the state is "merely the means for realizing whatever social purpose," the two being identical,[1] therefore the essence of the state no longer provides a single point of connection for the personality ideal and its principle of autonomy:

> Hopeless, therefore, is the perennial attempt to deduce a minimum or a maximum in the competence of the state from either the essence of the state or the essence of the individual. It is idle, today as ever, to try and demonstrate that an absolute limit can be drawn somewhere against the expansion of the state versus the individual. It is also irrelevant whether one views this limit as deriving from an innate and inalienable freedom of the individual, as the old teachers of natural law once taught, or whether one regards certain state interventions and certain legislative competencies – that is, the connection between specific situations and acts of coercion – as incompatible with the essence of the individual as a free, self-determining personality, as is held by modern teachers of government and law who reject natural law and think they are standing on the basis of positivism.[2]

Thus writes Kelsen, and correctly, on his standpoint. So correct, in fact, that one can barely understand what purpose this more or less melodramatic "rebuttal" of his opponents can serve, once it has been settled that state and law are one and the same. The explanation of this pathos can be found in this, that Kelsen's standpoint, like that of Bergbohm earlier,

---

1 Kelsen, *Allgemeine Staatslehre*, p. 40.
2 Ibid., p. 41.

is inspired by the relentless struggle of the science ideal, which is essentially based in the humanist worldview, against its spiritual mother, the personality ideal. Kelsen's entire standpoint demonstrates to what extent the naturalistic science ideal leads to *political* consequences (as was already the case with Hobbes): with both it leads to a boundless absolutism, which is never based on positive law but on a logicistic foundation. Kelsen even trumps Hobbes, as Hobbes still reserved a natural right of self-preservation for the individual.

With Kelsen, the personality ideal no longer serves as a counterweight against this consequence of the science ideal. Is such a boundless dominion by the state desirable? Referring the question to politics by no means suggests that in this area Kelsen believes in firm yardsticks derived from the humanist personality ideal. After all, in regard to "ethical-political postulates" he embraces a skeptical relativism.

The undermining of the personality ideal in the idea of the just state goes hand in hand with the logicistic emasculation of the concept of law for constitutional political theory. In an important paper about the concept of law in the Constitution of the Weimar Republic, given in 1927 for the Association of Professors of German Constitutional Law, Hermann Heller remarked:

> The current political degeneration of the idea of the just state stands in the way of a clear understanding of the meaning of the concept of law in the just state. In 1910 Thoma had to discover the concept of the just state for political theory all over again![1] Prior to this rediscovery, the meaning of the classic conception of the just state had been forgotten, and today contemporary science of constitutional and administrative law distinguishes between two concepts of law in the same way as it distinguishes between a *formal juridical* idea of the just state and a *material* one, which it calls "political." At bottom, it knows no more how to deal with the material idea of the just state than how to deal with the material concept of law.[2]

Indeed, the distinction between law in a formal and a material sense, which became common property in today's dominant theory of constitu-

---

[1] See Richard Thoma, *Rechtsstaatsidee und Verwaltungsrechtswissenschaft* (Tübingen, 1910).

[2] H. Heller, "Der Begriff des Gesetzes in der Reichsverfassung," *Veröffentlichungen der Vereinigung der deutschen Staatsrechtslehrer* 4 (1928): 115.

tional law after it took a radical turn towards positivism with Laband, Anschütz and Jellinek, is bereft of all meaning.[1]

In the classic idea of the just state, the concept of "material law" had significant content, stamped as it was by the humanist understanding of natural law. In line with Rousseau, the concept of the just state demanded that the law be an expression of the general will (in distinction from the will of all). A just state was to manifest, on the one hand, the postulate of *freedom* as a people's autonomous self-determination,[2] and on the other, the postulate of *equality* in the sense of equal treatment of all citizens as measured by the public interest, without distinction of a person's rank, position, and so on.[3] This natural-law content of the concept of law was derived from the humanist personality ideal. Tied in with this was a more technical, organizational effort, rooted in the postulate of legal security,[4] at delimiting a material sphere of competency as a prerogative for the legislative power.[5] For this formula, the *trias politica* theory of Montesquieu took on fundamental significance. The rationalist spirit of the times demanded of laws that their stipulations meet the criteria of universality and constancy, since the concept of universality was taken to be of "higher value" than that of individuality.

When Laband's famous book on budget law came out in 1871 it provided a new basis for the distinction between law in a formal and a material sense. Laband rejected the criterion of universality and with "logical necessity" wished to acknowledge as positive law only the expression of the inner will of the state. The substance of the latter was "a legal stipulation or norm regulating or determining legal relationships." It is known that with this criterion Laband specifically meant to character-

---

1 From a different standpoint Krabbe argues against this distinction in his *Het wetsbegrip* (1927), pp. 1 ff. The distinction is also opposed by Raymond Carré de Malberg, *Contribution à la théorie générale de l'État, spécialement d'après les données fournies par le droit constitutionnel français* (Paris, 1920), 1:276 ff., 314 ff., and by Heller, "Der Begriff des Gesetzes in der Reichsverfassung," *passim*. See also the literature mentioned by Duguit in his *Traité*, 2:140 ff.
2 Cf. Rousseau's and Kant's ideas of freedom.
3 A notion still found in Robert von Mohl, *Encyklopädie der Staatswissenschaften* (Tübingen, 1859), p. 327.
4 On this, see the extensive treatment by Carl Schmitt, *Verfassungslehre* (Leipzig, 1928), pp. 138 ff.
5 The French National Assembly of 1789 meant to denote by "le loi" (the law) only the highest legal norms governing the political life of the state as a whole. In the German states, the struggle between the territorial princes and the estates about a prince's independent right to initiate legislation occasioned the formula of Baron von Stein, according to which "the new general laws of the land" had to be concerned with the "freedom and property of the citizens." No attempt was made, however, to arrive at a more precise definition of this criterion.

ize budget laws as purely formal laws in order to uphold a government's competence to spend funds not contained in the budget, or even if no budget were ever approved. In fact, it was to uphold the undivided sovereignty in the person of the king, in connection with his theory that "sanction alone is legislation in the constitutional sense of the word."[1]

Laband's entire theory is essentially an expression of the idea of the just state in its second phase. It considers law a merely formal limitation of the sovereign will of the state as concentrated in the king and based in the essence of the state, and it expects this limitation to guarantee freedom.[2] According to this theory, when a government's actions conflict with a purely formal law, there is as yet no violation of law, since the formal law merely has the *form* of a law and has but an administrative regulation for its *content*.

Even this last trace of a connection with the personality ideal has collapsed in the concept of law as defined by the logicistic identity theory. This theory can no longer speak meaningfully of a limitation of state activity by legal means, since the state and the logicist-positivist legal system are completely identified with each other. The concept of law in identity theory is of course purely formal. Kelsen recognizes as "law in a material sense" only the relative criterion of the universality of its content,[3] a content, however, which in keeping with his law-idea is purged of all "ethical-political postulates."

In his work on constitutional theory Carl Schmitt writes:

> All other characteristics of law as a substantial, rational, just and wise command have today become relative and problematic; the *natural-law* faith in the law of reason and the rationality of law has largely collapsed. What saves the constitutional state from utter dissolution into the absolutism of shifting parliamentary majorities is a mere lingering remnant of respect for this general character of law.[4]

I should think this is small comfort for the defenders of the just state! Should it surprise us that in this general crisis of the humanist personality ideal the logicist, idealist view of law, through the thin wall of its world of forms, meets up with its twin sister, its ancient antipode: power naturalism? To quote Kelsen's own words: "those who lift the veil with-

---

1 Heinrich von Marquardsen, *Handbuch des öffentlichen Rechts der Gegenwart* (Tübingen, 1921), 1:72; 2:6-10.
2 See Lorenz von Stein, *Die Verwaltungslehre*, 2nd ed. (Stuttgart, 1869), 1:116-17; Hugo Krabbe, "Het wetsbegrip," in *Staatsrechtelijke opstellen* (The Hague, 1927), 1:1; and Heller, "Der Begriff des Gesetzes in der Reichsverfassung," pp. 106 ff.
3 Kelsen, *Allgemeine Staatslehre*, p. 235 ff. See also Carl Schmitt, *Verfassungslehre*, pp. 151 ff. and Léon Duguit, *Manuel de droit constitutionnel*, 4th rev. ed. (Paris, 1923), p. 97 and *Traité de droit constitutionnel*, 2:145 ff.
4 Carl Schmitt, *Verfassungslehre*, p. 156.

out closing their eyes see the Gorgon head of power staring them in the face."[1]

At this juncture, idealist humanism is separated from naturalist humanism by mere hollow, meaningless terminology. The entire ideology that the humanist personality ideal, from Grotius to Hegel, had offered to political theory finds itself in a condition of relativistic, skeptical decomposition. And so a large portion of the European states has proved ripe for the new ideology of dictatorial power.[2]

Kelsen has already addressed the question of how to define even the Bolshevist dictatorship as a legal theory free of all forms of ideology.[3] He attempts this in spite of the fact that Bolshevism denies the normative meaning of law on every occasion, and that Lenin bluntly describes the essence of Bolshevism as "unlimited power, not restricted by any laws or any general rules and resting directly on force."[4]

Unless the "pure theory of law" is willing to abandon its logicist-positivist claims, it will not be able to avoid tackling this question. All it needs to do, basically, is to abandon a certain ethical-political terminology which Kelsen still has retained in memory of the old personality ideal. Should norm-logic, with its theory of levels (*Stufentheorie*), wish to comprehend within its logicist system the collection of Bolshevist ordinances that are invariably inconsistent since they categorically deny the normative validity of formal decrees, it would, in carrying out this program, not get any further than formulating the original norm. And as one of the most authoritative official commentators on Soviet law has testified, that original norm is the "driving force and basic law of this state," namely that *force must be exercised under all conditions which the ruling party may decree in the economic interest of the ruling class*.[5]

But no, in order to adhere strictly to the logicist doctrine, norm-logic would even have to scrap the only thing that still imparts any substantial consistency to the activity of the Soviet bosses: namely, the "ethical-political postulate" of the "interest of the ruling class." But once it had "purged" this original norm, it would be able to conclude its account of Russian constitutional law with the observation that now all individual

---

1 Hans Kelsen, "Comment," in *Veröffentlichungen der Vereinigung der deutschen Staatsrechtslehrer* 3 (1927): 55. Kelsen aimed this statement at natural law; see also his work *Der soziologische und der juristische Staatsbegriff. Kritische Untersuchung des Verhältnisses von Staat und Recht* (Tübingen, 1922), p. 95.
2 *General Editor's note*: The reader is reminded that after Italy had become fascist a decade earlier, Germany would follow suit within two years of this writing!
3 Thus Kelsen in his Foreword to Boris Mirkine-Guetzévitch's *Die rechtstheoretische Grundlagen des Sowjetstaates* (Vienna, 1929).
4 Vladimir I. Lenin, *Zur Frage der Diktatur* (Vienna, 1921), p. 15.
5 Georges Gurvitch, *Vvedenie v obscuju teoriju mezdunarodnogo prava* (Prague, 1923), p. 12, quoted by Mirkine-Guetzévitch, *Die rechtstheoretische Grundlagen des Sowjetstaates*, p. 3.

actions of the Soviet authorities are understood, on strict logic, as delegated from this original norm. For the Bolshevist dictatorship also knows no juridical boundaries of competence that hold for "state organs," despite the letter of the Constitution of 1925, no more than it knows even a formalist-positivist concept of law. Concerning this, Mirkine-Guetzévitch observes:

> The principle of dictatorship on the one hand, and the structure of government organs on the other, lead not only to the negation of all legislation but even to the dispensing of the concept of objective right as such. In the Soviet state, fact and right are simply one.[1]

Indeed, the "pure theory of law" cannot spurn anything for weaving it into the system of its "norm-logic" – no murder, no robbery, no violence, no arbitrary use of power – unless it opens the windows to the *meaning* of law, as was recently done by Alfred Verdross and Fritz Schreier.[2] But that system can here be summarized in two sentences.

Whether this formalistic norm-logic may still be called *science* is a question that will be hard to answer in the affirmative by anyone who still demands of scientific thinking that it provide us with meaning-synthetical *knowledge* about the object under investigation.

5. The modern reaction to the crisis in humanist political theory. Attempts to reconstruct it on the basis of a dialectical phenomenology. The Berlin School and the Integration Theory. The new humanist view of reality and epistemology in this theory

Our diagnosis of the crisis in humanist political theory presented thus far – tracing it back to three causative factors: the essentially naturalistic and individualistic view of reality; the functionalist position in epistemology; and the skeptical dissolution of the personality ideal – is accepted as correct by all political theorists who are adherents of the contemporary *geisteswissenschaftliche*[3] school of political theory.[4]

---

1 Ibid., p. 13. On page 66 the author remarks: "Soviet constitutional law does not know the concept of a *hierarchy of norms*, and therefore, as the Russian critic [Timashev] puts it, factually the constitution is not superior to any ordinance."
2 See Fritz Schreier, *Die Interpretation der Gesetze und Rechtsgeschäfte* (Leipzig, 1927), p. 9.
3 *General Editor's note*: The German designation of the *natural sciences* and the humanities is known as *Naturwissenschaften* and *Geisteswissenschaften*.
4 Cf. e.g. Rudolf Smend, *Verfassung und Verfassungsrecht* (Leipzig, 1928), § 1; Hermann Heller, "Die Krisis der Staatslehre," *Archiv für Sozialwissenschaft und Sozialpolitik* 55 (1926): 289–316; Gerhard Leibholz, *Das Wesen der Repräsentation unter besonderer Berücksichtigung des Repräsentativsystems* (Berlin, 1929), pp. 13

This fresh school is making a resolute attempt at surmounting the crisis without abandoning the immanence standpoint of humanism's worldview. Its representatives certainly do not form a closed phalanx, nor have they offered a worked-out political theory. Yet in a certain sense we may speak of a "school" here because they share certain methodological premises and accept a common theory of integration, which we may call, after the father of "integration theory," the school of Smend, or the Berlin School.

For the rest, when speaking of the Berlin School we must not lose sight of the fact that its most important spokesmen, the professors Rudolf Smend and Hermann Heller from Berlin, and Carl Schmitt, Gerhard Leibholz and Leo Wittmayer from Bonn, often defend very different viewpoints. Hence their intellectual affinity is located more in their point of departure and their method than in their results. We might also mention Siegfried Marck, who is a Marxist, as a philosophically kindred spirit of this school: although he may not be counted among the integration theorists, Marck is still similar to them in a methodological sense.[1] It is in particular this school's view of reality and theory of knowledge that we wish to submit to an examination as to its value for political theory.

Smend and Schmitt are trying to introduce a new political theory under the name *Verfassungslehre*, a "constitutional theory" that would grasp the state in its full spiritual reality and at the same time avoid both the rock of naturalism and the reef of monistic norm-logic. They have adopted a fresh vantage point from which to address the problem of the many-sided meaning-synthesis of the various meaning-functions of the state. This problem, as we saw, was the central problem of political theory on which both the naturalistic and the norm-logical monism, as well as the so-called two-sides theory, ran aground. Smend in particular has tried to introduce a method which stands in opposition to the sharply defined methodology of Kelsen's norm-logical school and which he (Smend) derives from Litt's phenomenological sociology.

Theodor Litt belongs to a school of phenomenology that is rapidly gaining in influence. This school attempts to break through Husserl's one-sided orientation of the method of *Wesensschau* (the contemplation of essences) to the logical function of consciousness, the pure *cogito* (in

---

ff. Of course the norm-logical school *per contra* hails the dawn of overcoming the crisis precisely in the rise of the "pure theory of law"; cf. e.g. S. Rohatyn, "Die verfassungsrechtliche Integrationslehre," *Zeitschrift für öffentliches Recht* 9 (1930): 261: "In truth there is no crisis in the general theory of the state, although one is justified to speak of a crisis among a few German theorists of constitutional law."

1 Cf. Siegfried Marck, *Substanzbegriff und Funktionsbegriff in der Rechtsphilosophie* (Tübingen, 1925). Smend, however, repudiates Marck's concept of the state.

a Cartesian sense). Litt advocates a much broader orientation to the totality of the functions of consciousness, including the emotional and evaluative ones, to which cognitive value is therefore ascribed as well. The school relates Husserl's phenomenological method to the broad concept of the "pure," spiritual "I" that Wilhelm Dilthey introduced into psychology in its turn to the humanities. Max Scheler, Martin Heidegger, Hans Freyer, Richard Hönigswald, Theodor Litt, Eduard Spranger, Johannes Volkelt, Paul Hoffmann and various other phenomenologists must be counted among this Diltheyan school, whose adepts have also adopted (some more than others) the peculiar historicist trait of Dilthey's philosophy of life.

Litt elaborated his *geisteswissenschaftliche* sociology in his important work on "the Individual and the Community."[1] This sociology belongs to the "formal school" founded by Georg Simmel, which consciously abandoned the program of the "universalist school" and tried to delimit for sociology its own formal field of investigation. This field nowhere overlaps with the other "social sciences" (history, linguistics, economics, law, ethics, and so forth), yet in a formal sense it is to serve as a foundation for all these disciplines. Litt, however, in opposition to most of the other adherents of the school (Simmel, Leopold von Wiese, Alfred Vierkandt, and others), chooses a standpoint that is very much his own. He operates with a distinctive view of the relation between an "individual I" and a community. Based on his phenomenological analysis of the structure of the spirit, his formal sociology is intended, as a philosophy of culture, to furnish all the humanities with what he calls the "methodological and metaphysical" *a priori* basis.

In what way, according to this philosopher, is thinking in the humanities different from natural-scientific thought? The difference is this: in the humanities there is a relation of perfect identity between subject and object, while in the thinking of the natural sciences the I, as the subject, has to place its object, as being foreign to the thinking I, in opposition to itself, and must strive to purge knowledge of all subjective factors. Natural-scientific thought aims at knowledge of *objective spatial reality* while eliminating the structure of the "I" as subject. Essentially this knowledge is based on the *isolation of elements*, such that the scientific determination of the coherence between these elements only occurs afterwards.[2]

> What, however, is the deepest reason for the fact that the spirit, in drawing close to an objective world [*scil.* that of the humanities] which ap-

---

1 Theodor Litt, *Individuum und Gemeinschaft. Grundlegung der Kulturphilosophie*, 3rd ed. (Berlin, 1926).
2 Ibid., pp. 10–11.

parently it is compelled to resign itself not to know in light of the spirit's own self-examination, actually does draw closer to it thanks to this very self-examination? The reason is none other than the fact that this object is . . . *himself*, the scientist's own world, the very sphere with which the scientist as a thinking and knowing being feels solidarity. Whatever he does here in order to make transparent the imperfections inherent in his own being only serves to clarify his being and thereby to illuminate that object which the scientist seemed compelled to relinquish as the conclusion of his self-examination. In the sharpest distinction from the knowledge of spatial reality, the subject-object relation must be kept free of every shadow of representation which the subject sees as something *over against* itself, as a foreign object that it must deal with from the outside. Once this has become clear, once the identity of subject and object (which cannot be compared to anything else) is recognized as the core of these relationships, the notion is no longer strange that reflection on one's own shortcomings at the same time signifies victory over these shortcomings and conquest of the object.[1]

In this sense the phenomenological analysis of consciousness is the "self-illumination of the spirit." It cannot, like the spatial orientation of natural-scientific thinking, dissect the "spiritual reality" into isolated "elements," placed side by side. Rather it must always start out from the totality, the coherence, from which the "moments" can be understood in their relative independence. Nowhere in the thinking of the humanities may a provisional "conceptual boundary" be viewed as *definitive*. The boundaries must always be breached dialectically, not in order to let all moments flow together again without distinction, but to allow the boundaries to count as mere dialectical moments in the spiritual totality. The moments may therefore not, like the "elements" in natural-scientific thought, be connected purely externally, but must be seen in a spiritual unity of structure,

> . . . which connects everything with everything, not through a mechanical bringing together, but through a meshing rich in tensions, through a reciprocal penetration of attraction and repulsion.[2]

Now what does the "spiritual reality" consist of, whose spiritual structure will be clarified by a phenomenological analysis of essence? It consists of the dialectical unity of psychic experiencing in time and the timeless ideal sense or meaning (*Bedeutung*) intended by this experience. With Litt, the sphere of meaning is in no way identical with the sphere of normativity or value of the Neokantians.[3] On the one hand,

---

1 Ibid., p. 16.
2 Ibid., pp. 21–22.
3 The followers of Litt in political theory largely lose sight of this fact. Both Smend and Heller often equate the "domain of meaning" with the "domain of normativity

Litt argues, the sphere of "that which is meaningful"[1] covers much more ground than "that which is normative." The norm-conformative and the anti-normative alike fall within the sphere of what is meaningful. That which is bereft of all meaning lies outside the "spiritual world" and cannot be referenced to notions of norm or value.

On the other hand, the phenomenological analysis of structure is also *indifferent* to any normative distinctions. For, according to the essential character of their structural insertion within the totality of spiritual reality, the valuable contents of consciousness are in no way preferable to those that are anti-normative and objectionable from an evaluative standpoint.[2] The theory of structure knows only one distinction that delimits its area of judgment: that between what is meaningful and what is meaningless. It is an analysis of a spiritual reality and has to leave the normative value judgment of this reality to the normative sciences. But as a science of essences, which clarifies the essential principles of the structure of the "spiritual world," it yields the basis for all the humanities, including their epistemology and methodology.[3]

In order to make room for this phenomenological analysis of the structure of spiritual reality, the narrow natural-scientific bounds of Kant's concept of experience must of course be breached. In its aim to offer a *descriptive* analysis of essence, phenomenology does not want to be reproached that it is guilty of constructing an *a priori* reality beyond all possibility of experience. It claims to be describing exactly what is most certain about spiritual "experience" and demands the title *experiential knowledge* for the manner in which it wishes to provide knowledge of spiritual reality.[4] Even the Kantian form-matter scheme proves to be useless for this phenomenology.

> What the phenomenology of spiritual reality entails is not a doctrine of categories in the original Kantian sense, nor a theory of logical forms that permits spiritual life to enter as something recognizable, but a theory of the directing principles of this life.

The scheme of a doctrine of transcendental categories, accommodated to the relation between thinking spirit and a "nature" external to it, does

---

and value." Heller in particular, one of the best and most productive thinkers of this school, sometimes mixes natural-scientific, normative and phenomenological thinking in a way that prompts the question whether he has really understood the thought of Litt; see e.g. his work *Die Souveränität*, p. 35, where the dialectical method in legal theory is sought in the dialectical connection of a causal and a normative mode of viewing! On p. 79 he speaks of what we intuitively combine into a "dialectical unity of sensitivity and meaning"; and so on and so forth.

1 The sphere of "das 'Sinnhaften,' desjenigen also was eine 'Bedeutung' hat"; ibid., p. 28.
2 Ibid., pp. 28–29.
3 Ibid., pp. 36–37.
4 Ibid., p. 26.

The Crisis in Humanist Political Theory

not permit being transposed to the relation between the thinking spirit and a "material" that is essentially identical with it.[1]

Nor may we equate the "phenomenological I" as a center of experience with the "epistemological I" which constitutes merely a "moment" in this I,

> ... for the spirit can recognize itself only insofar as it stands, as the "subject" absorbed in the pure act of knowing, *opposite* itself as a living totality.[2]

This phenomenological I is not a substance which remains constant *behind* the fluctuations of its experienced moments and which functions as bearer of these experiences, but in its essence it is, in the sense of an intimate dialectical union, identical with every one of these temporal experiences.[3]

All across the board the objectivizing, opposing scheme of natural-scientific thinking is useless for a descriptive structural analysis of the experiencing I. Corporeal experiencing should never be explained in terms of the natural-scientific scheme of space, time and causality. Experiential space and experiential time do not stand opposite the I; the I lives in them. The I lives in every moment of life and for that reason it cannot mechanically separate present, past, and future in experiential time. All moments penetrate each other here. Only a "perspectivist" dialectic is able to grasp this structure in a continuous reciprocity of the relationship between I and body, and between body and I. Prominently visible at the same time is the *individuality* of every experienced moment, and with that of the I. Although the phenomenological analysis of structure as an analysis of essence only looks for *general* determinations, that is, for *essential* law-conformities, it is driven with logical necessity to postulate what is uniquely *individual* about each moment. For, Litt argues, essential law-conformity cannot be discovered by an inductive comparison of concrete moments in life from which common traits are abstracted; it can only be discovered through a dialectical traversing of every individual moment to the structural totality within which alone it can reveal its individuality.

> Logically speaking, too, that which is particular is not separation from the general, abstraction from the general, but intimate unity with what is general. The logic of true individuality is at the same time the logic of the most encompassing universality.[4]

---

1 Ibid., pp. 26–27.
2 Ibid., p. 49.
3 Ibid., p. 90.
4 Ibid.

Just as phenomenological structural analysis finds the I and the world as dialectically interwoven in the experienced moment in a real "reciprocity of perspectives," so it finds the experienced moment of "I" and "you."

> Living in you and me are not just similar, comparable perspectives but kindred ones, perspectives that determine each other and interlock with each other; and my/your immediate knowing about them is simultaneously a knowing about their interlocking nature.[1]

Here, too, the investigation, directed primarily at the *eidos*, the general essence, is automatically driven to acknowledge the individuality of the "I" and the "you."

> Whenever I and you, understanding each other and understood by each other, approach one another in experiencing the "same" situation, this sameness expresses itself in an interweaving of perspectives that comes close to removing any (also partial) veil over the content of the experience.[2]

The reciprocity of perspectives between me, you, and the world is first realized in the symbolic expression movement in which the temporal experience and timeless meaning are tied together in dialectical fashion through the very sensory corporeality of the form of expression. Here, all objectifying mode of thinking, which isolates the "sides" of the symbolical expression from one another, is shown to be inadequate for grasping the structure of this life phenomenon.

Just as little as the expression movement is initially perceived as a purely sensory phenomenon, behind which the psychic event would have to be traced, so little can sensory perception and understanding its meaning be grasped in isolation.[3]

Meanwhile the meaning and the symbolic form in which it is embodied are not themselves located in the structure of experiential time. Rather, in their dialectical unity they are clearly exempt from all temporal change.

> Form and meaning can assert themselves as such only when all shifts and turns that fill experiential time remain external to them.

The big question now is: how can experiential, temporal consciousness absorb timeless meaning? In fact, how can any relation exist at all between a consciousness which in its deepest essence finds itself in the

---

1 Ibid., p. 110.
2 Ibid., pp. 111–12.
3 Ibid., p. 158.

movement of experienced time, and a symbolic meaning which stands timelessly above it?

Litt's phenomenology of consciousness does not give us any satisfying answer to this crucial question. With a few convoluted sentences the author glosses over the insoluble antinomy implicit in his humanist, immanence standpoint. He assures us:

> Since experiential consciousness extracts and differentiates from its own living movement "form" and "meaning" and takes distance from them, it establishes a relationship with that which differentiates it from its own structure as timeless. It would not have been capable of this if it had not already within itself overcome linear time [*scil.* the objective space/time of natural-scientific thought]. To a person who merely existed "in time," whose being exhausted itself in the fleeting passage of a present without extension, whose past and future were a nothing – to such a person any conceivable relation with something timeless would be a closed book; for in the "punctuality" of the moment neither form nor meaning can find shelter. On the other hand, to a person whose experience continually transcends external succession, to whom the non-present is yet present – to such a person the overcoming of succession, which is already present in the structure of his experience, offers not just a possibility but a stimulus to arrange the content of his experience – not in order to replace this somehow with a timeless object . . . but to arrange it in such a new light that, in the very experience itself, a "something," something objective, begins to stand out.[1]

But with this assurance Litt obviously does not resolve the antinomy implicit in his view of a symbol-bound meaning as a timeless product of an I that is changing in experiential time. Simply to contrast "linear time" with "perspectivist time" cannot help us overcome this antinomy. The contradiction is implicit in the immanence standpoint itself, which gives short shrift to the many-sidedness of cosmic time for the sake of certain absolutized functions of consciousness (in this case the psychic-historical ones).

Indeed, only "dialectical thought" in the tradition of Fichte, Schelling and Hegel, which desires to put aside the cosmic order by proclaiming the sovereignty of *geisteswissenschaftlich* thought which is rooted in the freedom postulate of the personality ideal and which sanctions the antinomies in which it must embroil itself by constantly transgressing the meaning-functional boundaries – only this kind of dialectical thought can find satisfaction in the line of reasoning reproduced above.

Proceeding from this whole train of thought – which we could only outline here in an extremely schematic form – Litt now chooses his po-

---

[1] Ibid., pp. 161–62.

sition in regard to the basic problems of current sociological theories: namely, the relation between individual and community, individualism and collectivism, personalism and trans-personalism. In sociology the individualistic view of society assigns reality only to the individual. Trans-personalism can assign true reality only to the bond, to the community, and can treat the individual only as a dependent member. Litt now believes that the whole dilemma is caused essentially by an erroneous application of objectifying, non-dialectic natural-scientific thinking within the domain of the humanities. Both these basic trends of thought make independent (that is, *reify*) one of the two sides of the spiritual universe: either the individual experiencing I, or objective social meaning. As long as the I and the social world are placed, in the manner of objectifying thought, in opposition to each other in a rigid, impenetrable substantiality, the problem will remain insoluble.

The phenomenological structure of the I of the humanities, according to Litt, is not an element of spiritual life that can be made into an object that supposedly is related to this life in a causal fashion. The category of inter-individual interaction as introduced by Simmel and adopted by most of the adherents of the formal school of sociology (von Wiese, Vierkandt, Max Weber) fails to appreciate this structure by reifying the individual. The I cannot be reduced to an "individual" that exists prior to social life, but its essence consists only in "social interwovenness" (*sozialer Verschränkung*).

This concept of social interwovenness, which plays such a central role throughout this phenomenological sociology, can only be understood in connection with another central concept of Litt's sociology, that of the "closed circle." In Litt's opinion the elementary structure of the closed circle is present in pure form

> wherever a plurality of two or more living centers [of I's] stand in a significant relationship one with another, so that each one rounds out his contours with respect to all the others, just as all the others, conversely, experience his formative influence upon them.[1]

In this sense the closed circle is essentially connected with the system of symbolic forms of expression which in the spiritual reality are required for mutually understanding one another.

To the extent that the I seeks a psychic connection only with the you, exclusively with you, a connection that strives for mutual "understanding" on the basis of meaningful symbolic forms of expression, to that extent the ideal contents of meaning, which are symbolized in sensory forms, remain too much tied to the vital content of this one living con-

---

1 Ibid., p. 239.

nection – too much for them to be able to separate themselves sharply and objectively from the matrix "of the shared special corporeal-mental event." Only in a "closed circle" does the symbolic form, denoting meaning, obtain a sharply objective character that rises above the simple movement of expression (*Ausdruckbewegung*). Only then does the spiritual objectification in *meaning* and symbolic *form* indeed become transpersonal. This comes about in that the forms of expression no longer change from person to person and from moment to moment but remain available as the objective symbolism of a social living totality, a supra-individual spiritual unity. Such a closed circle is not the sum total of the relations between individuals, and even less the sum total of the individuals themselves. It is a spiritual, supra-individual structure, one in which the individual I's point to *essentially* social connections, and one in which the transpersonal connections, which by virtue of the fundamental structural principle of the "reciprocity of perspectives" are oriented to the objective meaning, interpose themselves in an essence-shaping way in the individual experiences of all the members.

Every I of a closed circle shares in the total experience (*Gesamterlebnis*) of that circle. And this experience, too, cannot be constructed from isolated elements. The experiences and actions of all the members are embodied here in the indivisible unity of a totality that knows nothing of an absolute opposition between its own experiences and actions and "foreign" experiences and actions.

According to Litt, the ideational analysis of essences can demonstrate this structure of the *Gesamterlebnis* in every communal activity of a closed circle (for example, a deliberation, a pronouncement, a decision, and so on). Now this structural relationship, which inseparably connects the life of the I with the transpersonal life in the closed circle, Litt calls social interwovenness (*soziale Verschränkung*).[1]

With this characterization of the relation between individual and community, Litt chooses a position that is as much opposed to individualism as it is opposed to the universalist school in sociology which has its most militant modern representatives in the person of Othmar Spann and which is generally embodied in the Organism Theory. This entire school, to which Gierke too belongs, assigns a supra-individual I-ness to the communal bond, a "collective I" which is conceived as an activity center that is to be sharply distinguished from the individuals composing it. Litt rejects this universalist conception because the spiritual unity whose basic principle is called "reciprocity of perspectives" would be

---

1 Ibid., p. 248.

altogether canceled by the introduction of a supra-personal I-ness.[1] The spiritual unity in structure of the closed circle coincides with the dialectically unified structure of the experiences which find their center of activity only in individual I's. It is the social interwovenness that braids together the differences of the individual I-structure and the social structure.

> It is precisely this co-dependency which makes the I so sure that its utterances transcend the circle of its particular existence. If it manages to indicate properly what is general and essential in the structure of one's I, then it calls up, as the necessary correlate of itself, the composition of the spiritual world in which that person is taken up.[2]

The difference between the structure of the individual I and a social structure is also evident in that the living unity of the I consists of a *single biotic body* which cannot be spatially divided without disrupting the living entity. But the "closed circle" has no individual body, and its dissolution has no analogy in the somatic-psychic structure of the individual.[3]

* * *

In the foregoing we have very briefly recited the view of reality and individuality in Theodor Litt's phenomenological sociology. Now it is on that basis that Rudolf Smend has erected his new, albeit extremely schematic, political theory,[4] which has gained a following as "integration theory."

Smend intends to defend the reality of the state as an organized community of wills [*Willensverband*] in opposition to Kelsen's norm-logical school. He notes, however, that the *theory of the three elements of the state* which is still not entirely vanquished can never be the point of departure for a political theory that would be part of the humanities. It bundles nation, territory and government into a corporeal or, still murkier, a psycho-physical unity and chooses the nation, united in a territory, as its starting point, viewing it simultaneously as the object of a psychical ruling power. Kelsen has criticized this theory, and Smend fully accepts his critique because it leads astray into "static spatial thinking."

---

1 Ibid., pp. 246–47.
2 Ibid., p. 248.
3 Ibid., pp. 249 ff.
4 Smend is even more modest about his book, for he does not call it a "Political Theory in Outline," but merely a work that lays out the presuppositions of a constitutional theory. This restriction happens to correspond exactly with the one Litt attaches to his phenomenological sociology in its fundamental relation to the particular disciplines of the humanities.

With Kelsen, Smend also rejects the theory of sociological interaction[1] which tries to understand the state as a system of causative interactions between isolated individuals. Nor does he accept Jellinek's sociological theory of the state as a "purposeful community" (*Zweckverband*). For both theories fall into the familiar trap of constructing, in a non-dialectical fashion, the spiritual reality of the state out of the reified individual.

Concerning the teleological view of the state as a social reality, Smend remarks that the purpose of the state is located outside the social arena and that this view can therefore not serve to clarify the structure of the state:

> Rationalism, by means of its teleological manner of thinking, has clarified and then threatened all the humanities. In its legal and political theory the teleological orientation only compounded the other sources of error by working with an individualistic manner of thinking which has never yet been entirely overcome. It conceived of individuals in isolation, alongside one another, and then connected them in spatial images by means of juridical relations and elevated them by means of a personified State – and all that for purposes that lie beyond the goals of law and politics, purposes which, as principles of explanation, frustrate each of the special disciplines in their primary task, which is to penetrate to the distinctiveness of their scientific object. Particularly the liberal mind, which is foreign to the state, is prone to see the state merely as a technique of civilization, and it is liable, owing to such a teleology, to neglect the primary and essential question of the structural law of the state.

Naturally, Smend also rejects the universalist view of the state as a substance: ". . . there are also no substantial points of support for the power connections of spiritual and social life."[2] To the extent that Kelsen critiques the "social reality" of the state as defined in the sociology of Simmel, Vierkandt and von Wiese, and rejects every kind of reifying organological theory, Smend is in complete agreement with him. But insofar as Kelsen bases himself on a long since conquered epistemology in order to combat any possibility of understanding spiritual reality, Smend writes that Kelsen's "nihilism in the humanities belongs to a happily closed chapter in the history of science."[3]

---

1 Of course Kelsen, in his work *Der Staat als Integration*, makes grateful use of Smend's rather unstable terminology which causes him to speak repeatedly of the reality of the state as a "spiritual interaction." Although Smend radically rejects the interaction theory (see his *Verfassung und Verfassungsrecht*, p. 11), he is of the opinion that this theory nonetheless comes closest to understanding the spiritual-social realty.
2 Ibid., p. 11.
3 Ibid., p. 13.

Let us examine whether Smend's optimism about conquering the crisis in political theory with the aid of Litt's *geisteswissenschaftliche* sociology is indeed justified.

Following in the footsteps of Litt, Smend tries to understand the social reality of the state as that of a *closed circle*. The structural unity of such a closed circle is, as Litt already argued, forever in motion, however much it may be "captured in symbols, forms and laws."[1] For it is real only to the extent that it forever actualizes – or rather realizes – itself anew.

The reality of such a closed circle may not be doubted just because it has been argued by Kelsen that the sum total of all individuals who juridically belong to the state, including children, the insane, those who are asleep and those who are not at all conscious of belonging to the state, is not identical with the circle of those who are factually relating to one another in that psychological interaction in which sociology attempts to locate the reality of the state; that therefore the concept of the state wielded by a sociology of the state can never be a view of reality but merely a conceptual form of a purely juridical and normative nature.[2] This whole argument, Smend notes, is founded on a naturalistic psychology which views consciousness mechanically as the sum of momentary states of consciousness and lacks insight into the spiritual structure of the I and of experiential time. The real experience of membership in a state does not depend on momentary points of consciousness, "since the human being is not the 'punctual' I of his momentary consciousness, but the indivisible unity of the whole of his being and experience, also while asleep or not thinking about it."[3]

The real interconnectedness of citizens consists first of all in a sense of "having the possibility of understanding their political milieu."[4] Litt has given an elaborate exposition of the operation of "social mediation" by means of which the spiritual interconnectedness can be extended in all directions.[5] Mediating factors that deserve special attention in political life, according to Smend, are "reports on the state of affairs in the political community, and reports on public opinion which are continually adapted to the individual's need to understand and which provide him with the only possible image of the community as a whole and thus with the possibility of actively participating in it," and, finally, with all the many other means of "social mediation" that may be reckoned among "integration factors."[6] We shall discuss these factors later.

---

1 Ibid., p. 14.
2 See Kelsen, *Der soziologische und der juristische Staatsbegriff*, pp. 8 ff.
3 Smend, *Verfassung und Verfassungsrecht*, p. 14.
4 Ibid.
5 Litt, *Individuum und Gemeinschaft*, pp. 252 ff., 276 ff.
6 Smend, *Verfassung und Verfassungsrecht*, p. 14.

Smend intends to demonstrate the reality of the state as a structural "coherence of experience." To that end he points out the basic significance, fundamental for all spiritual life, on the one hand of the "perspectival limits of the human capacity for understanding," and on the other of the "limitless capacities for understanding on the basis of this same perspectival conception."[1]

Of course all this provides Kelsen with an easy target for a razor-sharp counterattack. It will be difficult to deny the efficacy of this counterattack when Kelsen points out that the "capacity for understanding" on which Smend bases his proof for the reality of the state is indeed "limitless," and thus does not stop at the bounds of the state. No more can we deny its effectiveness when Kelsen, with his characteristic spicy humor, asks Smend whether terminating membership of the state would cancel the capacities for understanding "which, as we know thanks to phenomenology and the metaphysics of time, continue to function even during sleep." Where Smend argues that [legal] membership in a state means a strong "factual" embeddedness in the coherence of the organized political community, Kelsen counters, correctly on his standpoint, that "since this [embeddedness] disappears without a trace when legal membership is cancelled, one will doubt its 'factuality' and view the questionable 'community of wills' as a purely *legal* one."[2]

Indeed, the onus was on Smend to demonstrate that the community of those who make up the state embraces only those members who *rightfully* belong to the state. He should have given account of the cosmic coherence that obtains here between the juridical and the psychical structure of experience. But dialectical phenomenology is incapable of doing so because it fails to grasp the reality of the state itself as a cosmic meaning-structure. In its very starting point it betrays its functionalist disposition which forces it to place meaning as an ideal, timeless domain in opposition to experience in time.

Dialectics cannot clarify for us the cosmic coherence of meaning that obtains between the law-spheres. In order to maintain the absolute sovereignty of phenomenological thought it redefines the systatic coherence of our temporal cosmos as a dialectical coherence, a coherence that can only be viewed as being identical with "spiritual reality" by a synthetic mode of thinking that fails to recognize its own meaning-boundaries.[3]

---

1 Ibid., p. 15.
2 Kelsen, *Der Staat als Integration*, p. 41.
3 Cf. e.g. Litt, *Individuum und Gemeinschaft*, p. 245: "Precisely in the encompassing interwovenness of perspectives which are not simply factual fusions but which as

Why does this dialectical phenomenology have to take "meaning" as "an ideal, timeless structure," in contrast to experience in time? Because it cannot grasp the universality of the cosmic temporal order as long as it remains rooted in the immanence standpoint. And hence it has also shut the door to clarifying the cosmic coherence of all meaning-functional sides of reality that are given to us only in this order of time. Its phenomenological conception of time bears the stamp of functionalism on its forehead.

Thus, as Kelsen has rightly pointed out, we see Smend once again irretrievably falling back on fictions when he tries to understand the reality of the state detached from jural norms. Whenever such fictions are resorted to, they testify to an inadequate view of reality. Smend writes:

> When an utterly mindless person [!] cannot share in the state as a spiritual entity since such a person is not a spiritual being [!], that person will nevertheless, out of respect for the fragment of humanity he represents, be treated juridically and factually as if he did share in it.[1]

But already this single fiction is fatal for the phenomenological view of reality, exposing its utter failure.

The heart of Smend's phenomenological political theory is located in its view of the social reality of the state as a process of integration. The word *integration* is the true magic wand of his theory. Smend himself observes: "Here lies the political hinge in the field of reality from which political and constitutional theory will have to proceed."[2]

If this concept of integration is indeed to contribute to the clarification of the meaning-individual structure of the state, it will also have to possess a meaning-individual delineation, which is still entirely foreign to Litt's concept of the closed circle. With Litt, after all, the closed circle is merely the general structure of every social connection.

According to its program, then, integration theory is supposed to provide a meaning-individual application of Litt's basic concept to the state structure. But this would require a rigorous analysis of the meaning-individual structure of organized communities in order to establish the structural coherence between their various meaning-functional sides. The phenomenological concept of meaning and of time is altogether inadequate for this purpose.

such are experienced and known to consciousness, such that their existence coincides with their being experienced, precisely here we have before us the classic paradigm of the effective reality of the world . . ." This is the old logic of Hegelian metaphysics which generates temporal reality itself from the dialectical concepts of thought.

1 Smend, *Verfassung und Verfassungsrecht*, p. 16.
2 Ibid., 17.

From the immanence standpoint it cannot be admitted that cosmic reality is enclosed within meaningful law-spheres and that every one of its sides is bounded by its own functional meaning.[1] Nor can it admit that the cosmic order of time courses through all these meaning-functions and weaves them together in a certain order.

The way in which dialectical phenomenology views reality suffers from the fundamental ailment of every immanence philosophy. It chooses its absolute Archimedean point from which to survey the coherence between all meaning-functional sides of temporal reality *within time itself*. Consequently it must tear cosmic reality apart into a timeless *noumenon* and a temporal *phenomenon*.

Following in the footsteps of the post-Kantian freedom ideal, dialectical phenomenology orients its study of the humanities to the humanist personality ideal. For this reason it wants to construct the relationship between both "worlds" in a dialectical fashion by which timeless, ideal meaning permeates natural reality, which in itself is meaningless.

The mode of thought in the human sciences finds its prototype in Fichte's dialectical theory of science. Basically, it originated in a version of the humanist worldview that wanted to carry through the continuity postulate of the personality ideal at the expense of the continuity postulate of the mathematical science ideal. To interpret "nature," the product of the science ideal, as being itself a product of the personality ideal is the deepest tendency of all humanist thought engaged in the human sciences.

This explains the deep aversion displayed by the Berlin School to the political theory of the school of Laband and Kelsen. It is the old polarity between the personality ideal and the science ideal which here manifests itself in a new form. And it is not surprising that Kelsen's sharpest arrows against Smend and his followers are directed at the "ethical-political postulates" that permeate their entire political theory.

A curious and more or less shady side to all this is that phenomenological political theory tries to hide its ethical-political postulates, which are derived from the personality ideal, behind a seemingly *exact method of analyzing essences*. Edmund Husserl, the father of modern phenomenology, has already advanced the thesis that all normative sciences are grounded in purely theoretical sciences directed at the study of essences.[2] And as we saw above, Litt adopted this thesis when he taught that normative qualifications become irrelevant for phenomenological sociology. It is in this fashion that research methods in the humanities

---

1 Husserl already teaches that this meaning is generated through the phenomenologically purified I who *assigns* meaning; see his *Ideen zu einer reinen Phänomenologie*, 1:106 ff.

2 Edmund Husserl, *Logische Untersuchungen*, vol. 1, *Prolegomena zur reinen Logik*, 2nd ed. (Halle an der Saale, 1913), pp. 37 ff.

try to come to terms with Kant's postulate that the personality ideal is withdrawn from the domain of scientific thinking.

To a sleuth like Kelsen, trained in discovering the admixture of "ethical postulates" in theoretical thought, this natural-law attitude could of course not remain hidden. And he is undoubtedly correct when he repeatedly brings to light the thinly veiled postulates of the humanist personality ideal behind the so-called pure theory of this *geisteswissenschaftliche* doctrine of the state.[1]

Smend's concept of integration presents itself as a phenomenological concept of essence, gained by a purely descriptive analysis of spiritual reality. And to that extent it is marked off as sharply as possible from all juridical norms. He begins the exposition of his integration theory as follows:

> Political theory and constitutional law deal with the state as a part of spiritual reality. As parts of reality, the spiritual structures of collectivities are not static substances; they form the meaningful unity of real spiritual life, of spiritual activities. Their reality is one of a functional actualization, reproduction, or, more precisely, an enduring spiritual mastery and expansion (whose value may be progress or regression) – only in and through this process are they, or do they newly become, real in every moment![2]

We really do not learn anything more substantial about this phenomenological concept of the essence of the state, and it is hard to maintain that this convoluted description has made us any the wiser.

Smend had already introduced the term *integration* in his 1923 article on "political authority in the constitutional state and the problem of forms of government"[3] And Wittmayer, in his article on "the statelike character of the Reich as a logical and national form of integration," defined this integration as "the sum-total of all political representations of unification and unifying forces."[4] But this definition obviously remains useless as long as it does not accurately establish what is meant by "political."

The word *integration*, as is well known, stems from infinitesimal calculus and hence has nothing whatsoever to do with political theory. Following in the footsteps of Spencer,[5] the concepts of differentiation and

---

1 See e.g. Kelsen, *Der Staat als Integration*, pp. 49 ff.
2 Smend, *Verfassung und Verfassungsrecht*, p. 18.
3 Smend, "Die politische Gewalt im Verfassungsstaat und das Problem der Staatsform," in *Festgabe der Berliner Juristischen Fakultät für Wilhelm Kahl zum Doktorjubiläum am 19. April 1923* (Tübingen, 1923), 3:16 ff.
4 Leo Wittmayer, "Die Staatlichkeit des Reiches als logische und als nationale Integrationsform," in *Fischer's Zeitschrift für Verwaltungsrecht* 57 (1925): 145 ff.
5 Herbert Spencer, *Principles of Sociology* (London, 1882), pt. 5, *Political Institutions*, §§ 440 ff.

integration took root in universalistic sociology and were given meanings that were clearly derived from the natural sciences. Understandably, these were sharply rejected by Smend. It would therefore not have been superfluous for Smend to have given us a genuine *geisteswissenschaftliche* definition of the process of political integration

It indeed makes sense to speak of integration and differentiation in all of organized communal human life. But what is the typical meaning-individual structure of integration in the organized community that we call a state? In vain do we look for an answer to this pressing question in Smend's "definition" of integration. We observe here how this phenomenological theory of politics, which sees the core of its scientific method in the synthesis of *experienced reality* and *meaning*, does not trouble to introduce even a minimal delineation of the meaning of its concepts.

Not until he deals with the constitution of a state does Smend somewhat firm up his concept of integration. He endorses a dynamic view of a constitution. For him a constitution is the principle of the dynamic *genesis* of political unity from a spiritual force and energy underlying this unity.[1] He defines a constitution as "the juridical ordering of the state, or, more precisely, of the life in which the state finds its vital reality, namely its integration process."[2]

The comprehensive nature of the integration process can of course "not be fully grasped or regulated from a few schematic constitutional articles that are based on ever fresh information received from third or fourth parties. Instead, it is merely hinted at and, as far as their integrating power is concerned, it is only set in motion.[3]

This is followed by a very characteristic passage from which it becomes apparent that for Smend constitutional law must indeed draw its meaning-individual character from the state itself:

> Whether and in what way the required result of a satisfactory integration arises from these [articles of a constitution] depends on the operation of all the vital political forces of the nation as a whole. In the flow of political life, the required result may often not be obtained in exactly constitutional ways. In those cases, despite such incidental deviations, the fulfillment of the integrating task will, thanks alike to the value-conformity of the spirit and the articles of the constitution, sooner satisfy the spirit of the constitution than a constitutional practice that is true to the letter of the constitution yet poor in its effect. Thus it is the intention of the constitution itself not to be a stickler for details but rather to look at the totality of the state and the totality of the integration process, which do

---

1 Thus Carl Schmitt, *Verfassungslehre*, pp. 5–6.
2 Smend, *Verfassung und Verfassungsrecht*, p. 78.
3 Ibid.

not just allow but actually encourage those flexible and broadening interpretations of the constitution that deviate widely from every other legal interpretation.[1]

It is obvious that Smend here places constitutional law and politics in the closest possible relationship, and in so doing takes a strong stand against the complete separation between the two such as has been introduced by Gerber, Laband and Kelsen.[2]

Thus it becomes even more important to find out what Smend really means by "political unity." It is indeed not easy to find a consistent answer to this question in Smend's muddled and often contradictory trains of thought. We get the first hint of an answer, curiously, in the *theory of state goals* for which Smend otherwise has so little respect. He writes that the theory of state goals "quite rightly and at every turn is pervaded by the old doctrine of the tripartite goals of justice, power and well-being." The second goal turns out to be paramount: it is "the basis for understanding all the pertinent phenomena, primarily the constitution and its meaning."[3]

Carl Schmitt has demonstrated this essential goal of the state in the *peculiar character of dictatorship*, particularly in the profound difference between the exceptional measures of Article 48 of the Weimar

---

1 Ibid., pp. 78–79.
2 This strict separation of constitutional law from politics is of course also rejected by the "teleological" view of the state. Jellinek already, in his *Allgemeine Staatslehre*, pp. 13 ff., warned against a "purely juridical method" that intends to separate constitutional law from its *material*, "teleological" connection with politics. Most recently, Heinrich Triepel, in his rectorial oration *Staatsrecht und Politik. Rede beim Antritte des Rektorats der Friedrich Wilhelms Universität zu Berlin am 15. Oktober 1926* (Berlin, 1927), and Ernst von Hippel, in his *Untersuchungen zum Problem des fehlerhaften Staatsaktes. Beitrag zur Methode einer teleologischen Rechtsauslegung* (Berlin, 1924) as well as in his important treatise "Über die Verbindlichkeit des Gesetzes," *Archiv des öffentlichen Rechts*, n.s. 18 (1930): 86 ff., have expressed themselves in a similar vein.

Of course the connection of constitutional law and politics is also found in the Neokantian political theory of the Baden School and in the neo-Hegelian political theory of Julius Binder, Erich Kaufmann, and others.

In the meantime everything depends on what these writers mean by "politics." The "teleological" theory naturally has a "teleological conception" of politics. A case in point is Jellinek's *Allgemeine Staatslehre*, which on p. 13 defines politics (in the sense of practical political science) as "the theory about state goals and the study of political phenomena from teleological points of view that furnish the criterion for evaluating political conditions and relations." As we shall see below, integration theory has a different view. For modern uses of "politics" consult *Die Grundlagen der Politik*, vol. 1 of *Handbuch der Politik*, ed. P. Laband (Berlin, 1912).

3 Ibid., pp. 82 f.

Constitution and "in a certain sense lawful norms and actions of the state."[1]

Arthur Wegner has convincingly pointed at this essential goal in the special nature of certain "juridical functions," which, however, do not serve justice so much as uphold state power, such as punishment for spies, franc-tireurs, those guilty of high treason, and so on.

> However [writes Smend], its scope extends much farther: it is the state as "ruling value," as Jellinek calls it, its "maintenance and reinforcement," its integration . . . which besides the values of justice and well-being (or the value of administration) factors in as the third value in the same order . . .[2]

To these remarks Smend immediately adds some indications as to the criteria that distinguish the state from other organized communities:

> This orientation of a state's constitution as an integration order according to its integration value is its first and basic distinctiveness, as opposed to the constitutions of other organized communities.[3]

His next sentence is very disappointing:

> The criteria that distinguish the state from other organized communities will not be thoroughly elucidated here.

Indeed, that would be major feat for a phenomenological theory of the *essence* of the state! But we do get at least a bit more light.

In the first place we are told that the existence of the state is not, like that of most of the other [sic!] organized communities, guaranteed by a power located outside itself, but instead that the state "by virtue of an objective 'value law-conformity' simply integrates itself in a self-gravitating integration system." And in the second place, essentially inherent in the state community and its continuously unfolding integration system is the sovereign unity of territorial decision-making power as formal dominion and ultimate ordering power, whereas all other organized communities generally [!] are optional means for attaining special practical ends.[4]

And so it turns out in the end that the entire integration concept rests on the ancient view of the state as an organized community of *power*. And we soon see the adherents of the Berlin School slipping onto absolutistic paths, leaving no room for sphere-sovereignty in non-state organized communities. The method of the humanities, too, backed by the humanist view of reality, renders impossible a genuine analysis of the individual meaning-structure of organized communities. On this

---
1 Schmitt, "Der deutsche Föderalismus: Die Diktatur des Reichspräsidenten," *Veröffentlichungen der Vereinigung der deutschen Staatsrechtslehrer* 1 (1924): 96–101.
2 Smend, *Verfassung und Verfassungsrecht*, p. 83.
3 Ibid., p. 84.
4 Ibid., pp. 84 f.

point the integration theorists all agree: the sovereignty of the state is *absolute* as against all other organized communities.

Heller, for example, has once more reinstated Bodin's concept of sovereignty. Against every attempt to maintain the sphere-sovereignty of the internal communal law of organized communities other than the state, he posits the thesis:

> To the juridical examination of the present-day state it appears that the positive character of the community regulations coordinated under it derives from the positivity of the legal order of the state.[1]

Similarly Carl Schmitt teaches:

> Basic rights for a natural or organized community cannot exist within the state ... The modern state is a closed political unit and by nature has *the* status, that is to say, the total status that relativizes every other status within it. It cannot recognize within its bounds any public-legal status prior to or above itself and endowed with equal rights.[2]

In another place Schmitt calls sovereignty "true state omnipotence."[3]

Operating behind the entire integration theory is the conception of the *power-state* in the trans-personalistic sense of the humanist freedom ideal. Its ideology is that of the personality ideal according to the trans-personalistic type introduced into philosophic thought by Schelling, Schleiermacher and Hegel.[4] Connected with this, however, is the peculiar irrationalist trait of all "philosophies of life," namely to highlight the typically irrational element in the power of the state that is not bound by norms, and on this point to absolutize individuality at the expense of the law. Schmitt is the best example of this. He adopts Kelsen's manner of drawing a parallel (albeit with a reverse accent on values) between reifying the state and theology and builds his concept of sovereignty on a "political theology." He holds that sovereignty lies with the person who decides in exceptional circumstances not governed by

---

1 Heller, *Die Souveränität*, p. 57.
2 Schmitt, *Verfassungslehre*, p. 173. Schmitt recognizes only "institutional guarantees" for organized non-state communities, by which he understands guarantees granted by the state itself and dependent upon its sovereign decision. The same view is found in the thought of the neo-Hegelian Julius Binder, *Philosophie des Rechts* (Berlin, 1925), pp. 538 ff.
3 Schmitt, *Politische Theologie. Vier Kapitel zur Lehre von der Souveränität* (Leipzig, 1922), p. 9.
4 Smend, *Verfassung und Verfassungsrecht*, p. 70, emphatically highlights the connection of integration theory with the dynamic concepts of the state held by Fichte, Schleiermacher and Hegel. Purely Hegelian as well is Schmitt's statement in his *Verfassungslehre*, p. 22: "Viewed juridically, what exists as a political entity is worthy of its existence."

norms, observing that "exceptional circumstances are for jurisprudence what miracles are for theology."[1]

This irrationalistic, decisionistic theory of sovereignty is completely oriented towards the modern concept of dictatorship,[2] and in this regard forms the diametrical opposite of humanism's rationalist idea of the constitutional state. It is a clear example of absolutizing subjective individuality at the expense of law, such as we can continually detect in the irrationalist types of humanist philosophy.[3]

But we find that Smend, too, consciously links up with irrational, mythological motifs as he expounds on the various integrating factors. Thus he refers to the literature of fascism with its mythology (derived from Sorel) of direct mass action, calling it "a goldmine for research into this area."[4]

It is well known how Georges Sorel in his *Reflections on Violence* openly followed Bergson's philosophy of life and viewed *myths* as the core of all social and political power, myths that arise from the depth of the vital instincts and take hold of the masses and inspire them.[5]

Smend differentiates between personal, functional, and material integrating factors, although in the reality of states these factors as a rule work closely together. As vital processes of the spirit they can never be explained by reducing them to causal regularity. They can only be understood by ordering them in their meaning-coherence as realizations of the "value law-conformity of the spirit."

Personal integration issues from leaders whose personalities are symbols of national unity. They represent the nation in their person, but they can only do this if their persons symbolize at the same time either a community's enduring historical values or its more transitory, material and political values.

Functional factors of integration, according to Smend, include

all events whose meaning is one of social synthesis,[6] enabling a spiritual content to be commonly shared, or reinforcing the experience of its commonality, with the double effect of an enhanced life for both the

---

1 Schmitt, *Politische Theologie*, p. 37.
2 In his work *Die Diktatur, von dem Anfängen des modernen Souveränitätsgedankens bis zum proletarischen Klassenkampf* (Leipzig, 1921), Schmitt has traced dictatorship from the beginning of the modern concept of sovereignty up to the proletarian class struggle.
3 Although acknowledging its merits, Heller too opposes Schmitt's theory of sovereignty; see his *Die Souveränität*, pp. 66 ff.
4 Smend, *Verfassung und Verfassungsrecht*, p. 42.
5 Georges Sorel, *Réflexions sur la violence*, 4th ed. (Paris, 1919). On Sorel, see Schmitt, *Die geistesgeschichtliche Lage des heutigen Parlamentarismus*, pp. 78 ff.
6 In the sense of Hans Freyer, *Theorie des objektiven Geistes. Eine Einleitung in der Kulturphilosophie* (Leipzig, 1923), p. 81.

community and the individual members.¹ Such functional integrating factors can occur in the area of the senses and can accompany as well as symbolize the spiritual content. A march or a demonstration is an application of functional integration in the life of the state. Events like that may be of a purely spiritual nature and then serve especially the continuing integration of a people into a "community of wills." Particularly suitable for this are elections,² parliamentary debates, cabinet formations and plebiscites.

Given their fundamental significance, all these integrating factors should not be seen as purely juridical procedures, nor superficially, from a teleological, sociological viewpoint, as simply means for making good decisions and choosing good leaders.³ Their primary meaning is the integration of the people into a political individuality.

> It is not so that in a parliamentary state the people are "politically available," to be given a special political quality from election to election and from one change of government to the next. Rather, the people has its very existence as a political nation, as a sovereign community of wills, in the first place by virtue of the prevailing political synthesis in which it continually renews its existence as a genuine state.⁴

The operation of this factor, as well as of all the other factors of functional integration, depends on two elements: first, its principle (here the majority principle) must generally have integrating power; and in the second place, it must have this power for the entire nation.

Concerning the second point, Smend remarks that the state and its form, as well as the juridical order, thrive on the "approval" of the subjects. Hence the proper operation of functional integration depends on the submission of the subjects to the operation of the most important factors of integration.⁵

In full agreement with Leibholz,⁶ Schmitt,⁷ and Heller,⁸ Smend once more takes up the old natural-law notion of the reality of the *volonté*

---

1 Smend, *Verfassung und Verfassungsrecht*, p. 33.
2 Though not by "secret ballot." Proportional representation, moreover, lessens the "integrative force" of universal suffrage (which, for that matter, Smend calls "individualistic") (*Verfassung und Verfassungsrecht,* p. 91). Of course these are all political judgments, and assessing them will depend on one's political point of view.
3 Cf. the ideas of Max Weber.
4 Ibid., p. 39.
5 Ibid., p. 41.
6 See Gerhard Leibholz, *Das Wesen der Repräsentation*, pp. 58 ff., which traces it back to Hobbes.
7 *Verfassungslehre*, p. 207.
8 In his work *Die Souveränität,* Heller restricts the "approval" to the "total" political order only.

The Crisis in Humanist Political Theory 61

générale, which Hauriou[1] already tried to show had an essentially sociological meaning.

Wherever the general approval of the integrating methods in parliamentary democracies no longer exists, modern political theory and practice wishes to replace these methods with "direct integration," to use fascist terminology. Smend explains that according to Sorel,

> only by direct action is the individual directly involved and politically alive; fascism is based on direct integration through corporatism, militarism, mythology, and untold other techniques.[2]

Besides integration through the constitutionally regulated contest as found in parliamentary or plebiscitary democracy, Smend sees a second form of functional integration in *dominion*.

The irrationalist turn in humanist political science is very much in evidence in Smend's sociological theory of dominion. Dominion must here be understood *geisteswissenschaftlich* as the realization of communal values: its legitimacy hails from irrational values; only the administrative activity of the state, in which Smend does not see its real essence, is justified by rational values.

Dominion is the most general form of functional integration to the extent that "all constitutional life under every form of government has the exclusive goal to build and express the ruling will."[3]

The norm-logical method understands dominion as the "enforcement of juridical norms,"[4] and the causal-scientific method, pursuing an objectification inadmissible within the humanities, defines dominion as the "opportunity to obey."[5] Neither method, according to Smend, is able to understand the spiritual reality of dominion as the "form of life of the state."

It is the common and essential trait of all formal integrative processes that they cannot be understood in rational terms of expediency. Rather, we may compare them "to an army's peacetime drills that weld it into a unity, or to gymnastic exercises, or to games and dances."[6]

But this *geisteswissenschaftliche* political theory, much as it opens up important points of view with its "dynamic-realistic" view of the state, displays nowhere more clearly than here how it ends up in word-games when it lacks the discipline of an exact meaning-analysis of the structure of the state. From all his discussions Smend has completely eliminated the essential *juridical* side of the state, and his picturesque analo-

---

1 Maurice Hauriou, *La souveraineté nationale* (Paris, 1912), pp. 18 ff.
2 Smend, *Verfassung und Verfassungsrecht*, p. 42.
3 Ibid., p. 43.
4 Kelsen, *Allgemeine Staatslehre*, pp. 38 ff.
5 Cf. e.g. Max Weber, *Wirtschaft und Gesellschaft*, p. 122.
6 Smend, *Verfassung und Verfassungsrecht*, p. 44.

gies with "marching troops" and "games and dances" turn into a scientific mystification as great as the famous biological analogies of the metaphysical-organic political theories.

Material integration is the third type of integration discussed by Smend. The first material integrating factors to present themselves are those communal values which the reigning political theory, in un-dialectical fashion, has dismissed from the definition of the state as mere "political goals." In opposition to this, Smend posits that the state is not a "real entity in itself" which is then employed as a means toward attaining ends outside itself: the state, rather, "is only real to the extent that it realizes meaning; it is identical with this realization of meaning." This holds for its goal of power as well as for its so-called juridical and cultural goals or ends: "only on the strength of this fullness of values does the state rule, that is to say, is the state an enduring, unifying, motivating coherence of experience for those belonging to it." Since the activity of the modern state has become incalculable in this regard, the historical and current value of the state is symbolically represented by flags, coats of arms, heads of state (especially monarchs), political ceremonies and national celebrations. It is especially in this way that the state's fullness of value can be experienced as a totality "with intensive and consciously integrating action."[1]

In this connection Smend again refers emphatically to Sorel's political myth and to fascist methods: "by political myth I mean, in the usage here proposed, integration formulated through symbols and thereby adapted to a fullness of political values experienced as an intensive totality"; and in line with Schmitt's political theology he even sees an affinity between "the integrating binding to the state and the religious binding to God."[2] Smend whole-heartedly agrees with Paul Yorck von Wartemburg's remark that the rationalization of constitutional thought, which excludes "taking any political values as faith values," at the same time "makes every politically binding value questionable."[3]

From all this we can see how the humanist personality ideal has withdrawn from the bulwark of rationalism's faith in reason to retreat into an irrationalist philosophy of life. Faith in the "natural order" has been converted into belief in a "political mythology."

In this context Smend finally deals with the integrating factors of territory and history. According to him, the territory of the state is perhaps the most important material factor for integration in the state community. For the purpose of understanding the reality of the state Smend as-

---

[1] Ibid., pp. 45, 47, 50.
[2] Ibid., p. 50, n. 2.
[3] Ibid., citing a letter by Yorck to Wilhelm Dilthey, dated 13 Jan. 1887.

signs a high value to the science of geopolitics, founded by Friedrich Ratzel. Understandably, he rejects the causal method of natural-scientific research.

State territory, then, must be seen in the first place as an integrating element of the political community insofar as it is an element of shared political fortunes, especially so when it imposes tasks for defense, reclamation, colonization, and so on.

The second integrating function of territory lies in the fact that the political domain is a cultural domain, the visible sum-total of the spiritual values held by a state and its people. To that extent it is usually qualified as "fatherland" or "homeland" (*Heimat*). For instance, during a time of war it represents in common speech and the world of emotions, more than anything else, the life and values of the political community. Just as the by-laws of an association formulate its purpose in its first paragraphs, so the constitution indicates the indefinable content of national life which it regulates, because it puts first and foremost the symbols of this content: "territory, colors and coat of arms, form of government and character of the state."[1] In this sense any changes in territory are not quantitative but qualitative changes in the essence of the state.

If we have followed Smend thus far in the exposition of his integration theory, the question forces itself upon us with increasing urgency: what *meaning* does our author really ascribe to the reality of the state? And what place does he give to the *jural* side in the meaning-structure of the state?

We have already seen how Smend sees the reality of the state as an ongoing integration of the nation into a sovereign "community of wills" on a given territory. Next, he assures us that the state's reality cannot be understood properly "unless it is taken as the unified operation of all integrating factors, which in conformity with the spirit's 'law-conformity of values' (*Wertgesetzlichkeit*) automatically work constantly toward a unified convergence."[2]

We learn, finally, that in the relation between functional and material integrating factors, the history of a state's political life shows that the material factors can crowd out the functional factors, and vice-versa. It also shows that in modern national life the functional factors especially play the main role as a result of the collapse of faith in the traditional values of the community. Furthermore, a situation of political integration, exclusively through integrating material content, can only be the object of a "no-state theory" or of a utopia, an indictment which is di-

---
1 Ibid., p. 56.
2 Ibid., p. 57.

rected against the classical liberal theory of the just state[1] as well as against the Marxist view of the state.[2]

However, what cannot be deduced from all this is the kind of meaning-structure that Smend ascribes to the state as a spiritual reality. No light is shed on that question until he begins to speak of the integrating significance of history. He writes in so many words:

> The qualitative meaning of political life is historical reality, [and] a true qualitative meaning, in contrast to an ideal one, is meaningful and understandable only when grounded in history and pointing to the future. Its totality is one of a historically flowing and concrete whole, not that of a theoretically frozen one.[3]

When we see this pronouncement in connection with the earlier one – that the spiritual power constitutes the integrative value of the state – the historicistic trait in Smend's view of reality becomes as clear as day. In our thetical exposition below, we shall see how "spiritual power" is indeed a real element of the historic meaning-function.

In the final analysis, the reality of the state as an organized community is again seen by Smend in a *meaning-functional* sense, namely *historically*.[4] But no matter how fundamental the historical meaning-function may be in the meaning-structure of the state, that meaning-structure can never be resolved on its subject-side into one specific meaning-function. A state's structure is fundamentally falsified when conceived in functionalist terms. By choosing its Archimedean point *in time*, however, the humanist view of reality is forced to deny the cosmic many-sidedness of reality and to reduce its meaning-functions, which are sov-

---

[1] The adherents of the Berlin School also agree that the liberal, rationalist view of the just state is most to blame for the crisis in political theory; cf. e.g. Heller, *Die Souveränität*, p. 73: "The crisis in the concept of sovereignty and state community, a concept that is based on the fictional and abstract representation of the state, is more deeply rooted in the general state of intellectual history than in Germany's political history. Whenever the monarchical principle is politically repudiated in favor of thinking in terms of liberal democracy – and especially then – it becomes apparent that the deeper roots of this crisis are found in liberalism's rationalistic notion of the just state . . ."
[2] Ibid., p. 61.
[3] Ibid., p. 53.
[4] Since the real historical function of reality, as we shall see later, can only be understood in subjection to *historical norms*, we need not be surprised that Smend regards "integration" not just as a dynamic reality, but also as a *normative* one, as a *mandate*, a *task*. To Kelsen, with his static and naturalistic view of reality, this is absurdity itself; see his *Der Staat als Integration*, pp. 58–59. This shows once again that a "neutral" critique is impossible.

ereign each in its own sphere, to one or more meaning-functional basic denominators.

In phenomenological dialectics this basic denominator is the historical one,[1] grasped in synthetic fashion, because its view of reality is essentially historicistic. And at bottom this view of reality is determined by the humanist personality ideal of the type of post-Kantian freedom idealism, which finds its only shelter for the subjective reality of human freedom vis-à-vis the determinism of nature in the historical function of reality.[2]

This meaning-functional manner of viewing the reality of the state in principle decides how Smend thinks about the relation between state and law.

The basic problem that has occupied humanist political theory since Jellinek concerns the relation between the so-called sociological concept of the state and the juridical one. From the humanist standpoint, which is responsible for the modern crisis in political theory, this problem could not be solved, not even by the dialectic of a phenomenological approach.

Smend sees state and law as two "inseparably connected yet enclosed (*in sich geschlossen*) provinces of spiritual life that serve the realization of a special idea of value."[3] This view sounds almost identical to that of Gierke, whose manner of reifying the state is so sharply rejected by Smend and to whose theory of organized communities we must return in our positive exposition below. Gierke sees the relation between state and law as follows:

> State and law are two independent and distinct sides of communal life. The state manifests itself in the powerful execution of desired common goals and culminates in political action; the law manifests itself in the demarcation of spheres of activity for the wills for which it is binding and culminates in the acknowledgment of right. . . . As different as are their social functions, state and law are dependent upon each other and find their fulfillment only through each other.[4]

The affinity between Smend and Gierke goes deeper than Smend himself is aware of. Beneath the surface of their methodological differences lies the historicist view of reality whose deepest root we discovered in

---

1 This is also the case in the thought of Martin Heidegger, *Sein und Zeit*, where the essence of *Dasein* is sought in what is *historical*.
2 Evident also in Heinrich Rickert, who tears the cosmos apart into *natural reality* and nonreal, timeless *values*, leaving no place for individual subjectivity except in *history* as a "realization of values."
3 Smend, *Verfassung und Verfassungsrecht*, p. 98.
4 Gierke, *Die Grundbegriffe des Staatsrechts und die neuesten Staatsrechtstheorien* (Tübingen, 1915), p. 105.

the humanist personality ideal in the post-Kantian type of the humanist freedom idealism. *To juxtapose state and law as two "enclosed" sides of spiritual life indicates a total lack of insight into the meaning-structure of reality.*

On the historicist standpoint, however, this impossible juxtaposition is understandable. After all, if the "real meaning-content" of all spiritual reality is of a historical nature, then law as to its subject-side is historical as well.[1] In that case, the state as a real communal unity of wills on the one hand, and the reality of law on the other, ultimately become specific sides of social-historical life, which one can *set side by side* as comparable entities, even while acknowledging an intimate bond between the two.

The juxtaposition is worked out in great detail by Smend. He sees the life of the state as "integration" and as an "ordering and formative unfolding of power." The reality of law is seen by him in "positive enactments, legal security and the administration of justice by means of law-making, the courts, and life itself." Just as the integrating factors in the life of the state, so in the world of law the great integrating factors of juridical life carry, complement and facilitate each other. And again, these factors form a system "which, by virtue of the spiritual law-conformity of values, likewise converges into a positive reality of the concrete legal life of the juridical community, similar to the way in which the integration factors converge into a system in the reality of the state – in both cases partly prescribed, partly encouraged, and partly allowed by written law."[2]

In this sense, legislation and the judiciary together form, as parts of the justice system under the constitution, the closed system of juridical functions, insofar as they are regulated by written law. For this very reason they are "in a certain sense," says Smend, "foreign elements" in the constitution:

> They belong to it because they too [!] are forms of political life. But after overcoming the medieval jurisdictional state [!] their center of gravity is no longer located here, that is to say, in its political quality.[3]

The judiciary as part of the *trias politica* (of course the un-dialectical, objectifying theory of the three powers is rejected by Smend) is, as

---
1 Thus also Heller, *Die Souveränität*, p. 47: "Law as an intersubjective normative binding of the will has *gegenständliche* objectivity; of course it does not display this as a sensory phenomenon of nature *but as a historically unique reality*." On the same page he states even more clearly: "[Positive] law always forms part of the individual nature of historical reality."
2 Smend, *Verfassung und Verfassungsrecht*, p. 98.
3 Ibid., p. 99.

Montesquieu remarked, indeed "in some ways worthless,"[1] that is, it does not serve the value of integration but of law.

> This value crosses state boundaries – hence the solidarity of single states in a confederation, just as the solidarity of "culture states" in juridical matters insofar as these are true juridical matters in distinction from executive and administrative matters. The judiciary should also integrate – but integrate the juridical community, not the state, *which in principle at least is another sphere*.[2]

This last sentence is most telling. As is evident from the entire design of his constitutional doctrine, forming its inner value, Smend is on the track of the basic structural difference between constitutional law and the integrating nature of public law, which we shall discuss later in the thetical part. Yet the view of reality from which he starts makes a proper meaning-analysis of this structural difference impossible. And so he arrives at his impossible juxtaposition of state and law as fundamentally different spheres of spiritual life.[3]

Smend detects a closer relationship with the state structure in legislation, since it occupies a central function in both the political and the juridical system, whereas jurisprudence presumably is only of marginal importance in the constitution. This is an incomprehensible distinction between legislative and judicial decisions, considering that jurisprudence too is not "uniform" but exhibits the same fundamental differences in structure as legislation, depending on whether or not it relates to the internal structure of the state. (Think of the basic difference between civil and administrative law!)

Finally, as for what "*the* juridical community" means in contrast with the state community, Smend leaves us altogether in the dark.

In this way the integration doctrine, with its distorted construction of the place of law in the structure of the state, collapses irretrievably under the razor-sharp critique of Kelsen. Nothing can counter Kelsen's critique as it reduces this political theory to an absurdity:

> In Smend's view of state and law as two "enclosed" spheres, it is an act of law, not an act of the state, when a court condemns an accused to death and carries out the sentence. On the other hand, it is an act of the state, not an act of law, when an administrative organ imposes a speed-

---

1 *General Editor's note*: Cf. Montesquieu, *The Spirit of the Laws* (1750), 11.6: "Of the three powers mentioned above [the legislative, the executive and the judiciary], the judiciary is in some ways "en quelque façon nulle."
2 Ibid.; emph. mine, H.D.
3 This explains why Kelsen directs his sharpest criticism at this vulnerable position; cf. *Der Staat als Integration*, p. 60. Of course all structural differences are eliminated in Kelsen's own "pure theory of law."

ing fine on the driver of an automobile in an administrative process differentiated according to specific cases. For according to Smend's treatise the administration once again belongs to the state system as determined by the integration value.[1]

The merit of Kelsen's *Allgemeine Staatslehre* is that it has demonstrated once for all the impossibility of any political theory that wants to gain a concept of the state apart from law. A historicist sociology, which seeks to grasp the state as an integral, sovereign organized community of power, independent of the legal order, must in spite of itself constantly appeal to the legal order, but in so doing it vitiates the meaning of both law and state. This sociology, even as one of the "human sciences," remains caught in the crisis of the humanist science ideal which, because of its functionalist orientation, cannot find a way to a genuine meaning-synthesis between the jural function and the remaining meaning-functions of the structure of the state.

Might and right are the two functional poles within the structure of the state. In his book *Die Idee der Staatsräson*, Meinecke has given us an insightful account of how the old antinomy between *raison d'état* and abstract natural law developed. This antinomy spelled the fiasco of every functionalist position in political theory which is no longer able to grasp these meaning-facets in their harmonious, meaning-individual coherence.[2]

Given its historicist attitude, the *geisteswissenschaftliche* concept of the power-state cannot but end up in the pole of *raison d'état* thinking, which Hegel adjusted in an idealist sense whereby the meaning of the jural, in the fashion of historicism, is absorbed into the meaning of spiritual power. No matter how impassionedly it proclaims the sanctity of "the idea of law" on the basis of the trans-personalist, idealist type of humanism's personality ideal, it has set this idea politically adrift on the waves of the historical unfolding of power. Erich Kaufmann's notorious formula for the idea of law – "The victorious war is the social ideal"[3] – is but a particularly crude and ominous accentuation of historicizing the meaning of law in politics.

The same conclusion, basically, is reached by Carl Schmitt. Schmitt sees the essence of the state as a sovereign and integral organized community of power, the meaning of which lies in the political integration

---

1 Ibid., p. 63, quoting Smend, *Verfassung und Verfassungsrecht*, p. 98.
2 Friedrich Meinecke, *Die Idee der Staatsräson in der neueren Geschichte* (Munich and Berlin, 1924). Eng. trans. *Machiavellism: The Doctrine of Raison d'État and Its Place in Modern History* (1957).
3 Erich Kaufmann, *Das Wesen des Völkerrechts und die Clausula Rebus sic stantibus* (Tübingen, 1911), p. 146.

of the nation in terms of its relation to friend and enemy (the sole criterion for politics, according to Schmitt!).[1] He also teaches that constitutional law ultimately derives its force of law from a political decision which preempts all jural norms and which is made by an existing political power. He writes:

> Every existing political unit has its value and the justification for its existence, not from whether its norms are correct or useful, but from its existence as such. Compared to this existential decision, all normative rules are secondary [!]. Also, all concepts used in jural norms that presuppose the political existence . . . receive their content and meaning not from a norm but from the concrete reality of an independent political existence.[2]

The historicist view of the meaning of state and law could not be demonstrated more clearly. Law has become a secondary form, by means of which the goddess of power writes the bloody decrees of history.

Herman Heller, most level-headed and keenest thinker of the Berlin School, may seemingly have broken the spell of historicism in his important distinction between "fundamentals of law" and "rules of law," and his grounding of all positive law in *legal principles*; he may have penned the fine words, "Transcendent norms and individual wills are equally the *sine qua non* of positive law";[3] yet his more-than-formal "jural-logical" principles and his "ethical fundamentals of law" at the end of the day turn out to be dependent exclusively on recognition by "cultural circles," while he expressly recognizes the possibility of violating these material principles by positive law. They are but "juridical possibilities" over against the reality of positive law, which as spiritual reality is subsumed under a historicistic basic denominator.[4] And Heller quotes with approval the ethical nominalist Hobbes:

---

1   See Schmitt, "Der Begriff des Politischen," *Politische Wissenschaft* 5 (1928): 1 ff. The following is another characteristic statement: "As a consequence of being prepared to face the possibility of a serious situation calling for effective war against an effective enemy, political unity is essential, either a unity that defines who are friends and who is the enemy, thus a unity that is in this (not in some absolute) sense sovereign, or there is no unity at all . . ." (ibid., p. 11).
2   Schmitt, *Verfassungslehre*, pp. 22 f.
3   Heller, *Die Souveränität*, p. 49.
4   In a similar sense Leibholz, *Das Wesen der Repräsentation*, p. 21 (ital. mine, H.D.): "The fact that the legal force of theoretical insights into the state may be limited in a temporal and spatial sense does not nullify their *a priori* character. Their spatial-temporal limitation merely indicates that these essential cognitions, whose obviousness was not lost, have not yet connected with *historical reality* in concretely observable shapes, or else that their connection has again been severed. 'What is es-

Theft, murder, adultery and all injuries are forbidden by the laws of nature, but *what* is to be called *theft, murder, adultery, injury* in a citizen is not to be determined by natural but by civil law.[1]

Already in my series of articles "In den Strijd om een Christelijke Staatkunde"[2] I showed that such a view of natural law issues directly into positivism.

Has the Berlin School succeeded in overcoming the crisis in humanist political theory? When we finally review its political theory as a whole we must answer resolutely in the negative.

No matter how much the school is right in combating the formalism and juridical monism of the norm-logical school of political theory, it remains itself in every respect in the thrall of the crisis between humanism's science ideal and personality ideal.

On the one hand, the dialectical method itself is no more than the hypertrophy, and, at the same time, the debacle of a functionalist manner of thinking, one that thoroughly falsifies the meaning-structure of reality and attempts to carry through the sovereignty of the personality ideal even at the price of sanctioning the antinomy. On the other hand, this school causes the personality ideal to end up in a full-fledged crisis of a trans-personalist historicism which, given the collapse of the rationalist faith in a natural order, must resort to an irrationalist philosophy of life which degrades political theory to "political mythology."

---

sential and what has existence' relate to one another as 'possibility and reality.' Therefore it is also possible for positive law to deviate from, or even completely ignore, the essential concepts that capture the essential cognitions." A similar account is found in the thought of the Husserlian phenomenologist Adolf Reinach in his work, "Die apriorischen Grundlagen des bürgerlichen Rechtes," *Jahrbuch für Philosophie und phänomenologische Forschung* 1 (1913): 685–847, at 813 ff. In a slightly different sense Fritz Schreier advances this idea in his work *Grundbegriffe und Grundformen des Rechts: Entwurf einer phänomenologisch begründeten formalen Rechts- und Staatslehre* (Leipzig, 1924), p. 92. Compare my criticism of this entire conception of an *a priori* phenomenological theory of law in my oration *De Beteekenis der Wetsidee*, pp. 95 ff. where I also have demonstrated (see p. 96) that this view contradicts Husserl's own view regarding the relationship between "essential" and "factual" disciplines; see Husserl, *Ideen zu einer reinen Phänomenologie*, 1:18.

1 Thomas Hobbes, *Elementa philosophica de cive* (Amsterdam, 1647) 6.16.
2 *Anti-revolutionaire Staatkunde* (quarterly) 1 (1927): 142–86. Eng. trans. *The Struggle for a Christian Politics*, pp. 232–77.

Part II

A Calvinist view of the state versus the crisis in humanist political theory

1. The meaning-structure of cosmic reality in light of the Calvinist idea of law and subject

We saw how behind the crisis in humanist political theory a view of reality and an epistemology are operating which are deeply rooted in the basic structure of the humanist worldview. We also noticed how the humanist view of reality shifts depending on the relation between the science ideal and the personality ideal in the various types of humanist ideas about law and subject. The epistemological concept of "experience" followed suit in this. It turned out to depend on the choice of Archimedean point in certain functions of our consciousness as they are interwoven in the cosmic order of time. Time and again this concept of experience turned out to be rooted in an absolutization of meaning-synthetic thought which elevates certain functions in reality to be the common denominator of all of empirical reality.

One should not suppose that the irrationalist "philosophy of life" would be an exception here. Bergson's "intuition" was to make us feel the "durée" (duration), the "stream of life," which would directly reveal to us the "essence of reality." However, this was essentially nothing but a reification of the psychical subject-function of consciousness, a function which we first abstract, by means of a laborious meaning-synthetical *psycho*-logical analysis, from the organic-cosmic coherence of full reality. Bergson's "metaphysics" as the science of what is "absolute" in reality, would have us *feel* reality instead of *representing* it. As a result, this only furnishes us with vague and confused "sensations" instead of clear concepts. Bergson writes:

> If metaphysics is possible, it cannot be anything but a *difficult and painful effort* by placing oneself directly, through a sort of intellectual expansion, into the matter which one studies, in order to progress from reality to concepts, not from concepts to reality.[1]

But, as already appears from his concept of time, the whole of Bergson's irrationalist metaphysics rests on reifying the (subjective and actual)

---

1 Henri Bergson, "Introduction à la métaphysique," *Revue de métaphysique et de morale* 11 (1903): 21–22 (emph. mine, H.D.).

sensory function of consciousness, which he has abstracted from full reality. And *this abstraction is only possible through meaning-synthetic thinking*, through theoretical thought which, as we shall see, consciously sets apart temporal reality by establishing an opposition within it. But it can never perform this abstraction through psychic feeling itself, which is direct and actual and which is certainly not capable of a "difficult and painful effort" in the sense demanded by Bergson.

To that extent all immanence philosophy, which necessarily has to bring reality under the sovereignty of meaning-synthetic thought, is primarily founded on a quasi masked reification of the logos. This holds equally for the rationalist and irrationalist view of reality.

The natural, naive and pre-theoretical picture of the world is now interpreted in accordance with this essentially functionalist attitude, and so is drastically falsified. Immanence philosophy usually interprets the naive attitude toward temporal reality according to the scheme of a so-called "copy theory" (*Abbildtheorie*), which holds that observation furnishes us with an "image," a type of "photograph" of real things.[1]

This is a theoretical falsification of the naive-realist attitude.[2]

The true nature of this attitude is rather that in its temporal functions our consciousness is not placed *in opposition* to reality as a copying or as a constructing agent, but is seen, rather, as an organic part *of* and *in* temporal reality. Wherever, and in whatever way, a dualism is accepted

---

1   See e.g. Paul Natorp, *Die logischen Grundlagen der exakten Wissenschaften*, 2nd ed. (1921), p. 8, where he fingers as the "basic error of naive realism" the notion "that entities are given to us by way of observation in a kind of *mirroring* of objects in our representation." Windelband, too, writes in his *Einleitung in die Philosophie*, 2nd ed. (1920), pp. 197–98: "This most common meaning of truth was no doubt first derived from naive empirical thought and there applied to the representation of things and their activities. This concept of truth presupposes that there exists a relation of *reflexibility* between human representation and reality, to which it ought to relate as its object. We have here perhaps the most complete expression of the naive view of the world which assumes that the representing mind is surrounded by a world that somehow ought to repeat itself within this mind . . ."

2   The naive experience of reality, too, has a *religious foundation*. We emphasize this in particular, in order to preclude from the outset the idea that cosmology, if not in theoretical thought then surely in what is considered to be *given* by "naive realism," possesses the basis for a genuinely neutral attitude. Our thesis, that there is no religiously neutral experience of reality, is the statement of a truth that will be conceded by every person who compares the pre-theoretical experience of reality of a simple Christian with that of a simple non-Christian. One can also phrase it as follows: With the apostate attitude of one's consciousness the human person no longer penetrates to his or her true transcendent selfhood. The apostate self-consciousness *clings* idolatrously to what is temporal; it is *dispersed* in the meaning-diversity of the cosmos and *lacks true concentration in the focal point of existence*: the service of God!

between "consciousness" and "reality," it is *not the naive view of reality that is speaking, but rather a philosophic theory*.

Humanistic epistemology begins by misinterpreting naive experience in accordance with its functionalist, meaning-synthetic starting-point and then looks down on this attitude with arrogant self-sufficiency. Typical in this context is Rickert's attitude toward "naive realism." It is true that he, a neo-Kantian, acknowledges that naive realism is not a scientific theory that can be *contested* scientifically. He also knows that therefore the "copy theory" does not belong in the naive experience of reality either. Yet he believes he does full justice to "naive realism" when he interprets it in such a way "that the components of the sensory world of space and time, familiar to us all, constitute the only reality," and he believes that the transcendental-idealist epistemology deviates from naive realism only to the extent that it adds to this position "that the being of all reality must be looked at as an immanent being, as a being within consciousness or as an object, to which necessarily belongs a conscious subject." And following this misinterpretation of the naive experience of reality Rickert feels warranted in appraising it as no more than "a complex of opinions which are vague and not thought through, and which suffice for life and may quietly be left to those who merely wish to live."[1]

Against this altogether arrogant and distorted representation of what naive realism stands for, I wish to posit an entirely different appraisal. Every attempt at interpreting the naive experience of reality in terms of the view that certain real functions of a physical-psychical nature make for full reality, is based on a functionalist misunderstanding of the *given* of naive experience. Naive, pre-theoretical experience is positioned in an *en-static, not synthetic* fashion within full reality with all its functions, which are woven together in the cosmic order of time, including both those of a natural and a spiritual nature. And this experience intuitively resists every attempt by absolutized synthetic thought to rob it of one or more meaning-sides of its reality.

One has only to try and interpret the naive experience of, say, a landscape, a painting or a table in the manner in which Rickert sees "naive realism," to realize at once that in so doing nothing whatsoever would remain of the naive experience of reality. Pre-theoretical experience raises an intuitive and irrepressible *protest* against any tearing apart of full organic reality into a temporal *phenomenon* and a timeless *noumenon*. That same "naive realism"[2] sees reality in the structure of individual things, whose meaning it does not, on principle, close off in

---

1 Rickert, *Der Gegenstand der Erkenntnis*, 3rd ed. (Tübingen, 1915), p. 119.
2 The label is actually misleading since it creates the impression that it refers to a "theory" of reality.

any one of the functions of reality. It knows no natural reality in and by itself, *an sich*, detached from the spiritual functions. *It does not yet distinguish the meaning-functions of things in meaning-synthetic knowledge*, but it has a *systatic and en-static* awareness of the meaning-coherence in reality. That is why it reacts negatively to removing any meaning-functions from that full meaningful temporal reality. The naive concept of a thing may still cling passively to its sensory appearance, but systatically it belongs, as the objective-logical meaning-function of the thing that is actualized by naive logical subjectivity, to the naive experience of reality, just as does the objective function of language.

Remark : From the outset the "copy theory" played its metaphysical role also in the view of language. Plato already observed a shortcoming in language symbols insofar as the "sign" is necessarily inadequate to the signified "idea." Leibniz, the father of the idea of universal signs for all domains of knowledge, misled by the same metaphysical theory, talked about a *cogitatio caeca* (blind reasoning) obtainable only through signifying symbols, as opposed to *adequate knowledge* that flows from immediate intellectual intuition.[1] The mistake in this essentially *metaphysical* line of thinking is that it views the linguistic sign as a kind of "copy" of the signified meaning. In other words, it fails to appreciate the *unique sovereign structure of the lingual function*. In light of our law-idea and subject-idea, lingual meaning, as "symbolical signification of meaning," is a sovereign meaning-function of full reality which can be reduced neither to the substrate of nature nor to the signified meaning-function. Mentally eliminate lingual meaning, and all meaning-functions that appear later in the cosmic order lose their meaning.[2]

As well, a scientific concept, in its meaning-synthetic nature, can only exist through the anticipated *hypothesis* of the lingual function. On the other hand, the mistake in the view here criticized lies in a view of the objective symbols detached from the actual lingual subjectivity. In its *objective* lingual function the *sign* does not exist in itself but is constantly dependent upon a normed *actualization* and *objectification* of lingual subjectivity. "Symbolic signification" as a spiritual subject-function is just as actual and direct a function as any other. Furthermore, with the exception of the first boundary sphere (that of number), objectification is necessarily found in all the law-spheres and is therefore not a defining feature merely of symbolical signification.

Like the psycho-sensitive side of reality, this naive concept of a thing is embedded in the full organic coherence of natural and spiritual functions of the cosmic order of time.

Naive experience sees reality as a world of things, whose reality is not exhausted in certain functions but rather participates in the organic totality of cosmic reality. Precisely because of this, it does not hesitate to assign also to so-called "natural things" sensory, logical and post-logical, normative properties; yet it remains conscious of the fact that there is a big difference between "dead" objects and animated things, between

---

1 Gottfried Wilhelm Leibniz, "Meditationes de cognitione, veritate et ideis," in *Philosophische Schriften*, ed. Gerhardt, 4:422 ff.
2 See also Ernst Cassirer, *Philosophie der symbolischen Formen* (Berlin, 1923), 1:51.

human beings and animals, and so on. That is also why naive realism unhesitatingly accepts spiritual realities such as a state, a church, a work of art, and so forth, in a *systatic thing-structure*. And it will never exchange this organic view of things for the absolutized, synthetic view, as is done by the so-called critical approach. That approach takes the reality of such spiritual things in purely functional terms and would even want to accuse naive experience of reifying such abstracted functions!

All attacks on the naive experience of things by functionalist epistemology (including phenomenological epistemology) are senseless. For the naive attitude accepts reality in the way it presents itself, and precisely as naive experience it is fully within its rights to do so. It is not the task of philosophy arbitrarily to reinterpret naive experience or to write it off, but rather to clarify it in deepened meaning-synthetic thought and to give an account of it (cf. the *logon didonai* of Platonism). Naive experience is not a *theory* which one can contest; it is a *given*, nay more, it is *the great datum* of all theoretical-philosophical reflection. A cosmology or epistemology that is unable to do justice to this given stands fundamentally condemned. But what has humanist epistemology in all its varieties done? Cosmologically, it has committed the mortal sin of accepting as *given* the very thing that should have been its greatest *problem*, namely, to account for the functions of consciousness which we can isolate only by means of meaning-synthetical abstraction from the fullness of reality. *After all, nothing is given us in a meaning-functional synthetic way.*[1] What is given to us is but the cosmic meaning-systatic coherence of reality, in which our temporal functions of consciousness are organically interwoven with all other meaning-functions of reality. Kant teaches that the only *given* in the "Gegenstand" are *Empfindungen* (the as yet unorganized sensory matter of experience) and that everything in the representation of a thing which transcends the impressions ordered by the transcendental-psychic forms of intuition is the product of an interfunctional transcendental synthesis. All this implies that the naive concept of a thing, too, is taken to be the product of synthetic *oppositional* thinking, in the sense of thinking *that sets apart* or *separates*. For however much Kant's epistemology was primarily intended to track down the transcendental conditions for natu-

---

1 Cf. e.g. Kant, *Prolegomena to Any Future Metaphysics*, Preamble 1.4, where he writes: "In the *Critique of Pure Reason* I have treated this question ["Is metaphysics at all possible?"] synthetically, by making inquiries into pure reason itself and endeavouring to determine the elements as well as the laws of its pure use according to its principles. This is a difficult task which requires a determined reader to penetrate gradually into a system *which is based on no data except reason itself* and which therefore seeks, without relying on any fact, to develop knowledge from its original germs" (emph. mine, H.D.).

ral-scientific thought, his discourse claims to be valid for *all* experience, and therefore also for *pre*-theoretic experience.

As we saw above, from the outset Kant, in line with the tradition of immanence philosophy's metaphysics, limited the pillars for our knowledge to the psychic and logical functions of our consciousness. Once he adopted these functions as *given*, he used this pseudo-given to put the following question to epistemology: "How are 'synthetic judgments a priori' possible?"

What Kant could not see from his functionalist, immanence standpoint was this, that the psychic and logical functions of consciousness themselves can be isolated from the temporal systatic coherence of cosmic reality only by means of a meaning-synthetical cognitive act. Thus this epistemology, borne of a false "metaphysics," became the entryway for humanist philosophy, even before one had accounted for the cosmological problem of meaning that is *pre*-supposed in the synthetic isolation of certain functions of consciousness.

Obviously, from the immanence standpoint the primary synthesis, in which this standpoint itself is grounded, could not possibly become *the problem to be accounted for. For this synthesis is already contained in the a priori ideas of law and subject of immanence philosophy*.

This dogmatic bias of all humanist epistemology is ultimately based on a worldview. And it has found its succinct expression in the functionalist "law of consciousness" (*Satz des Bewusstseins*) or "law of immanence" (*Satz der Immanenz*), according to which the *given* is limited to functional contents of consciousness. This is a thesis that even convinced critical realists such as Alois Riehl and Oswald Külpe cling to as a dogma.

In opposition to this dogmatic position of epistemology, which falsifies the *given* in accordance with the bias of the immanence standpoint, we must state first of all that the *given* is never that which results from an act of *synthetic binding*, since it is already *bound systatically*.

In naive, pre-theoretical experience we apprehend reality in the full systasis of its meaning-functions, which as such display an organic, unbreakable coherence. The problem of knowledge arises only in the attitude of deepened, oppositional (*tegenoverstellend*) thought, which, through a synthetic abstraction from full reality, turns the non-logical meaning-functions into a *problem*. Thus the basic question of epistemology should not be: How is objectively valid knowledge of the *Gegenstand* possible? but rather: How is the primary synthesis possible *which first gives rise to the problem of what is put in opposition*? In other words: How does synthesis relate to systasis?

From the immanence standpoint, systasis has to be reinterpreted as synthesis, even when a serious attempt is being made to ground the problem of knowledge ontologically, as in modern critical ontology. For, so long as one keeps looking for one's Archimedean point in the temporal functions of consciousness, one is forced, in one's ontological quest, to assume a common denominator for temporal reality which is itself derived from synthetic thought (a case in point is the abstract concept of *being*). And one can only note that philosophic thought by itself has never succeeded in overcoming this immanence standpoint.

Greek idealist metaphysics, with its reification of ideas, is the conclusive proof of the thesis that apostate human consciousness, as it attempts by its own means to climb up to what is eternal, supra-temporal and divine, necessarily begins to look for the eternal *within* time. The reification of ideas, which absolutizes the *noumenon*, was rooted in the reification of the *nous*, the absolutization and deification of the functions of human reason. *The God of this pagan metaphysics was apostate philosophy's pseudo-god, its idol.*

It was the fall of Christian philosophic thought, starting with the patristics, that failed to see clearly through this state of affairs. Time and again it strove for compromises with this idolatrous philosophy. The Christian religion had revealed a truth which once and for all had placed the Christian worldview in an unbridgeable antithesis over against all philosophy from the immanence standpoint. This truth was that the supra-temporal creational unity of temporal reality is not located in the *nous* – not in the immanent functions of reason or consciousness – but in the religious root of the human race in its creational relation to the sovereign will of the Creator God and its subjection to the eternal meaning of the divine order of creation: namely, to serve by glorifying His Name. Christianity had taught that this religious root of our temporal creation was corrupted by the fall into sin and restored again by Christ's meritorious death on the cross – that in Christ, therefore, as the Head of the reborn human race, is found the supra-temporal religious fullness of all temporal reality. The Christian religion had taught mankind that all temporal activity of the human race that does not issue from this sinless religious root is idolatry. It had learned not to ground any activity in this world "by itself" (*an sich*) as neutral, apart from that root.

In this way Christian thought possessed the key to a genuinely Christian philosophy. And yet, from the very first, in its views of reality, individuality and knowledge, we see Christian philosophy resorting again to Platonism, Aristotelianism, Stoicism, and so on, and in modern times to the standard-bearers of humanist immanence philosophy,[1] with the result that internal conflicts and antinomies constantly arise between Christian faith and Christian-pagan thought, and that Christian philosophy has given birth to a veritable family tree of heresies.

To this day I have not been able to explain this decline and fall of Christian thinking. Could one not see that every attempt at giving independence to the *naturalis ratio* – to natural reason, to "knowledge of the flesh" as the apostle Paul characteristically called it (Col. 2:18) – in essence amounted to apostasy in the face of God's sovereignty and His awesome revelation in Christ Jesus?

How could anyone believe, like Thomas Aquinas, that in keeping with the maxim *"Gratia naturam non tollit sed perficit"*[2] the Christian doctrine of grace would peacefully allow itself to be placed as a capstone on a purely idolatrous and pagan foundation? If Christians confess that all temporal theoretical truth is merely the temporal refraction of the absolute, supra-temporal truth regarding the relationship between Creator and creation as revealed to us in Christ, how then can Christian thought adopt from immanence philosophy the neutrality postulate for theoretic thought? But in the present context I shall not ponder this question any further.

Here I merely start by establishing that the Archimedean point of a Christian philosophy, the absolute point from which it wants to show us the origin, unity and coherence of meaning in all temporal reality, cannot be provided by philosophy itself. It can only be found in the absolute *religious a priori necessary for every philosophy*.

Immanence philosophy too has its religious *a priori* in this sense. On the humanist standpoint it is located in the idolatrous personality ideal, which also determines its entire philosophical position in the way it conceives of science.

Consistent with Calvin's own intentions, a Calvinist cosmology and epistemology cannot aspire to be anything else but a strict application of the Christian starting-point in all philosophic thinking, guided by God's Word and averse to all compromise with immanence philosophy. This starting-point guarantees a harmonious insight into the unity of our tem-

---

1 Most telling in this connection is the altered attitude of Calvin in opposition to the philosophy of antiquity. Whereas in medieval scholasticism mention is made repeatedly of the "divine Plato and Aristotle,"when Calvin mentions Plato, the philosopher for whom he has (relatively speaking) the most sympathy, he refers to him as "le pauvre payen"; see also his assessments in the *Institutes* 1.5.5.5, 1.8.1.9 and 1.15.6.7 (about Aristotle); 1.16.8 (Stoicism); 3.8.9 ("Christian Stoics"); 1.15.11 (apostate philosophy in general); 1.13.1, 2.1.1 and 2.2.3 (the false view of self-consciousness), etc. etc. Surely this should give one pause!

2 "Grace does not cancel nature but perfects it."

poral cosmos, directed toward its meaning-totality. By no longer choosing our Archimedean point for philosophic thought *within* the cosmic order of time, we are able to do full justice to the many-sided meaning of the order of time, to the many-sided interwovenness within this time-order, and so to the many-sided meaning and cosmic meaning-coherence of temporal reality.

Our Archimedean point determines our *self-consciousness* (the crux of all humanist epistemology) and makes us see temporal reality as an exceedingly differentiated refraction of the religious fullness of meaning of our cosmos via the prism of cosmic time, which time we *transcend* in the religious root of our self-consciousness, in our supra-temporal selfhood, but in which we at the same time dwell *immanently* with all our temporal consciousness and other cosmic functions.

The common denominator with which we grasp the deeper unity and coherence of all meaning-functions, which are refracted in cosmic time, is the religious supra-temporal fullness of meaning. This is not a synthetic abstraction of thought, but the concrete consummation of temporal reality itself. For this reason not a single meaning-side of temporal reality is brought under the denominator of another one.

Since we see the *sovereignty of God* as the only absolute sovereignty, therefore the key to our cosmology and epistemology, the basic principle of our philosophy, is found in the principle of *meaning-sovereignty within its own sphere*.

We now see this temporal reality as a religiously grounded, unbreakable cosmic coherence of sovereign meaning-spheres. Each sphere is delimited by means of a meaning-structure which cannot be reduced to any other meaning-function. Within each meaning-sphere a specific meaning-side of reality is, as subject-function, *subjected* (*sujet*) to a meaning-functional law-conformity.[1] In this sense each meaning-sphere is a law-sphere, which is interwoven with all other law-spheres into an unbreakable meaning-coherence by the cosmic order of time.

Thus this cosmology is rooted in a truly harmonious *idea of law and subject*, which in principle answers the question regarding the deepest origin, mutual relation, and coherence of all temporal meaning-sides of reality, both according to its law-side and its subject-side. From this

---

1 *General Editor's note*: Throughout his philosophical development Dooyeweerd never abandoned the position he took in respect of *wet* and *wetmatigheid* (law and law-conformity). He continued to treat "law" and "law-conformity" as being identical, without taking into account that law-conformity is not a property of the law but represents the *universal side* of *factual* reality. Only that which is subject to a law can function in *conformity* with it. Dooyeweerd thus actually denied the existence of universality at the factual side of reality, which explains his consistent reference to the *individual* subject-side.

standpoint, meaning is no longer a merely subjective realization of timeless, ideal values in a temporal reality of nature (thus Rickert). No more is meaning the product of a subjective assignment of meaning through an absolutized phenomenological I (thus Husserl and with him the entire school of phenomenology).[1] Meaning is not limited to the spiritual functions of reality, but *all of reality*, from top to bottom, is *meaning*, and it issues from the religious fullness of meaning. The natural sides of reality, too, are functional meaning-sides; they are refractions of the religious fullness of meaning in the root of the human race. The cosmic coherence between the law-spheres, as given in the cosmic order of time, reveals itself primarily in a cosmic order, by dint of which the law-spheres "found" (are a foundation for) each other according to the structure of their general meaning.

The numerical sphere of discrete quantity serves as the foundation of the spatial sphere of continuous, dimensional extension. The latter founds the kinematic sphere that lies at the foundation of the biotic sphere. This sphere forms the foundation of the sensory function of consciousness, which provides the foundation for the analytical sphere of logical thinking. The analytical sphere lies at the foundation of the historical sphere of cultural development, which in turn founds the lingual sphere of symbolical signification. That sphere is the basis for the social sphere of sociation and interaction, which itself is the basis for the economic sphere of the frugal balancing of values. The economic sphere in turn founds the aesthetic sphere of beautiful harmony, which founds the jural sphere of retribution. The jural sphere lies at the basis of the moral sphere of the disposition of love, which lies at the basis of the temporal sphere of faith.

In the general structure of meaning, which is the single defining criterion of every law-sphere, the coherence in cosmic time with all the other general meaning-structures is reflected in a specific *law-conforming structure*. Such a general meaning-structure possesses a meaning-nucleus which guarantees the sovereignty within its own domain of the law-sphere concerned. Inseparably connected with this, this nucleus guarantees the meaning-moments that are qualified by this core as *analogies* (or *retrocipations*) which point back to the meaning of (cosmically) *earlier spheres* (substrate spheres), or as *anticipations* which point forward to the meaning of (cosmically) *later spheres* (anticipated

---

[1] That this "phenomenologically purified" "pure I" is a meaning-functional reification appears from the essentially functionalist method of the *epochè* or "suspension of judgment" which in Husserl leaves only the "pure cogito" as Archimedean point. In the case of the phenomenologists of the school of Dilthey, the Archimedean point is obtained through the phenomenological *epochè*, in other words through the meaning-synthetically fixated, actual subjective psychic function of experience!

spheres).[1] For example, in the meaning-moment of dimensionality within the general structure of space we already find an analogy of number, while this analogy is nevertheless sovereignly qualified by the core meaning of space (continuous extension). Conversely, in the "infinite" function of number we find an anticipation of spatial continuity, which anticipation nevertheless bears a numerical meaning. "Projective geometry" has discovered the meaning-anticipations of space upon motion, and biochemistry has discovered the meaning-anticipations of the physical-chemical function to the biotic function, and so on and so forth.

Only the two terminal functions of our temporal cosmos, namely that of number and the most complex function, that of the temporal function of faith, deviate from this cosmic structure to the extent that the general structure of the first points to no analogies and the last points to no anticipations. (Faith is the open window to eternity.)

The anticipatory functions deepen the general structure of a law-sphere by *approximating* the meaning of the cosmically later spheres; in the final analysis they point forward to the religious fullness of meaning, of which all temporal meaning-spheres are merely *refractions*.

In synthetic thinking, which we shall discuss later, we may thus obtain a *concept* and an *idea* of the general meaning of each law-sphere. The *concept* grasps the meaning-structure in a "restrictive function," that is to say, in a meaning which is not yet deepened, not yet *disclosed*, in the systatic coherence of its *nucleus* and its *analogies*. The *idea*, on the other hand, grasps the structure of meaning in an "expansive" or "deepened" function in the disclosing of its "anticipatory" spheres. The *idea* of a functional meaning always points to the totality of meaning, which in the final analysis is never actual *in time*, but only in the supra-temporal, religious fullness of meaning in Christ.

When we thus grasp the structure of a functional meaning, say of the spatial, the lingual, or the jural, then it must be obvious that a "pure" meaning-structure does not exist, and also cannot be grasped in a meaningful concept that yields knowledge. To postulate such "purity" for concept-formation would involve the impossible task of understanding the meaning of a law-sphere "by itself," outside of its cosmic-temporal

---

1 *General Editor's note*: Dooyeweerd views *time* as an encompassing dimension of reality, guaranteeing an order of succession (earlier and later) between the different aspects. Initially he called references to modally earlier aspects *analogies* and references to modally later aspects *anticipations*. Eventually he simplified this distinction and used the term *analogy* to encompass both these "inter-modal moments of meaning-coherence" – implying that we have to distinguish between *retrocipatory analogies* and *anticipatory analogies* (cf. *A New Critique of Theoretical Thought*, 2:75).

coherence with the other law-spheres. But the structure of any law-sphere, including that of the logical sphere itself, is meaning only *within the cosmic coherence of meaning*. With its analogical and anticipating functions it is itself rooted in that coherence of meaning; it would lose its meaning as soon as its connection with the other law-spheres were mentally severed.

Not a single special science has managed to furnish real knowledge of a law-sphere by attempting to grasp that law-sphere "purely" in thought, detached from the spheres founding it. That holds first of all for mathematical physics! This science, as the science of the physical meaning-function of reality, was only born after the cosmic coherence between the law-spheres of number, space and motion was discovered. And all physical concepts grasp the physical functions in an inseparable coherence with the mathematical ones. The meaning-structure of every law-sphere reflects the totality of meaning within its own sphere. Sphere-sovereignty finds its mirror image in the *universality* of each law-sphere, each after its kind.

The entire criticistic postulate of a "pure theory of law," a "pure logic," a "pure sociology," and so on, stems from the epistemology of Kant with its self-contradictory form-matter scheme. With that, we return to this epistemology.

We already saw that humanist epistemology, because of its functionalist approach, is unable to account for the primary meaning-synthesis of thought, which it takes as the "given" from which to proceed. Recall that all thought that yields knowledge is based on an interfunctional meaning-synthesis between the analytical function of thought and the non-logical meaning-functions to be investigated. But once a meaning-synthetic standpoint is absolutized, it is impossible to answer the question, How is this interfunctional synthesis possible? By the very standpoint of immanence philosophy, the basic problem of *cosmological self-consciousness*, which as a supra-functional agent accomplishes the meaning-synthesis, is functionally falsified. Obviously this also happened when Descartes reified the thought function into a thing-substance, a "res cogitans."

In the final analysis Kant, too, understood self-consciousness in a logical-functional sense. As a transcendental condition of all categories of understanding Kant assumed a primary synthetic form of the understanding when he remarked:

> Only because I can understand the multiplicity of them (*scil.* of the representations) in a consciousness, do I call them altogether *my* conceptions, for otherwise I would have such a multicolored, multiple self as I have representations of which I am conscious. Synthetic unity of the

multiple intuitions, given *a priori*, is therefore the basis for the identity of apperception itself, which precedes all *my* specific thinking. However, this connection is not located in the objects and cannot somehow be derived from them through perception and so be absorbed in the understanding. Instead, this connection is solely an accomplishment of the understanding, which is no more than the capacity to connect *a priori*, and to bring the multiplicity of the given [!] representations under the unity of apperception, whose basic proposition is the highest in all of human knowledge.[1]

This *purely functional* understanding of self-consciousness contains in a nutshell the entire internal antinomy of this *critical* theory of knowledge. Self-consciousness necessarily bears at once a time-transcending and a time-immanent character. The deeper identity, which is experienced in the *selfhood*, is a trans-functional one; it is the experience of *knowing to be one and the same* in and above all cosmic meaning-functions, and *having an awareness of the temporal meaning-functions as one's own*.

If the experience of identity in self-consciousness were purely a logical-functional one, as Kant *had to* assume by virtue of his starting-point, the common denominator for comparing the meaning-functions would also have to be merely logical-functional in nature. The *self* would then itself be logical-functional and would have to fend off all non-logical functions of reality, including the psychical one, as *not-its-own*, not belonging to the *self*.

Obviously, with that the possibility of synthetic knowledge would have been cut off; in other words, once a functional apparatus for knowing is declared to be "*an sich*," to be independent, epistemology dissolves.[2]

Kant may have thought that the transcendental unity of self-consciousness as a basic logical function, as the *basic form* of understanding, was of necessity *related to* the multiplicity of intuited impressions, just as he conceived of the categories *as related to the* object of experience, yet by itself this relation was not yet a *meaning-synthesis* but simply a *problem* in need of cosmological elucidation, a problem which Kant formulated in a most uncritical manner.

As is well known, Kant addressed the problem of how a synthesis between the transcendental-logical forms of thought and psychic phenom-

---
1 Immanuel Kant, *Kritik der reinen Vernunft*, ed. Wilhelm Ernst, 3:125.
2 In his own way Richard Kroner has come to this insight as well; see his *Von Kant bis Hegel* (1921), 1:85. He formulates this antinomy as follows: "If the I is understood solely as a unity in opposition to multiplicity (as understanding in opposition to intuition, as thinking in opposition to knowing), then it can never be known synthetically; gone, then, is the possibility of experience."

ena is possible in his *Transcendental Doctrine of Judgment*. And he tried to solve the problem with his theory about the *transcendental schema of the concepts of understanding*. But this "solution" rested on an obvious *petitio principii*. Kant formulated the problem as follows: How is a synthesis between purely mental concepts and (psychic) phenomena possible? And his answer was: By means of the *schema*, as an *a priori* (interfunctional) synthesis of the category and the psychic form of intuition called *time*. However, in this transcendental schema the interfunctional synthesis has already been completed, albeit in an *a priori* sense. To the question, How is *this* interfunctional synthesis possible? we get no answer at all. In other words, Kant explained the possibility of the interfunctional synthesis between understanding and sensibility by means of the interfunctional synthesis, accomplished in the *a priori* schematized category. Which means that he begged the question.

Kant does try to make the possibility of this synthesis plausible by pointing at the "similarity" of time (as a psychic form of intuition), on the one hand with the mental category insofar as both are *general* (!) and rest on an *a priori* rule, on the other hand with the sensory appearance insofar as time is contained in every empirical representation. However, in a discourse which is intended to be critical and which starts from a fundamental difference between the psychic and logical "pillars of knowledge," this "similarity" (the equivocal term serves to overcome the gap in the argument) is just not adequate for clarifying how the interfunctional synthesis is possible.

Kant sensed that beyond the logical category and the psychic phenomenon a *third factor* is needed in order to make the interfunctional synthesis between the two possible. But in his train of thought *time* is not *a third* something, since it is already contained in the empirical representation. Kant knows time only in the functionalist sense of a psychic form of intuition. The multiform *cosmic order of time*, in which all meaning-functions are mutually interwoven organically and which has its own *function of time in every law-sphere*, each of which is qualified by the sphere-sovereign meaning-structure of the law-sphere concerned, is altogether unknown to Kant. *And yet, the cosmological problem of time is the core of both the problem of reality and the problem of the possibility of knowledge.*

According to Kant the interfunctional synthesis between the logical category and the psychic form of intuition is performed by the "transcendental imagination." In his important study *Kant und das Problem der Metaphysik* (1929), Heidegger has attempted to prove, using the first edition of the *Critique of Pure Reason*, that this transcendental imagination used by Kant was originally meant as the common root of thinking and intuiting. In doing this Heidegger raises a problem that Fichte had indeed raised first. Yet in the context of Kant's epistemological position this interpretation is unacceptable. It interprets Kant in the sense of Heidegger's own metaphysics of being and time.[1] For that matter, Heidegger himself admits that in the second edition of Kant's *Critique* the transcendental imagination has been absorbed completely into the logical function of understanding.

Kant calls this imagination the "synthetic influence of understanding upon the inner sense,"[2] and everyone senses that the word "influence" obscures the problem of synthesis. According to Kant the "inner sense" (the psychic-sensitive function of consciousness) is affected by the transcendental synthesis of the imagination. But that is exactly where the problem lies!

Thus, on the one hand the possibility of the interfunctional synthesis cannot be clarified by Kant, while on the other hand as well, the entire scheme of form and matter is self-contradictory. Kant conceived of the categories as *pure forms of thought*. These forms were to demonstrate the sovereignty of the epistemological subject as law-giver of nature (the postulate of the science ideal). But insofar as they seek to provide natural-scientific "knowledge" there is no way they can be "pure" since they must themselves contain an interfunctional meaning-synthesis between the logic-analytical meaning and the mathematically founded physical meaning. And even to the extent that one would want to take them *logically*, they bring to expression analogical meaning-moments in the analytical meaning-structure which cannot even reveal their logical meaning outside of their connection with the mathematical and physical meaning-structures. Thus, the logical unity, multiplicity and totality in

---

1 In my book *De Wijsbegeerte der Wetsidee* I shall elaborate my rejection of Heidegger's interpretation of Kant extensively with reference to the first edition of the *Critique of Pure Reason*. In connection with the present brief and schematic account of my epistemology and cosmology I have to refer throughout to this [not yet published] book for a more detailed and elaborate explanation. [Cf. *A New Critique of Theoretical Thought*, 2:492–536.] Heidegger's interpretation is also questioned by Cassirer in his article "Kant und das Problem der Metaphysik," *Kant-Studien* 36 (1931): 1–16. Heidegger's metaphysics of time, which locates time in the *being* of "Dasein," in the essence of the transcendent selfhood of our consciousness, at bottom rests on the same phenomenological-functionalist attitude towards reality that we found in Theodor Litt. The many-sidedness of the cosmic order of time can never be understood in this way. Heidegger's view of time is essentially historical-phenomenological in nature. The extent to which it is rooted in the humanist personality ideal appears prominently from his treatise *Vom Wesen des Grundes* (1929), esp. pp. 31 ff.: "Freiheit allein kann dem Dasein eine Welt walten und welten lassen." (Only through freedom can human existence realize and dispose of a world.)

2 *Kritik der reinen Vernunft*, 3:128.

its *logical sense* cannot exist outside of the meaning-substrate of number, and likewise the logical "substance" in the sense of constancy in the movement of thought cannot exist outside of the meaning-substrate of physical motion; and so on, and so forth.

However, Kant is wedded to the dogmatic bias that our knowledge has only two functional pillars and for that reason he can acknowledge at most only *one* type of interfunctional meaning-synthesis. He conceives of the categories as *merely logical functional syntheses*[1] of a multiplicity in psychic intuition. By themselves they remain *logical* forms which merely bear a *relation* to psychic sensibility, a relation which Kant cannot clarify: only in its synthesis with *time* as a transcendental form of intuition can it be of an interfunctional nature.

And what is the "material" of experience in Kant? By itself it is undetermined, according to him. But this "material" is nothing but the psychical objectification, based upon its physical analogies, of the physical function, which as a *psychical* object is qualified by the meaning-nucleus of the sensory function and is governed by psychical law-conformity.

However, although physics as natural-scientific *thought* cannot break the bond with its psychic substrate (experiments must continue to be oriented to sensory observation!), its intention is *not* to grasp what is objective-psychical, but to understand the *physical* meaning-functions. That is also why Kant's concepts of time and space, which in essence are understood in an objective, psychological fashion, are not useful in physics, as the *modern theory of relativity* has demonstrated. In other words, the form-matter scheme is completely devoid of any insight into the cosmic meaning-structure of the law-spheres and is self-contradictory insofar as it attempts to bring "*psychic* sensitivity" under a "categorical legislation" which, although " purely logical," is supposed to be

---

1 Kant's entire contrast between a *formal* and a *transcendental logic* is essentially unclear because he does not sufficiently distinguish between the merely logical synthesis (in the sense of the logical combination of an analytical multiplicity of conceptual elements) and the *knowledge-yielding interfunctional* meaning-synthesis.

   General Editor's note: It is clear that by1931 Dooyeweerd had already arrived at his epistemological view of the *Gegenstand*-relation and at the idea that this theoretical opposition of the logical and the non-logical functions requires an interfunctional meaning-synthesis in order to arrive at knowledge of the "Gegenstand." This position eventually prompted Dooyeweerd to develop his transcendental critique of theoretical thought. For an in-depth analysis of the problems entailed in this transcendental critique, see D. F. M. Strauss, "An Analysis of the Structure of Analysis – The Gegenstand relation in discussion," *Philosophia Reformata* 49 (1984): 35–56.

the "form" of all *physical* law-conformity!¹ A cosmological confusion of meaning-structures reigns here, which essentially and basically falsifies the problem of knowledge.

One need not wonder what kind of chaos will arise in cosmology when this form-matter scheme is transposed – against Kant's intention, to be sure – to the area of the normative sciences. This occurs for instance when, in the manner of Stammler, socio-economic life (!) is promoted to becoming material for a *jural form*, which is purported to be purely logical!

The entire form-matter scheme is not born from a truly *critical* cosmological investigation, but from the dogmatic bias of the humanist law-idea with its two mutually antinomic factors of the science ideal and the personality ideal.

It is well to speak plainly for once, in view of the arrogant attitude of criticistic epistemology when facing naive experience, which it simply does not understand in its meaning and essence.

In the present context I do not wish to elaborate any further on the hypertrophy of the so-called transcendental critique of knowledge in the Marburg School (to which Kelsen's "pure law theory" is oriented). With its rationalism this epistemology wants to expunge the last trace of *synthesis* still retained by Kant in his scheme of the concepts of understanding and claims to grasp the epistemological synthesis "purely logically." An epistemology that thrusts aside the entire cosmic law-order by means of the dogmatic bias of the sovereignty of the *nous* as law-giver cannot lay claim to the honorary title of "critical" theory.

It was Fichte who introduced a dialectics into philosophical thinking, and behind it we saw the operation of the continuity postulate of the humanist personality ideal. However, all that this dialectics has achieved is to smuggle the scepter of the cosmic law-order into the hands of the kind of thinking found within the so-called "human sciences." It has laid the totality of self-consciousness in the absolutized moral function. The continual transgression of the boundaries of meaning by dialectical thinking can only be carried out by sanctioning the antinomy. And it is justified with the thesis that the *nous* itself has established all boundaries of meaning, so that this *nous* can also sovereignly transgress them.

Dialectical phenomenology, with which we made our acquaintance in the sociology of Litt, believes that it acquires an adequate understanding of spiritual life itself by means of its dialectics! From its lofty height it looks down on the naive experience of things in human society, and be-

---

1 *General Editor's note*: As pointed out earlier, Dooyeweerd here self-consistently equates *law* ("wet") and *law-conformity* ("wetmatigheid").

lieves that it can consider the naive view of organized communities as "structural entities" to be the product of a natural-scientific, objectifying, spatial way of thinking. As if the naive concept of a thing is based on meaning-synthetic thinking!

What is *meaning-synthetic thinking* in the light of the cosmic meaning-coherence of reality? It is nothing other than the anticipatory *deepening* – the unfolding of the meaning – of naive, syn-systatic thought which still clings to its connection with psychic sensibility. And this deepening is always *guided* by the meaning of historical development. The meaning-synthesis is founded in the meaning-systasis, and not the other way around! In meaning-synthetic thought the deepened analytical function of consciousness liberates itself from being *simply embedded* within full temporal reality; it *places itself in opposition* to the non-logical meaning-functions that demand to be known; it becomes "*gegenständlich.*"

This Gegenstand, this thing that is placed in opposition – this problem of knowledge – cannot be cosmic reality itself. For our analytic function of thought is itself systatically interwoven *within* that reality, and remains so in its deepened, theoretical activity.

The "*Gegenstand* of knowledge" arises only through a conscious *setting apart* of systatic reality, through performing an *analytic epochè with respect to the continuity of the cosmic order of time*, whereby the non-logical meaning-structures are fixated in logical discontinuity. That this deepening of systatic, naive thinking must take place by way of "being placed in opposition" can be explained from the analytic structure of the logical meaning-function itself. Only through an act of logical discrimination can the analytic meaning-structure reveal its universality in its own sphere!

The possibility of a meaning-synthesis can only be clarified in terms of the view we indicated earlier concerning the structure of self-consciousness. Self-consciousness *transcends cosmic time* insofar as the individual selfhood participates in the religious root of the human race, of whose fullness of meaning all temporal meaning-functions (both natural and spiritual) are only refractions of meaning in time.[1] The selfhood is *immanent in cosmic time* insofar as our functions of consciousness are interwoven in the cosmic order of time. The non-logical meaning-functions are not *foreign* to our self-consciousness. Together they are all

---

1 Therefore, as Calvin so clearly shows in his beautiful first chapter of his *Institutes*: all true self-knowledge, and with it all true knowledge of the world, is dependent upon the *knowledge of God*. The depths of wisdom found here are inaccessible to immanence philosophy.

proper to ourselves. Only because of this can we get to know them in their law-conformity.

Systatic cosmic self-consciousness is still only embedded with naive awareness in the meaning-coherence of the functions of reality.

Synthetic cosmological self-consciousness, which performs the *meaning-synthesis*, reveals itself in this opposing way of thinking. In the *deepened intuition* the cosmological self-consciousness observes the coherence of meaning in logically articulated discontinuity. (This deepened observation is a deepening of the purely "experiencing" intuition, by means of which our logical thinking submerges itself in the continuity of the meaning-boundaries that are at once fixed and overarched by the cosmic order of time). In this fashion the meaning-functions, which are articulated within the meaning-coherence, move apart and thus can become the "Gegenstand" of the meaning-synthetic and opposing manner of thinking. Every meaning-function as a function in the meaning-coherence is more than *merely* functional. *This "more" results from the continuity of the order of time, which overarches and pervades all boundaries of meaning.* The opposing manner of thinking cannot grasp this cosmic continuity in the meaning-synthesis, but performs an *epochè* with respect to it in order to acquire meaning-synthetical concepts.

We experience this cosmic continuity only in the naive cosmic experience, but without an articulated realization of the meaning-functions. For that reason *cosmological* self-consciousness always appeals to *cosmic* self-consciousness. For cosmological self-consciousness always remains founded in naive cosmic self-consciousness, just as meaning-synthetic thinking is merely a deepening of the meaning of rigid meaning-systatic thinking, just as, finally, the *cosmic meaning-systasis* provides the foundation for the cosmological meaning-synthesis and makes it possible.

An epistemology that is founded cosmologically in the manner outlined above acknowledges the many-sidedness and universality of the cosmic time-order and upholds the meaning of the sphere-sovereignty and sphere-universality of the law-spheres. At the same time it rejects the reified scheme of form and content, not just for the humanities (as phenomenology does), but *all across the board*. Such an epistemology is perfectly capable of taking on the methodological and the meaning-structural problems which the ongoing differentiation of academic disciplines poses for philosophy. In particular it is capable of shedding unexpected light on the boundary issues between the disciplines.

As far as the problem of time is concerned, our epistemology attains to the cosmological truth – which as far as I know has never yet been recognized – that the cosmic order of time is not exhausted in a single law-sphere and exactly for that reason possesses a *meaning-function* in *every* law-sphere, one which can only be grasped in terms of the meaning of that law-sphere. Modern philosophy knows at most a natural-scientific and a historic-psychological (phenomenological) concept of time (the *durée*, the *stream of life*). In contrast, the view we defend here advances to the insight that every special science, distinguished by a sovereign *gegenständliche* meaning-function, must employ its own meaning-functional concept of time. We are to view the relationship between the *cosmic* and the *functional* orders of time in this fashion: all functional meaning-structures exist *within* cosmic time; all functional orders of time, however, function *within the functional meaning of their law-sphere*.

For instance, number has a functional time-order within *numerical meaning*. *"Earlier"* or *"later"* in this series has the meaning of a quantitative *more* or *less*.

Space has a functional time-order in spatial simultaneity which in turn founds the analogy of *simultaneity* in the meaning of motion.[1] The general theory of relativity, which rejects any privileged static system of coordinates, has done no more than to grasp time *in the functional meaning of motion*, just as it conceives of space as an *analogy within the meaning of motion* correlated with kinematic time.

The meaning of the biotic has its functional time-order in the functional sense of biotic development. Similarly, the psychic meaning has its functional time-order in the functional "duration" of sensitive consciousness (in the sense of Bergson); the logical meaning has its functional time-order in the functional sense of the analytical *prius et posterius* [that which is logically earlier and later], in which the *logical causality principle*, too, is founded (the principle of sufficient reason); the historical meaning has its meaning-functional time-order in the functional meaning of cultural development (as when we speak of historical *time periods*); the linguistic meaning has its functional time-order in the functional meaning of the time of symbolical signification, and so on. Furthermore, in each time-order *after* that of number we find

---

1 This meaning-functional time-order of spatiality, in its anticipatory direction towards motion, is essentially the "absolute," mathematical time of Newton. However, Newton still clung to the untenable metaphysical view that *mattter in motion* is present in space by filling it. Space is rather, as demonstrated by the general theory of relativity, *analogical within movement*. How else, as Einstein has shown, would it be possible that the properties of *physical space* are determined by matter? It is true that the psychical image of motion appears within the psychical spatial image, but space and motion alike are only *analogically* present within the sensitive psychical consciousness.

an inseparable correlation between an *actual subjective* and an *objectively actualized* direction of time.

Kant understood the psychic time-order one-sidedly in the objective direction and Bergson in the subjectively actual direction.

In the social time-order, as the time of *sociation* and *social interaction*, "clock time" is the objective direction, which for every individual person, however, has its own individual-normative *subjective meaning*. Furthermore, the functional time-order displays the same anticipating, deepened elements as possessed by the meaning-structure itself. For instance, "overstaying one's welcome" during a first courtesy visit has a subjective sociative meaning, which is deepened when the economic time-order is anticipated in that such "staying too long" causes my host to lose economically precious time, and so on.

In this way, by abandoning the functionalist immanence standpoint, an entirely new light is shed on the problem of time. So the battle between Bergson and Einstein over the question whether *absolute* time exists emerges as a fruitless fight between two meaning-functional views of time (the physical and the actual-psychological) that argue over which of the two has grasped *true cosmic time*. Obviously, *neither of the two* has done so. For *all* meaning-functional time-orders are merely meaning-functions of cosmic time, which flows through all law-spheres. And of this cosmic time a meaning-synthetic concept is impossible, because all meaning-synthetic thinking presupposes cosmic time.

From our standpoint, and in opposition to the functionalist limitation of experience, we acknowledge that our ability to experience temporal reality fundamentally embraces all its meaning-functional sides; that not a single meaning-function transcends our experience, while our self-consciousness fundamentally transcends the cosmic time-order in its religious root. With that, the functionalist "proposition of consciousness" collapses.

What stops us, for instance, from joining Kant and dissolving all that is given in reality into the "material" of psychic sensory impressions? Answer: The *meaning* of the psychic function of consciousness itself. For that meaning refers backward and forward to non-psychic meaning-functions, not merely to the logical one but to the temporal organism of the meaning-functions *in which alone it can exist*; just as, conversely, the non-psychic and the non-logical meaning-functions appeal to the psychic and the logical.

For this reason we must say: Nothing is given to us *without* the psychic function of consciousness, but very much is given *outside* of the sensory function of consciousness, just as we cannot know anything *without* the logical function yet know very much *apart from* that function.

In observing a flowering apple tree we would rob it of its meaning as an apple tree if we were mentally to eliminate all its non-psychic and non-logical functions. Psychic sensitivity and logical thought are inseparably connected with the non-psychic and non-logical functions of reality.[1]

In the light of this cosmology, how are we to see the naive experience of an entity? What is the structural meaning of a "thing" in this naive experience? We emphasize once more that the naive experience of things has nothing to do with a metaphysical substantializing of its functions, or with a natural-scientific mode of thinking. Rather, temporal reality *gives itself only in the systatic structure of things. The thing-structure is the meaning-individual structure of cosmic reality.*

This point is obviously of utmost importance for a truly cosmological view, also for organized human communal life, including that of the state. Hence we must now pay special attention to the structural problem of things in connection with the cosmological problem of individuality.

From our standpoint, cosmic individuality is founded in a strictly religious, supra-temporal fashion. In the Christian idea of the *Corpus Christianum* this individuality comes to pregnant expression within the religious root of the human race. Earlier, we saw that this Christian view of individuality is strictly incompatible with that of immanence philosophy. As the totality of meaning, the religious fullness of meaning is at the same time the absolute meaning-individuality in the root of the human race. That is why all of temporal reality, from top to bottom, is a temporal manifestation of the supra-temporal religious individuality. Cosmic reality cannot be locked up in any single temporal law-sphere; it reveals itself equally in all the law-spheres.[2] Hence it is meaningless to search for a *principium individuationis* (principle of individuation).

Within the cosmic time-order, meaning-individuality has a structure which fundamentally reaches across the boundaries of the law-spheres.

---

1 This whole theory, which of course I have only sketched in brief outline here, is developed in detail in my soon to be published work *De Wijsbegeerte der Wetsidee*.
2 This is often denied with respect to the analytical law-sphere; cf. e.g. Johannes Volkelt, *Gewissheit und Wahrheit* (1918), pp. 506 ff. However, Duns Scotus already discovered meaning-individuality within the logical sphere when he designed his scholastically and metaphysically conceived theory of *formae individuantes* (individualized forms). Yet in doing this he did not generate a turnabout in the functionalist view of individuality, as Heinz Heimsoeth and Johannes Assenmacher mistakenly believe.

That structure is the cosmic structure of a thing, which exactly for that reason is a structure that *gives* itself immediately in the naive experience of reality, seeing as the latter is embedded in the continuity of the cosmic time-order.

Cosmological thought can illuminate and clarify this individuality-structure in a meaning-synthetic fashion by means of an *epochè* with respect to the cosmic time-order. Yet for cosmological thought the time-order is an entirely irrational *cosmological a priori*, which cannot be understood in a meaning-synthetical concept. For, as we saw, such synthesis is founded in systasis.

Let us begin, then, with an analysis of the meaning-structure of a thing in nature, such as a tree. Cosmological thought, as it analyzes the structure of this natural thing, will have to begin at once by synthetically establishing all its meaning-functions that are enclosed within sovereign law-spheres.

The tree, then, has a meaning-function in the spheres of number, space, and physical motion. But so long as we view the tree from these functional sides it does not yet make sense to speak of a tree. For algebra, only numerical relations are relevant; geometry knows only spatial figures; physics sees the tree as merely a mass of energy, which as such does not distinguish itself as a *tree*. Not until we consider the biotic, the organic vital function of the tree does it make sense to talk of a *tree*.

The biotic meaning-function is the *qualifying* meaning-function of the natural thing-structure of the tree. At the same time it is the last *actual subject-function* which the tree has in temporal reality. But in naive experience we do not functionally close off the reality of a tree. We see the reality of this tree as a thing also in its psychic and post-psychic meaning-functions, again without articulating these of course.

In principle the tree does indeed have meaning-functions in all these later law-spheres, but they are no longer *actual subject-functions* of the tree. Instead, as *object-functions* they *can only be actualized* by later subject-functions.[1]

---

1 The subject-object relation is therefore not found exclusively within the psychical and logical meaning-functions: reality displays object-functions in all law-spheres that contain in their general meaning-structure analogical meaning-elements (in all spheres, that is, except that of number). Already within the spatial sphere we encounter an objectification of a numerical subject in the spatial point. A series of numbers objectifies itself in the spatial points of a straight line. This object-function is founded in the numerical analogy within the general meaning-structure of space, namely in its *dimensionality*, which cannot be comprehended outside the meaning-coherence with number.
  General Editor's note: Eventually Dooyeweerd distinguished between modal

The tree is an object to our sensory-psychic awareness; it is an object in the formation of logical concepts, in historical development, in social interaction, in language, as an economic entity, as a legal object, as an object of beauty and an object of faith. Nevertheless, all these object-functions, which can only be actualized through animal or human subjectivity, belong to the *full cosmic reality of the tree*; they are not creations of human imagination or human thought. Object-functions reside potentially in the full reality of the tree and merely need actualization by the corresponding subject-functions which the tree does not possess.

Now what role is played by the qualifying meaning-function that we pointed at in the structure of the tree? In its meaning-individuality it is the "leading function" in its structure, which directs the earlier reality functions to the biotic destination of the tree.

But how is this "leading" possible? Surely the reality functions that the tree possesses in the earlier law-spheres follow their own meaning-functional laws according to the principle of sphere-sovereignty? Indeed; *but what comes into play here is that which is more than meaning-functional in the structure of a thing*.

We saw earlier how the cosmic order of time, as law for the refraction of meaning, founds the sovereignty of each law-sphere within its own sphere, but at the same time overarches and pervades them. In the physical meaning-side of the tree as a subject, nothing happens in conflict with the physical laws. But the subject-side of a law-sphere, as an ontic function, is thoroughly *meaning-individual*. And that functional individuality is a veritable *dunamei on* (potential being) for the leading function. Only the latter actualizes the functional individuality into a side of the individual reality of the thing we call a "tree."

How this "leading operation" is possible remains an inscrutable problem both for *cosmology* and *a fortiori* for *science*, since the continuity of the cosmic time-order in which this "leading action," this individual unfolding of the anticipatory spheres, takes place in the earlier meaning-functions of the tree is the *a priori* of cosmological thought itself.

In the internal structure of the tree the leading function accomplishes this process of unfolding so completely that in our naive experience we see the tree as a perfect unity that overarches the boundaries of the meaning-functions.

> analogies on the law-side and on the factual (subject-) side, and in terms of this distinction dimensionality represents an analogy of the meaning of number on the law-side of the spatial aspect, each different dimension representing a different *order of extension* (see *A New Critique of Theoretical Thought*, 2:86).

However much the sphere-sovereignty of the meaning-functions so "led" or "guided" remains intact *internally*, it is immediately evident again in the external relationships of the tree. When a fierce storm uproots the tree it falls down, obeying in its physical reality function the laws of motion, laws that are sovereign in their own sphere, even as this "physical motion" does not fall under the meaning-individual "leadership" of the biotic function.

As we saw, the individuality of things penetrates every one of their meaning-functions, but their individuality-structure can only be understood in terms of the meaning-individual leading function. For the special sciences, the functional meaning-individuality remains an *apeiron* (a boundless something), a *me on* (a non-being), unless and until these sciences discover the "leading function" among the law-spheres which they investigate and which determines the structural principles of things. Thus, modern physics, which had long discovered strict individuality on the subject-side of the physical law-sphere, discovered a structural principle within that individuality as a result of its study of radio-active phenomena.[1]

The discovery of the ongoing functional meaning-individuality present in physical micro-events at once meant the discovery of the impossibility to absolutize physical laws to the level of a natural necessity determining all of reality. The functional meaning-individuality, after all, refers beyond the boundaries of its law-sphere to the possibility of guidance by later meaning-functions.

This brief analysis of the structure of a *natural* thing highlights but one of the structural types occurring in reality. There are also complex structures of things which are qualified by a meaning-individual *object-function*. To this type belong all *cultural objects*, whose qualifying function is determined by human activity. Such an objective cultural thing, like a sculpture, a painting, a chair or a table, has a unique double structure. Here the objective meaning-structure rests on the substrate of a subjective natural one, whose qualifying subject-function can be none other than the physical one. But the individual structural unity of a cultural object is qualified by an object-function, which is made actual by

---

1 As a consequence of these radioactive phenomena all chemical elements are shown to have a certain "duration of existence" [half-life], in other words an individual structural law according to which they decay *from within,* at most arrested or accelerated by influences *from without,* in a specific rhythm and a set time period. Undoubtedly this points to an internal individual direction and leading or guidance which is inaccessible to a one-sided horizontal-functional view. It is hardly necessary to refer here to the significance of Planck's quantum theory for the discovery of the functional individuality of physical processes, which showed that the foundations of classical physics were no longer tenable.

human subjectivity. Human subjectivity gives all cosmically earlier functions (the subjective as well as the objective ones) a meaning-individual direction towards the qualifying spiritual object-function (for example, as a social, aesthetic, or economic object-function). Through this circumstance the natural thing-structure is opened up in a meaning-individual way, because the "leading" natural function itself is led in such a way that *it no longer determines the individual structure of this thing*.

The meaning-individual process of unfolding in such cultural things may take place perfectly or less perfectly. If, for instance, a duality asserts itself in a work of art between natural and spiritual functions, it means that the subjective aesthetic conception has not received a proper objective realization.

In his temporal cosmic existence the human being, too, has a thing-structure, but this structure lacks a "leading function"; it is *under the immediate dominion* of the individual supra-temporal religious root of the personality. All things that are qualified by a "leading function" lack an *independent* supra-temporal root; they are perishable and are bounded by their leading function in their activity. The human being lacks such a meaning-individual boundary. He thus shows his transcendence of time and all temporal things. This transcendence alone determines "the place of man in the cosmos." Since Scheler's book on this subject[1] this theme has been at the center of modern humanist philosophy.

2. The meaning-individual thing-structure of organized human communities. The refutation of the reasoning of dialectical phenomenology. A critical examination of the theory of organized communities as advanced by Gierke and Preuss

The organized communities found within human society display a distinct meaning-individual thing-structure. We have noted several times already that naive experience unreservedly takes these spiritual units, too, as structural entities, and that it is quite inadmissible to interpret this as a symptom of an "objectifying and spatially oriented natural-scientific" mode of thinking.

The structure of organized human communities has to be clarified by a cosmological meaning-analysis, and it is not advisable for theory to ignore any "given" of naive experience or to thrust it aside on the basis of a dogmatic misunderstanding.

It is self-evident that the naturalistic and individualistic view of reality must deny an independent thing-structure to these organized communities. On that view, reality is functionalistically closed off in the physi-

---

1 Max Scheler, *Die Stellung des Menschen im Kosmos* (1928).

cal and psychic functions of nature. The naturalistic view considers the human person a natural biological and psychological individual, oddly ignoring the results of natural science which, owing to its own meaning-functional attitude, can obviously not provide a criterion for individual things. For here the normative functions of the spirit are all *ideal* in the sense of law-conforming normative constructs, ideas or values. These have no sovereign subject-side, which forms an essential part of cosmic reality.

The naturalistic "functionalist metaphysics," of which Kelsen too turned out to be an adherent, must naturally reject as "metaphysical" any view that organized communities are real entities. And dialectical, phenomenological sociology, starting out with the primacy of the personality ideal taken as transpersonal and conceiving reality from top to bottom in a spiritual functional manner, must reject the view that organized communities are entities because it believes that this view of organized communities amounts to an objectifying conception of both the "I-ness" and the organized communities. This school of sociology admits only three possibilities: [1] an individualistic view which denies that organized communities are real; [2] a universalistic view which deifies the reality of organized communities into a supra-individual "I-ness" and honors the individual only as an element, a dependent part of the organized community; or [3] a view from the perspective of the human sciences regarding the reality of organized communities which assigns neither to the individual I nor to organized communities a thing-structure but wishes to understand the essence of organized communities in terms of inter-individual "social interwovenness."

But it is clear that this polemics against our view of organized communities as "structural things" likewise completely bypasses the cosmological view of the thing-structure as meaning-individual structure of temporal reality. And once we understand the "I-ness" in the sense of *individual selfhood* in the cosmic and cosmological self-consciousness, then a universalist view of a temporal organized community as a "supra-individual I-ness," as a "collective I", can simply not be considered. Such a view of organized communities can only be defended by an idealist immanence philosophy that seeks the root of the personality within cosmic time.

According to our understanding, the *Christian* view of the personality, the "individual I," cannot be sought in time; and so we are fundamentally opposed to a "humanist" sociology which, along with all immanence philosophy, does exactly that. The individual selfhood is thoroughly religious and is supra-temporal. *Within* the cosmic time-order neither an individual person nor an organized community can assume selfhood, I-ness.

This is the cardinal starting-point for any truly Christian view of temporal society. At the same time this means the definitive rejection of every "metaphysical" view that makes the cosmological thing-concept into a substance. The individual I-ness of the human being transcends all temporal organized communities because it shares in the religious root of the human race, of whose fullness of meaning all of temporal reality in its natural and spiritual functions is merely a temporal refraction.

Against the acknowledgment of the meaning-individual thing-structure the argument cannot be adduced that it would mean an inadmissible attempt to objectify communal life in its subjectively actual sense.

This entire argument comes from the corner of a humanist view of reality, which has thoroughly falsified the concepts of both subject and law and can only discern subjective actuality in a "phenomenological subject."

The truth is this: reality possesses *actual subject-functions* in *all* law-spheres. But the humanist view of reality has absolutized its meaning-synthetic position and degraded into *objects* all actual subject-functions outside of the reified functions of consciousness. As a result, it sees, say in nature, merely an *object* of knowledge governed by the rules of the absolutized epistemological subject-functions.

This can be explained from the absolutization of the meaning-synthetic and opposing direction of thinking, which, at least in the natural sciences, must make the actual subject-functions into a problem, a *Gegenstand*, and first objectify them in a meaning-synthetic logical fashion.[1] In the normative sciences of the humanities, synthetic logical thinking can indeed not objectify any post-logical subject-functions. For, as we saw earlier, all objectification within the structure of a law-sphere is founded in the analogies of the aspect under consideration. And of course, the logical, analytical meaning cannot point *back* to normative aspects for which it serves as a *foundation* in the cosmic time-order.

This cosmological insight *accounts* for the *kernel of truth* in the method of the human sciences. Yet, the human sciences cannot dispense with objectification, since they cannot grasp the post-logical aspects as "pure" but only in their *cosmological connection* with the *pre-logical* aspects.

In our previous section we already saw that the *objective* thing-structure consists of only one of many structural types of individual reality.

---

1 Already in the naive thing-concept we find a *systatic objectification* through which the sensory impressions are objectified within the logical meaning. But this differs from the *opposing meaning-synthetical objectification*.

The "natural thing" itself is a subjectively actual thing and human communities are *a fortiori* subjectively actual thing-structures. Hence it can never be an inadmissible "materialization" of temporal communal life when we, based on the *given* of naive experience, assign a meaning-individual structure also to organized communities. The cosmological thing-concept must be kept free of all the meaning-falsifications which it has suffered in immanence philosophy.

Before we submit the individual thing-structure of organized communities to a cosmological meaning-analysis, we shall first briefly pay attention to the organological theory of organized communities which, following in the footsteps of Beseler, has been worked out in a masterly way by Gierke, and besides him has been applied in political theory notably by Preuss.

As a theory of associations[1] Gierke's conception of organized communities hails from the Germanist wing of the Historical School, which, under the militant leadership of Beseler, began its fierce battle with the Romanist wing of Savigny and Puchta. Its philosophical foundation is the same as that of the Romanists: Schelling's romantic objective idealism gave rise to the historical theory of an organic (and initially subconscious) development of law from a supra-individual communal spirit or *Volksgeist*, a theory which Beseler and Gierke accepted without reservation. In back of this historicist mode of thought operated the humanist personality ideal of the trans-personalist type, which lodges the sovereignty of the human personality in the structure of a supra-individual organized community.[2]

The Romanist theory, however, which especially since Puchta began to see Roman law a-historically as "ratio scripta" (written reason), had taken over the juridical fiction theory of the Romans as applied to legal persons. This theory could see all of human societal life only under the dualistic juridical scheme of *universitas* and *societas*, and in both figures it concentrated only on the *external civil legal relations* of organized communities. In opposition to the rigid individualism of Roman private law, Beseler was among the first to place the Germanic view of law, which proceeded from the corporative bond of the entire field of law, thus doing full justice to the internal supra-individual structure of organized communities.

At this point I shall not trace the development of Beseler's and Gierke's corporative theory (*Genossenschaftstheorie*) any further. Here

---

1 *Translator's note*: orig. *Genossenschaftstheorie*, alternately rendered in extant English translations as "corporative theory" or "theory of fellowships."
2 For more details, see the second and third instalment of my article dealing with the "sources of positive law" in the light of the law-idea, published in *Antirevolutionaire Staatkunde* (quarterly) 4 (1930): 224–63, 325–62.

we are only interested in Gierke's organological theory of organized communities. Subsequent to publishing his grand historical and systematic foundation for this theory in his standard work on German corporate law, Gierke summarized his theory of organized communities in various monographs and most succinctly in his famous rectorial oration of 1902 on "the essence of human organized communities."[1]

Gierke acknowledges the historical and juridical origin of his theory. It arose in the first place from a study of the historical development of Germanic law. But he elaborates the theory cosmologically into a general theory of organized communal life, and he has this to say about that theory:

> It runs through the political theory of antiquity and the medieval doctrine of society; it accompanied every attempt at overcoming the atomistic-mechanistic end result in the intellectual world of natural law; but not until the nineteenth century has it undergone a scientific elaboration, under the impulse of the new ideas about human society.[2]

In Gierke's own words, the organic theory views the state and other organized communities as social organisms, of which individual human beings, as "single organs," are the *parts*.

However, Gierke opposes the excesses of this theory, both in a naturalistic and a speculative-metaphysical sense. He writes:

> We do not forget that the inner structure of a whole, of which humans are a part, has to be of a kind for which all of nature provides us with no example; that a spiritual cohesion takes place here, prepared, formed, realized and dissolved by psychically motivated action; that here the realm of natural science ends and the domain of the humanities begins. Only, we view the social whole, like the single organism, as something alive, and subsume the communal entity together with the single entity under the genus concept of a living being. Whatever may be included metaphorically beyond that stems in part from a need for graphic description, in part from the need for a linguistic stopgap.[3]

Gierke has astutely defended this view of an organized community as a real spiritual organism against the arguments adduced from the side of the individualists. When they object that to assume vital units beyond the vital unit of the individual would amount to "mysticism" because sensory perception only shows us individual people, he contends that this is simply untenable since [i] the individual personality, too, cannot be perceived by our senses, and [ii] this objection begins with a naturalistic view of reality that has stopped short of scientific self-reflection.

---

1 Otto von Gierke, *Das Wesen der menschlichen Verbände* (Berlin, 1902).
2 Ibid., p. 12.
3 Ibid., pp. 15–16.

Next, he rejects the argument that from the point of view of science the entire organism is an unsolved riddle and that therefore the concept "organism" cannot explain the unity of organized communal life. Its legitimacy, Gierke counters, does not depend on whether its underlying unity can be explained. The real essence of the unity in the multiplicity of organized communal life is hidden from us, but the same holds for the entire concept of life, a concept that biology nevertheless cannot dispense with. A direct proof for the real existence of social living entities can no more be provided than that for individual living entities. Nevertheless, we are indirectly justified in drawing the conclusion that organized communities exist from their supra-individual activities in history and society. As well, our "inner experience" confirms this conclusion insofar as we are conscious of the fact that our individual I fits in a social reality of a higher order. Gierke goes on to affirm that we

> experience ourselves as self-contained entities, but we also experience ourselves as parts of a living whole that is operative within us.

From this passage we see that Gierke, in contrast to Marck's statement,[1] most certainly accepts social structures in the individual I itself, and definitely does not see the I as a rigid element of the collective entity. Indeed, Gierke expresses himself in terms which could have been borrowed directly from the arsenal of phenomenological political theory:

> When we reflect on all this, it becomes clear to us that the issue is not merely that external chains and bonds encircle us, but that psychic connections reach into our innermost self and build integrating components into our spiritual being. We notice that a portion of the impulses that determine our actions issues from the communities that penetrate us. We become conscious that we participate in communal life. When we create the certainty of the reality of our self out of our inner experience, the certainty of this reality does not merely extend to the fact that we make up individual living units, but also that we are component units of higher living units.[2]

This explains why dialectical phenomenology's resistance to Gierke's theory of organized communities finds its *true* basis in the fact that Gierke attributes a supra-individual, collective consciousness, a collective selfhood, to organized communities, whereas the phenomenologists defend a "monadological, functionalist view" of organized communities, a view which assigns a center of experience, the *I-ness*, only to the "individual self" and sees an organized community only as a "supra-in-

---

1 Marck, *Substanzbegriff und Funktionsbegriff in der Rechtsphilosophie* (1925), p. 93. For a critical discussion of Marck's views, see my inaugural address of 1926, *De Beteekenis der Wetsidee voor Rechtswetenschap en Rechtsphilosophie*, pp. 109 ff.
2 Gierke, *Das Wesen der menschlichen Verbände*, pp. 21–22.

dividual totality without an I-ness."[1] For Gierke posits explicitly that "we are merely parts of the whole," so that the totality cannot be in our individual I.

This is the point where we must take issue with Gierke's theory of organized communities, albeit for entirely different reasons than dialectical phenomenology. As we shall demonstrate below, Gierke's realistic theory is not based on a proper cosmological meaning-analysis of the thing-structure of organized communities, despite the many merits earned by this noted representative of the Germanic wing of legal science for his discovery of an internal law of organized communities with his distinction between *Sozialrecht* versus *Individualrecht* (social versus individual law). His theory relapses into the romantic "metaphysics" of the Schellingian trans-personalist personality ideal by reifying[2] organized communities into spiritual super-persons, even though Gierke rejects the ancient and the modern forms of idealist universalism which allow the individual to function *only* as a dependent part of the political collectivity.[3]

We shall now further substantiate our thesis that Gierke, too, did not arrive at a cosmological meaning-analysis of the structure of organized communities. We shall do so by referring to the manner in which he applied his *Genossenschaftstheorie* to political theory.[4]

Gierke starts in a promising manner by positing that the state is not "human generality pure and simple." It is only one among many social organisms of human society, and "its true conceptual essence is deter-

1 See Marck, *Substanzbegriff und Funktionsbegriff in der Rechtsphilosophie*, p. 95: "Henceforth, the interweaving of I and You, the original correlative generation of both concepts, the overarching fusion of the I with the other, the connection of I and You through the medium of an objective meaning – these accomplish everything that the organic theory sought to accomplish with its concept of the 'collective I.' Community can be experienced only in the individual soul; only in the relativity of the opening and closing of the conquering and retreating I can the boundaries of individual and totality be understood. A new type of social universalism thus clearly emerges in opposition to the old dogmatic and ontologizing version, from which not even a penetrating thinker like Gierke quite managed to free himself. The conception of the social as a totality lacking an I-ness is taking hold. Although every I is a totality, the reverse is not possible, for not every totality can be viewed as an I." See also Litt, *Individuum und Gemeinschaft*, pp. 279 ff.
2 Waldecker, *Allgemeinde Staatslehre* (1927), pp. 296 ff., attempts in a fairly arbitrary way to interpret the theory of organized communities developed by Gierke apart from its metaphysical foundation, though he does acknowledge the subjectivity of his interpretation.
3 Gierke, *Die Grundbegriffe des Staatsrechts* (1915), pp. 88–89.
4 According to Gierke, the state as such is not a corporation (*Genossenschaft*) but a body (*Körperschaft*); a "Genossenschaft" is merely s *species* of "Körperschaft"; cf. Gierke, *Genossenschaftsrecht*, 2:83.

mined by only one particular side of mankind's existence."¹ Its essence is based on this: "The content of the state as an organized community is the powerful execution of the general will." The state is the community of political action. "Its substance is the general *will*, its manifestation is organized *power*, its task is the purposeful *deed*."² That does indeed sound altogether metaphysically romantic. The "general will" as *substance*, power as the state's *manifestation* – these are concepts which Puchta already derived from the arsenal of Schelling's organic political theory.

Next we hear from Gierke that it is an inborn desire of man to live in a state, and thus that "the state is just as old as the individual." Communal life in a state-like manner has always existed, but according to Gierke one speaks of a state only when a special organism has formed itself for state-life. An isolated family, a nomadic tribe or a sib also fulfills the function of a state, but in those cases the state has not yet arrived at an independent existence. Before one can speak of a state it must first exhibit . . .

> . . . a specific character and a series of qualitative differences from all other organized political communities. Its power is not hemmed in by a similar power above it; and it is superior to every similar power beneath it. For a power that is the *highest* power distinguishes itself from every other power by the defining characteristic that it is nothing but pure power. And a will that corresponds with such a power is distinguished from every other will as a sovereign, purely general, self-determined will. For this reason, among all the organized political communities that display *state-like* characteristics, only the highest organized communal powers are called "states."

It is clear that Gierke's analysis of the state's structure in no way rises above that of the current Berlin School. It remains stuck in the idealist historical view of reality. The romantic Schellingian view of history appears candidly in the organological view of the *origin of states*. As Gierke informs us:

> The single state is no free creation of the individual but the inevitable product of the communal powers that realize themselves in the individuals [cf. the Schellingian "potencies"]. Originally, states arise and grow without any cooperation of a consciously creative will, as a natural product of the unconscious communal drive.³

In our critical examination of the political theory of the Berlin School we already saw how Gierke remains stuck in a view of reality which

---
1 Ibid., p. 99.
2 Ibid., p. 96.
3 Ibid., p. 97.

proclaimed state and law, notwithstanding the many close ties between the two, to be sides of human society each of which is closed in upon itself as to its origin, essence and task. With that he capitulates before the basic problem of any political theory – the meaning-synthesis of the social and juridical aspects. And yet, Gierke teaches that constitutional law "is only concerned with a specific side of the state, namely with its hitherto neglected jural side."[1] How little Gierke has penetrated to the full meaning-structure of the state is apparent from the fact that he, in the abstract, puts the essence of law in opposition to the essence of the state. That kind of opposition proves that Gierke fails to see why the general meaning-structure of a meaning-functional law-sphere such as the jural can never be placed on the same level as an individual meaning-structure like the state.

Gierke's pupil Hugo Preuss already dropped the one criterion which with Gierke distinguishes the state qualitatively from other organized communities, namely that of being an organized community of sovereign power and will. According to Preuss, the sovereignty dogma hails from individualistic Roman law and as such is incompatible with a truly organic theory of the state community. He feels that the concept of sovereignty is inseparably connected with the *fiction theory* that Gierke so vehemently opposed. "In diametrical opposition to the idea of sovereignty," says Preuss, the state is "a congruent (*wesensgleich*) member in the chain of human communal life," which downwards and upwards is organically connected with all other communities.[2] It is a view that enables Preuss, in his theory of *political federations*, to preserve the independence of member states apart from the concept of sovereignty. From his entire scheme, however, it is clear that he is attempting to validate a conception of the *just state* over against the historicistic *power-state* embodied by Gierke's political theory (even though Gierke also moderated it with his view of law). The salient point of this just state, says Preuss, is the fact that state and association (*Genossenschaft*) are the same in their essence, and that the contrast between "leadership" and "state power" is of merely *secondary* significance in the authority structure of organized communities.[3] From this point the line runs easily to a *syndicalist view of the state*, a *"political pluralism,"* to use a term of Harold Laski's, a notion that we shall have to revisit later.

All the same, Preuss' view of the state is no less historicist in cast. As a *merely historical* defining criterion he indicates that the state must be a "territorial body" with "control of its territory," that is, a corporative

---
1 Ibid.
2 H. Preuss, *Gemeinde, Staat, Reich als Gebietskörperschaften* (Berlin, 1889), p. 208.
3 Ibid., p. 215.

community that has the exclusive power of decision over its territory (though he concedes that this criterion already does not hold for the medieval states and the absolutistic states of the *ancien régime*). This territory belongs organically to its personality and is not to be understood as a relationship of subject and object.[1] The whole concept of "territorial body," as Preuss himself admits, is "essentially modern" and finds its prototype only in the *medieval town*. In spite of his obvious striving to banish the Roman *imperial idea* from the state concept, and to carry the idea of the just state forcefully through against the idea of the power-state, the relationship between state and law remains unclear, just as it does with his teacher Gierke. Preuss writes:

> As soon as two people exist side by side, it becomes necessary to somehow delimit their spheres of will with respect to each other, and thus is born the idea of law. And as soon as the first communal entity, namely the family, rises above the single individuals to embrace them, the idea of the state is born . . . Individuals and families, and with them the archetypes of law and state, are born at one and the same time.[2]

How seriously this view, which sees the family as the "archetype" of state and law, misunderstands the meaning-structure of the state can only become clear in what follows.

* * *

We shall now try to apply our cosmological concept of the thing-structure to the analysis of organized communities.[3]

---

[1] Cf. esp. ibid., pp. 406 ff. Another adherent of the organic theory, Heinrich Rosin, in his well-known study *Das Recht der öffentlichen Genossenschaft* (Freiburg im Breisgau, 1886), p. 43, arrives at the conclusion that state and municipality distinguish themselves from other "associations" only as territorial bodies.

[2] Preuss, *Gemeinde, Staat, Reich als Gebietskörperschaften*, p. 205.

[3] *General Editor's note*: Later on Dooyeweerd differentiated between (unorganized) *communities* (which have a natural foundational function – such as marriage and the nuclear family) and organized communities that are designated as "verbanden." For that reason in *A New Critique* the term "verband" was translated by the expression "organized community" (*New Critique*, 3: 178 ff.). However, although Dooyeweerd employs both the terms "verband" and "gemeenschap" in the present work, he does not attach an articulated and distinct meaning to them. For example, on p. 124 (below p. 107) of *Crisis* he refers to the "verbandstructuur der gemeenschap" – showing clearly that he nonetheless does not identify these two terms. On p. 133 (below p. 116) he closely approximates his eventual distinction, for there he distinguishes between natural and historically founded "verbanden." The next step was to call the former type *unorganized* and therefore *communities* (*gemeenschappen*), whereas the latter (as *organized communities*) received the label "verbanden." Consequently, since Dooyeweerd does not identify "verband" and "gemeenschap" in

We already pointed out that all these organized communities together display a subjectively actual thing-structure. The leading functions of these thing-structures can only be located in the normative law-spheres. In distinction from all subjective natural entities, the realization of organized communities is assigned to human activity, *as a task*. They are not given in *static fashion*, but assigned *dynamically*.[1]

Here lies the kernel of truth in Smend's integration theory. But with this insight we have obviously not gained very much for the analysis of the meaning-structure. For this dynamically normative nature is shared by all organized communities.

We come closer once we establish that organized human communities, as dynamic normative meaning-individual thing-structures, possess specific individual meaning-substrates in which their meaning-individuality is ultimately founded.

The specific individual meaning-substrate of organized human communities *ultimately* serves as the foundation for the meaning-individuality of their thing-structure, just as their *leading function* in its meaning-individuality can only be grasped in its cosmological meaning-coherence with this specific meaning-substrate.

Take, for example, the nuclear family bond and the larger bonds which encompass the extended family, the sib, and so on. The nuclear family has a meaning-individual communal structure which is clearly founded in a meaning-individuality of the biotic meaning-function. It is *biotic bond* and *blood relationship* that lie at the basis of the meaning-individuality of the structure of this organized community in a meaning-functional sense. In none of the earlier law-spheres do we find a functional, meaning-individual substrate for its meaning-individuality.

Yet, the structure of the nuclear family cannot be understood from this meaning-individual natural function. With its discovery we still only know that the nuclear family is founded in *nature* and as such bears a *constant character*, as distinct from organized communities with a historical foundation.[2] Not until we discover this normative entity's "leading function" can we get hold of its structural principle in cosmo-

---

Crisis – just recall the phrase "verbandstructuur der gemeenschap" – the term "verband" is here translated as "organized community."

1 Of course this also applies to the category, discussed earlier, of objective-spiritual thing-structures such as art works, cultural artifacts etc. The only difference is that in their case their realization is again fixed in a static objective form. But that this does not remove them from the cosmic time-order, as Litt holds, already follows from our entire cosmological view.

2 Within the jural sphere we do in fact encounter *institutions and principles* of *natural law*; more on this in my article about "the structure of legal principles and the method of legal science in light of the law-idea," in *Wetenschappelijke Bijdragen*

logical meaning-coherence, For the nuclear family this "leading function" is none other than the *moral meaning of love*, which is not to be understood in the abstract but rather meaning-individually, in its cosmological coherence with the biotic bond and blood relationship.

As a real cosmic organized community, the nuclear family has actual subject-functions in *all* the law-spheres. But the internal thing-structure of the nuclear family is determined by the leading function in its meaning-individual coherence with the specific substrate function. Also a family's internal law, economy, social interaction, language, and so on, are *directed* in normative fashion by their "leading" function, in the meaning-individual disclosure of the anticipatory spheres of these meaning-functions.

Insight into the structural principle of organized communities with a natural foundation also enables us to give a satisfactory interpretation of the phenomenon of what is called the *primitive archetypal norm*, which sociology usually explains by making the boundaries between the normative spheres completely relative to time and place. In a certain sense we may say that the primitive archetypal norm is *still* present, and indeed first of all in the nuclear family as an organized community. There is no need to go back to the Code of Hammurabi!

How then should we view this primitive archetypal norm? It can never be interpreted in a *meaning-functional* way, as positivistic sociology has tried to do, but only *cosmologically*.

By virtue of the structural entity of this organized community, the bearer of authority in the family acts to uphold not only the *internal* social norms but also the norms for the family's economy, law, morality, and faith. In the structure of the family all these meaning-functional norms are so closely interwoven that without exception they bear the stamp of the internal structural principle. When a member of this community transgresses one of the internal normative domains, that person violates the spiritual unity of the family and at the same time violates the entire complex of norms that obtain in it.

The primitive original norm is the cosmic totality-structure of this organized community, which overarches its meaning-functional boundaries. This organized communal structure is given to us, not within the time-order of a meaning-functional sphere, but fundamentally in the cosmic order of time. We shall never understand this cosmic communal structure if, in keeping with the continuity principle of the humanist science ideal, we allow the meaning-boundaries between the law-spheres to functionally shade off into each other (for example, historically or so-

aangeboden door Hoogleraren der Vrije Universiteit ter gelegenheid van haar vijftig-jarig bestaan (1930), pp. 225–66.

cially). We shall only understand it by maintaining the sovereignty of each law-sphere.

Next to the family, an entirely different internal meaning-structure is displayed by organized communities with a *historical foundation*, such as the state and the business enterprise. The state has no specific meaning-substrate in natural functions but is founded *historically*.

In primitive times, it is true, organized communities with a natural foundation did indeed perform various functions which the state later took over. But this should not tempt us, as happened in the case of Preuss, Marck, Waldecker and others, to lose sight of the essential difference in structure between state and non-political organized communities. The state-structure has its foundation in a meaning-individual meaning-function, namely *dominion over subjects*. With this we touch on a typical meaning-function of the structure of the state, which, as we saw, is absolutized in the historicist idea of the power-state.

In view of the great confusion in humanist political theory regarding the historical concept of dominion, we must now proceed to a closer cosmological analysis of both the general meaning-structure of the historical law-sphere and the historical meaning-individuality revealed in the relationship between government and subject.

It can be demonstrated from the cosmological analysis of its general meaning-structure and its analogies that the historical law-sphere is based directly on the substrate of the logical law-sphere, which is characterized by the analytical meaning-structure. The same is true of all law-spheres which contain the normative element of *positivity* in their general meaning-structure (the spheres of language, of social interaction, of economy, law, morality and faith). They all *display a historical analogy*, which shows that they are *founded* on the historical law-sphere.

That the historical law-sphere indeed rests on the substrate of the logical law-sphere is already apparent from what we remarked earlier about the structure of meaning-synthetic thought which as *scientific* thought stands for an anticipatory meaning-disclosure of naive, *syn-static* thought (which is rigidly tied to psychic perception) and is clearly dependent upon guidance or *leading* by the historical meaning-function.

We consider *cultural development* to be the meaning-nucleus in the structure of the historical law-sphere, and by virtue of the meaning-coherence with the analytical law-sphere we accept the historical meaning-structure to be a *normative* one, a structure that *presents us with a task*.

Ever since Bernheim, Windelband, Rickert, Troeltsch, Simmel, Dilthey and others, there has been an increase in epistemological and methodological inquiry into the criterion for historical thinking. These investigations have mainly been oriented to the various types of humanist ideas on law and subject and therefore do not look for the *irreducible cosmic meaning-structure of history as a law-sphere* along the lines of our cosmological principle of *sphere-sovereignty*.

Formal, categorial criteria such as "becoming," "individual value-relatedness," the "concept of development," and so on and so forth, do not get at the problem of the meaning-criterion.[1] The numerous modern studies of the *historical concept of time* likewise presuppose the problem of the sovereign meaning-criterion of history as such.

It is indeed impossible to reduce the modal nucleus, *cultural development*, to that of other general meaning-structures.

> **Remark:** Neither can the historical meaning-nucleus "cultural development" in any way be formalized in line with Neokantianism into a subjective individual "value-relatedness" (*Wertbeziehung*). By viewing it as a mere *subjective synthesis* of natural reality and supra-historical "values" (social, political, aesthetic, moral etc.) its meaning-sovereignty is entirely eliminated. In addition, this alleged synthesis is clearly dialectical in the sense of being intrinsically antinomic. The post-historical law-spheres have their own individual subject-side which can never be reduced to historical subjectivity. The unbreakable meaning-coherence between the historical and the other law-spheres does not abolish the functional meaning-sovereignty of the former. The desperation in which logical thinking in Rickert's conception of history gets entangled is strikingly evident in his own observation regarding the synthesis between natural reality and values: "Thus we capture in a concept that which strictly speaking cannot be grasped in a concept."[2] This is the pure dialectic that aims at a *logical* relativization of the logical principle of non-contradiction in order to substitute it with meaning-synthetical thinking. But logical thinking is relative in a cosmic sense; it is never *logically* relative.

In their general meaning-structure the post-historical law-spheres contain only meaning-*analogies* of this meaning-nucleus, and they can only be grasped in their coherence with the historical meaning (think of "civilized language," "cultured forms of social intercourse," and so on, which, in their linguistic or social sense, obviously are based on the founding meaning-substrate of a higher historical level of culture).

Among the *analogical* moments found in the general meaning-structure of the historical meaning-function, qualified by the aforementioned meaning-nucleus, we find retrocipations to all the pre-historical

---

1 On these criteria, see the approach taken by K. Kuypers in his dissertation dealing with the cosmological view of Vollenhoven and myself, *Theorie der Geschiedenis* (1931), pp. 97–105. I have analyzed these criteria extensively in my book *De Wijsbegeerte der Wetsidee*, where I shall also elaborate and explain my view of history. [Cf. *A New Critique of Theoretical Thought*, 2:190–298.]

2 Rickert, *System der Philosophie*, p. 260.

law-spheres (see Appendix A). One of the most important of these meaning-analogies is the historical element of *power* (we may speak here of a "physical analogy" insofar as this analogy is ultimately founded in the law-sphere of energy). *Historical* power can obviously be understood only in connection with all the earlier meaning-functions enclosed in law-spheres. It bears the normative qualification of cultural development; it is the calling to cultural power formation.

Humankind must in the first place gain spiritual *power* over natural functions in a historical sense. The human race is already confronted with this task in the story of creation.[1]

Although man can obtain this power only with the aid of his thinking, power is present in the logical function only as an anticipatory element. The humanist science ideal, in an apostate sense, has accentuated this historical element of power in the sense of a Faustian urge of dominion. On both the law-side and the subject-side of the historical law-sphere the *element of power* is still only an analogy *within its general* structure (albeit heavily laden with all earlier structures). It can assume all forms of historical meaning-individuality. In the historical meaning-function, too, meaning-individuality is a veritable *apeiron*. However, in the cosmic coherence with later cosmic "leading functions" it is transformed into a *dunamei on*, a dynamic being or potency. Through an anticipating meaning-individuality directed towards a leading function, historical power becomes a state's *dominion over subjects*.

Political dominion, as a meaning-individual spiritual power, can never be understood apart from its meaning-coherence with physical force. It is essentially always power of the strong arm, which strives for the *monopoly of sword power* in its *territory*. This distinguishes political dominion sharply from other meaning-individual forms of spiritual power, such as those of intellect, capital, art, honor, or faith. These various forms of power were subjected to an extensive investigation by Hobbes in his *Leviathan*,[2] but he *naturalized* the concept of power and consequently failed to see either its general normative historical sense or the fact that the meaning-individual forms of power are directed in a typical anticipating fashion towards meaning-individual "leading functions." It is only in connection with the guiding function of the

---

[1] See Genesis 1:28 : "and replenish the earth and subdue it, and have dominion over the fish of the sea and the fowl of the air . . ." etc.

[2] Thomas Hobbes, *Leviathan* 1.10: "Of Power, Worth, Dignity, Honour and Worthiness." See my criticism of the concept of power in the thought of Hobbes in my "In den Strijd om een Christelijke Staatkunde," *Antirevolutionaire Staatkunde* (quarterly) (1927): 165 ff.; Eng. trans. *The Struggle for a Christian Politics* (Lewiston, NY, 2008), pp. 254 ff.

thing-structure of the state as an organized community that its dominion turns into a *directed* meaning-individuality.[1]

As soon as one tries to promote "dominion" or the governing function as the qualifying or leading function of the state, one founders on the rock of either the naturalistic or the idealist theory of *raison d'état*.

Smend elevates political power into a self-grounded and autonomous value, the "integration value."[2] This amounts to a historicistic reification of a meaning-individual (albeit *founding*) function of the structure of the state. This reification destroys itself, since this meaning-individuality acquires a well-defined meaning only when it is *directed*. Without a connection with the leading function of the state, it is as little capable of defining the thing-structure of the state as the biotic bond and blood relationship by themselves are capable of defining the thing-structure of the nuclear family.

What then is the "leading function" of the state as an organized community? It can only be found in the *jural sphere* – though not of course in the *general meaning-structure* of the jural, which is the perennial error in the humanist conception of the place of law in the structure of the state. Rather, the leading function is found in a *jural function* that is grasped only in a cosmological coherence with the *founding* function, in this case the *function of dominion*.

In light of our law-idea and subject-idea, this cosmological meaning-coherence is not a dialectical one. It would be dialectical only if the synthetic understanding of the meaning-functions were brought under a common (absolutized) meaning-functional denominator by dialectical *thought*. For the latter ignores the meaning-boundaries of synthesis, and thus sanctions the antinomy. (In the case of a historicist view of reality, the meaning-functional denominator is the *historical*.) However, on the basis of our earlier expositions we know that the meaning of the jural itself is only given in a cosmic coherence of meaning. Already in its general meaning-structure it displays that unbreakable meaning-coherence in the analogical and anticipating meaning-moments that connect the meaning of the jural with that of all earlier and later law-spheres. As we saw earlier, synthetic thought, rooted in the thinker's cosmological self-consciousness, does nothing but logically *articulate*, functionally

---

1 Here we find the key to understanding the intimate connection between the power side and the jural side in the Protestant, Anti-Revolutionary theory of the state, although we must immediately admit that various theoreticians in this school (including Stahl) allowed themselves to be infected by humanist romanticism.

2 In his work *Der Staat als Integration*, Kelsen signals the ambivalence present in Smend's "integration concept." Originally conceived of as a real process, it is suddenly elevated to the status of a "value." In light of Smend's dialectical standpoint, however, this is not surprising.

separate, and *analyze* this systatic meaning-coherence through a suspension of the continuity of the cosmic order of time.

It is the meaning-individual *jural* governmental function, normed by public-legal principles, that *qualifies*, in coherence with the meaning-individual historical function of *dominion*, the meaning-structure of the state as an organized community, *directing* all its other reality functions towards the meaning-individual unity of a dynamic, normative thing-structure.

In order to arrive at a proper understanding of this meaning-structure of the state, in contrast with the dilemma of political theories rooted in immanence philosophy, we must realize that the state as an organized community cannot be conceived one-sidedly either as a system of norms or as a merely subjective reality. As we saw earlier, rationalist and irrationalist theories oscillate between the horns of this dilemma. We noted that the *rationalist* types of immanence philosophy actually possess only a *law-idea*, the *irrationalist* types only a *subject-idea*. Yet in the entire cosmic order of time, reality is given to us only *in an inseparable correlation between a law-side and a subject-side*. There is no subjective real entity that is not subjected to laws. Conversely, there are no laws without a subject. Consequently, *the reality of the state as an organized community is only given to us in an inseparable correlation between a mutually irreducible law-side and subject-side*.

In the normative law-spheres, too, temporal cosmic reality has its meaning-sovereign *subject-functions*, which however are only given in subjection to the law-functions, in this case to the norm-functions. Its real subject-function, which is contained in the jural law-sphere, is *qua* subject-function not reducible to a social, historical or psychical reality! The meaning-nucleus of the general meaning-structure of the jural, namely *retribution*, qualifies also the subject-side with an irreducible sovereignty in its own sphere (see Appendix B).

Meanwhile, the law-side of the historical sphere and of those law-spheres founded in the historical sphere displays a most remarkable cosmic structure, which we do not encounter in the earlier law-spheres. In the natural spheres, the laws are directly brought to bear, in a meaning-functional way, on individual subject-functions; they are, if I may put it that way, completely positivized by God, without any human interference. But in the normative law-spheres of the so-called spiritual meaning-functions, the functional laws are only given *in the form of principles*. These principles themselves have a meaning-individual foundation insofar as they are internal normative principles of the organized communal structures of human society.[1]

---

1 See my elaboration of this idea in my treatise on "the structure of legal principles and the method of the science of law in light of the law-idea," in *Wetenschappelijke*

The Crisis in Humanist Political Theory 113

Normative principles require positivization through the activity of the human will, on the foundation of historical development. Thus the *element of positivity* within the meaning-structure of the normative law-spheres introduces a peculiar structural interweaving of law-side and subject-side. This interweaving consists in the fact that on the law-side itself the element of positivity is given as a historical analogy. Thus a concrete norm always shows an interweaving between a *principle* and the *formative will of a subject*. Not just any subjects are competent to positivize: this competence is founded historically in *normative power*, which implies a task, a calling. The juridical law-sphere demands *material competence*, which, in its connection with power as this is differentiated in meaning-individual ways, elevates the positivity in jural norms above discretionary actions by juridical subjects.

In the internal structure of the state the competence to positivize *jural* and other meaning-functional principles rests on the meaning-individual historical foundation of the *dominion* relationship. From this state of affairs we understand at once the dilemma of humanist legal theory, which consists of the fact that it *absolutizes either the element of principle* in the jural norm, *or the element of positivity*. In the former case it ends up in a *rationalist natural law*, in the latter in meaningless *positivism*. Similarly, the distinction between *absolute* and *empirical* norms,[1] as introduced in legal theory by Windelband, turns out to be untenable in light of the above. Purely empirical norms no more exist in the cosmos than do *absolute norms*. The only *absolute* is the law's religious fullness of meaning: the demand to serve God.

Even the logical norms for thinking are only given to us in the form of principles. They must be *positivized* by the activity of human thought in deepened scientific thinking, anticipating the historical meaning. This thesis is borne out by the entire historical development of scientific theories. (Historicism, in the manner of Spengler, will of course interpret such theories in the sense of a complete historical relativism where theoretical truth is concerned.)

Bijdragen aangeboden door Hoogleraren der Vrije Universiteit, pp. 225–66.
   Within the historical law-sphere I call these "normative principles" *cultuurdominanten* (dominant cultural factors). By virtue of the meaning of history they here display a strictly *dynamic* character and they are meaning-individually different and vary from case to case depending upon the cultural spheres in which they operate. They are positivized by those who, as the "shapers" of culture, are *called* to do so. When culturally dominant factors, once positivized, are violated in an anti-normative sense, we call it "reaction." The nature of any "historical period" can only be understood systematically in terms of dominant cultural factors.
1 See e.g. Bódog Somló, *Juristische Grundlehre*, 2nd ed. (1927), p. 59, and Windelband, *Präludien. Aufsätze und Reden zur Einleitung in die Philosophie*, 3rd ed. (1907), pp. 292–93.

Other so-called "absolute norms," too, such as those for *aesthetics* and *morality*, are given in the form of *principles* only, and thus they demand to be *positivized* into concrete norms. That is clear at once from a simple comparison of, say, medieval and modern aesthetics and morality. Think of economic ethics in medieval times, with its culturally dominant factors regarding the prohibition of interest and its doctrine of *justum pretium* (fair price).

With the foregoing we have clarified the *internal structural principle* of the state as an organized community. But this structural principle still affords no more than the *key* for a many-sided meaning-analysis. *Nevertheless we feel justified in establishing that in principle we have satisfactorily resolved the fundamental problem posed by the political theories based on functionalism: one after the other, these theories foundered on the relation between right and might in the structure of the state, a relation that is cleared up through a genuinely cosmological meaning-synthesis between these different sides of the structure of the state.*

What matters now is to use the key we have found above in further analyzing the structure of the state, in particular as it applies to the problem of the *territory of the state*, its *people* and its *sovereignty*. Such a full-orbed analysis, however, ought to encompass all functions of the state as an organized community. These aspects we wish to examine in our last section, but first we would like to dissect a few other communal structures in their *founding and leading functions* in order to shed more light, by way of contrast, on the structural type of the state as an organized community.

As our first example we choose the temporal *church as an organized community*. As a visible temporal institution the church community, too, has a temporal thing-structure which is founded in a meaning-individual historical function of power. In this instance the function of power does not have the meaning-individuality of state dominion but is essentially a spiritual power of the divine revelation in history, which finds its center in the appearance of Christ on earth. Christ as the Head of the born-again human race is the historical bearer of power *par excellence*. He is the Founder of His church, also as a temporal institution, and rules it by His Word. The leading function of the church as an organized community is found in the meaning-individual function of *faith*, which finds its central content in the proclamation of the Word and the administration of the sacraments.

As a meaning-individual organized community, the church also has an internal authority structure which receives its character from its meaning-individual leading function, which distinguishes it sharply from the internal authority structure of the state. Under the kingship of Christ all temporal authority of the church as an organized community is not a state-like authority in the political sense of ruling over subjects; it is an authority, rather, of *serving* in the communion of faith. The bearers of ecclesiastical authority have a historically founded *task* with respect to faith. They are to make concrete the church confession as a whole of positivized norms for faith, founded in Scripture and tested against Scripture, always in connection with historical development. They are to uphold the meaning-individual character of internal church law.

The church as an organized community also bears a dynamic normative character; it must continually be *realized*. A special feature of its thing-structure, which obtains in no other organized community, is the fact that as a temporal institution it is a direct meaning-individual structural manifestation of the supra-temporal body of Christ. This feature is located in its "leading function." Earlier, we referred to the pistic function as *the open window to eternity*, since it is the upper terminal function of our temporal cosmos, which displays no anticipatory spheres. The *historical law-sphere is the founding law-sphere*, and in that sense the *nodal point, of the entire spiritual-functional dynamic in our cosmos*. In the same manner the *function of faith* is the *terminal function* for human activity, from which the *entire process of unfolding in the anticipatory moments of the law-spheres ultimately receives its meaning-functional guidance*. Scientific thought, too, ultimately receives its meaning-functional guidance from *pistis*, from temporal faith.

When the function of faith receives its nourishment from the apostate root of the fallen human race, the entire process of spiritual unfolding in our cosmos is directed in an apostate direction *which absolutizes what is temporal*, on the basis of the historical power of the Anti-Christ.

When it receives its nourishment from the anastatic root of regenerated mankind as guided by the Spirit of God, then the spiritual unfolding process in our cosmos is directed to the religious fullness of meaning in Christ on the basis of the historical power of Christianity. This is the lasting value of Augustine's vision of the age-old struggle between the *Civitas Dei* and the *Civitas terrena*. History remains the battle-field between the kingdom of God and the kingdom of darkness.

* * *

We wish to point at a final type of communal structure. Tönnies, in his well-known book of 1926, *Gemeinschaft und Gesellschaft*, counts them among the *gewillkürte* (voluntary or discretionary) kind and in that sense subsumes them under the category of *Gesellschaft*, which is that whole world of *free associations in their immense meaning-individual differentiation.*

We do not deem it correct to speak here of "coordinate relationships," since these organized social entities, too, bear a true *communal* character and, in contrast to all coordinate relationships, possess an *authority structure*.[1] Yet they undoubtedly display this fundamental difference from naturally founded organized communities, as well as from state and church, in that they are not only joined by free consent, but can also again be dissolved by voluntary decision. In other words, they lack the character of supra-individual necessity.

Yet it is a completely formalistic way of thinking to conclude, as does Walther Burckhardt, that this is the only essential difference from the state as an organized community (see Appendix C). *Free* organized communities, too, possess a meaning-individual thing-structure, which needs cosmological clarification. They too have a "leading function" and a meaning-individual founding function which determines their structural principle, and no theory of organized communities can abstain with impunity from subjecting them to a cosmological analysis. In our final section we shall see the crucial significance which this structural principle has for determining the material competence of state authority.

A modern business firm has its meaning-individual founding function in the historical power formation of capital and its "leading function" (the meaning-individual entrepreneurial function) in the economic law-sphere.

A club finds its meaning-individual substrate in the historical power of one's *social position* and its "leading function" in a meaning-individual social function of social interaction. We could go on.

A number of organized communities that belong to this last type also possess the peculiarity that they interfere only to a very small degree in people's lives; also, that they are purposeful communities[2] in the sense that they are called into being for a discretionary and specifically cir-

---

1 Marck, *Substanz- und Funktionsbegriff in der Rechtsphilosophie* (1925), pp. 100 ff., in line with Tönnies, distinguishes sharply between *Gemeinschaft* and organized coordinational communities. In the former a truly *social organism* is found, while the latter, by contrast, display a technical-mechanical *organization*. He accuses Gierke of confusing these two configurations. Only within the sphere of a technical organization does he acknowledge an artificial collective I, a *substantialization* of the spiritual I-ness. On the basis of views developed earlier in the present work, we find such a conception of organized communities unacceptable.

2 The "leading function" that qualifies the thing-structure as such ought not to be viewed from a teleological perspective. Particularly in the case of the state a teleo-

cumscribed purpose. Yet this is certainly not true in all cases. Professional organizations, for example, enfold their members in essential aspects of their lives. In modern times they represent transitional types that lean toward *necessary* organized communities.

* * *

Differing from all the organized communities of human society are the *coordinated societal relationships* in their infinitely varied structure. Taken in a cosmological sense, coordinated relationships represent a form of grouping which does not integrate the cosmic human societal relationships into a supra-individual unity, but amounts to a *coordination* which knows neither authority structure nor internal solidarity.

Usually one sees *individuals* as the subjects of coordinate relationships. But in fact they are merely temporary individual subject-functions by means of which one enters coordinate relationships. Just as the individual "I" transcends the structure of all temporal organized communities, so it transcends all temporal coordinate relationships. These do not by themselves exhibit a genuine thing-structure, and thus can never exist apart from organized communal relationships.

In contrast to the structure of organized communities, the structure of coordinational relationships is founded in the social law-sphere (whose meaning we seek in *sociation*[1]), to the extent that the entire distinction between coordinate and communal relationships occurs here for the first time. In its modern development, however, this distinction is altogether historically conditioned, since "sociation" outside the natural communities occurs only at a level of culture where the rigid walls between *natural* communities are breaking down. Such walls used to exclude non-members from peaceful interaction with the community, regarding them as "the enemy," beyond the pale of the law.

Finally, in this context we must point at the extremely complex mutual interweaving of the structures of organized communities and coordinate relationships.

Individual natural entities do not occur by themselves, outside of a relationship to each other. Rather, in a true "enkapsis"[2] they enter into

---

logical theory of organized communities is totally incapable of clarifying its inner meaning-structure.

1 *General Editor's note*: The Dutch term "*omgang*" has no direct English equivalent. Therefore the term "sociation" is employed, which expresses less than "association" but is still intended to designate the core meaning of the social. The German word "*vergesellschaftung*" is sometimes also translated as "sociation."

2 Cf. Theodor L. Haering, *Über Individualität in Natur und Geisteswelt* (1926), p. 47. Haering derived the term "*Einkapselung*" from the biologist Heidenhain.

more complicated meaning-individual thing-structures without losing their own thing-structure. In the same way a meaning-functional intertwining also occurs between structures of organized communities themselves, and between the latter and coordinate relationships. For instance, in the state as an organized community all non-state organized communities have an individual structural function of their own without being absorbed as such into the state structure. The same holds for the mutual coordinate relationships between the members of organized communities. This insight into the "enkaptic" structure of meaning-individual reality, as will appear below, is of fundamental significance for political theory.

3. **The relation between political theory, the discipline of constitutional law and sociology in the light of our Calvinist cosmology. Political theory as a cosmological theory of the structure of the state. The cosmological principle of sphere-sovereignty as applied to the question of juridical competence. Rejection of pluralist (syndicalist) theories**

The first conclusion to be drawn from our preceding exposition is that *general political theory* can only be of the nature of a cosmological structural theory of the state. It must not be oriented to a scientific *concept of function*, and even less to a metaphysical (indeed untenable) *substance concept*. Instead it must be oriented to the *meaning-structural cosmological thing-concept*, which now can no longer be misunderstood in the sense of a humanistic "objectification" of human communal life.

This at once clarifies the relationship of general political theory, so defined, to the discipline of constitutional law. This discipline remains a *juridical discipline* which, in order to do justice to the meaning-functional structural differences within the juridical sphere, must itself be founded by a *general political theory* and in a broader sense by a *cosmological theory of organized communities*.

A science of law is impossible without a foundation in a cosmological theory of organized communities. Even Kelsen's "pure theory of law" turned out to be founded in a theory of organized communities (which, however, revealed itself as a naturalistic, individualistic metaphysics).

Every positivist theory of law which attempts to level the fundamental meaning-functional structural differences within the jural law-sphere through a pseudo-logical postulate regarding the systemic unity, starts out from that individualistic view of organized communities so brilliantly embodied in Jehring's work of 1923, *Der Zweck im Recht*.[1]

This casts a peculiar light on the pre-logical postulate of "methodological purity"! The naivety of the norm-logical critique consists in this, that it tries to hide its cosmological presuppositions behind a "pure logic." In this sense it is less critical than Jehring, who openly puts his cards on the table.

How, then, does general political theory as a cosmological theory of structure relate to sociology? In the present context we can deal with this problem of sociology only very briefly.

The universalistic, synthetic school,[2] which in modern times has found a *methodological* defender especially in Franz Oppenheimer, undoubtedly poses a meaningful problem: that of an encompassing meaning-synthesis of human society as it is investigated by the various "social" sciences, each of which deals with a specific side of human society from its own special viewpoint. Yet the school does not recognize that we are dealing here with a cosmological problem of structure that can never be approached with meaning-functional methods. Along the lines of Comte, who carried through the humanistic natural-science ideal, it tries to solve this problem in a natural-scientific way. (For Comte, the "historical method" is merely a "modification" of the general positive method of natural science.)

We learn from Oppenheimer that sociology, as the universal-synthetic science of the "social process," has the same integrating significance for the "social sciences" as biology has for the natural sciences (!). We also learn that this universalistic sociology has to bar all normative meaning from its field of investigation, and that it should aim at the discovery of "social laws" which, to the degree that they explain complicated phenomena, have no more mathematical exactness than the laws of meteorology and other natural phenomena, yet which in principle will always have the character of *laws of nature*.[3] Its causality principle will have to be built, like that of physics, on the principle of equivalence ("*causa aequat effectum*") – thus a meaning-functional method, but at the same time with three different ways of viewing society: "the mechanical, the biological, and the psychological."

---

[1] A more extensive analysis is found in my study "De Bronnen van het stellig recht in het licht der wetsidee,"*Antirevolutionaire Staatkunde* (quarterly) 4 (1930): 1–67, 224–63, 325–62; 8 (1934): 57–94.

[2] The older definition of sociology in social philosophy, which still finds a representative in Othmar Spann, *Gesellschaftslehre* (3rd ed., 1930) will not be discussed here. In my inaugural address (1926, pp. 84 ff.) I still followed Troeltsch in not distinguishing this school from that of Oppenheimer and his followers.

[3] Franz Oppenheimer, *System der Soziologie* (Jena, 1922), 1:199.

This pseudo-scientific method is essentially the "bad metaphysics" of the humanist science ideal, everywhere revealing the humanist personality ideal. Whoever might take offense at this qualification has only to read Oppenheimer's foreword to his *System der Soziologie*. What do we read there as to what the book will offer us in terms of a positivist system of sociology "devoid of all value judgments"?

> The questions that can be answered with complete certainty, however, together constitute the contours of a *worldview* [!], a worldview which recognizes what people have in common as well as what separates them, and which is consciously oriented to peace among the nations and the concept of Humanity that transcends nation and race, to a world citizenship which does not, however, end up in an odious attempt to make everyone the same but which understands humanity as the concert of nations in which each player is master of his instrument and all players together produce the most wonderful harmony. In this way the new ideal of Humanity ties in with the old one of the great masters of the 18th century. And so I hope to be able to make my modest contribution to the new age, which must and shall overcome the horrible brutality of these war years.

All this is the result of "honest, straightforward science," which is to distinguish itself from "social philosophy" by eliminating all value judgments and working along exact methods of natural causality! This "exact science" has transformed itself into a humanist worldview which is proclaimed in so many words as the continuation of the humanist metaphysics of the 18th century. In the very act, the humanist science ideal, with its continuity postulate[1] which blurs all meaning-boundaries, has exposed its deeper origin in the humanist personality ideal.

We have already made our acquaintance with one of the most important representatives of the "formal school" in sociology recently established by Simmel. Theodor Litt has abandoned the *form-content* schema (see Appendix D) which Simmel's school had introduced and which indeed created much confusion. Litt wants to proclaim sociology to be a *dialectic-phenomenological science*, to serve as *the foundation for all the human sciences*. In this connection we may confine ourselves to the thesis we expounded earlier at some length, namely that this very influential school in sociology, too, is essentially functionalistic in orientation and for that reason is unable to clarify the cosmological problem of structure. And as we demonstrated in the case of Smend's political theory, it too is unable to overcome the crisis in humanist political theory.

---

1 Another adherent of this universalistic sociology states in so many words that there are "boundaries neither for the natural sciences nor for the social sciences"; cf. Albion W. Small, *The Meaning of Social Science* (Chicago, 1910), p. 121.

In our opinion, sociology as a normative *special science* is possible to the extent that it tries to grasp human society functionally in the modal sense of *sociation*. In this sense we may speak of a social law-sphere, whose law-side is formed by that exceedingly differentiated set of norms for social interaction (norms for civility, propriety, fellowship, play, fashion, tact, and so on) which was investigated for the first time (albeit in a methodologically unsatisfactory manner) by Jehring in the second volume of his *Der Zweck im Recht*. But even in this functional sense a sociological discipline remains dependent upon the foundation of a cosmological theory of organized communities in the sense we discussed earlier.

In this sense of "sociation" the state as a structurally organized community undoubtedly also has a "social" side. The "social function" plays an integrating role both in a state's internal relations and in the external relations between states. Smend is correct in pointing out the significance of ceremony, folk festivals, and the like in the internal communal life of the state. And quite recently Dimitch has devoted a book to the connection between norms of international civility and international law.[1]

Should anyone still not be convinced of the intrinsic untenability of dissolving the state into a functional system of legal norms, he should test the explanatory power of the "pure theory of law" on just this one point, namely whether or not the state has a "social" side, and then try to explain the fact that observing courtesy when receiving, say, foreign heads of state is not imputed to private state organs which do the receiving, but to the state itself. Such an imputation can only be understood from the cosmological structural principle of the state as an organized community, in which the jural function plays the *leading* role. The inescapable consequence of Kelsen's ideas, namely that one would not be able to speak in this case of a social function of the state itself, is untenable.

Take the case of China. Its government continued for a long time to treat foreign diplomatic agents with mocking contempt for every norm of international courtesy, even after the opening of regular diplomatic relations with the European states after the Peace Treaty of Nanking in 1842 and despite China's recognition of the legal principle of equality. This was an important factor in the tense relations between the Chinese state and the foreign Powers. In its treaties with England, up until the Treaty of Tientsin of 1858, it was lack of courtesy on the part of the *state* and not private individuals that made the Chinese government refer to British subjects as *yi* (barbarians).

---

1 Velimir N. Dimitch, *La Courtoisie internationale et le droit des gens* (Paris, 1930).

On 26 May 1888 Count Tisza, the prime minister of Hungary, declared officially in the Hungarian parliament that France was not a country where Hungarians could travel in safety. This remark was generally taken as a serious lack of courtesy towards the *French state*.

At the same time, because of the cosmological structural principle of the state it is impossible to treat this social function apart from the coherence with its *founding* and *leading* function, since the concept of the state itself is not a functional concept but a structural *thing-concept*. The same holds for all other functions of the state.

In the same way the Swedish author Rudolf Kjellén has tried to present a non-functional structural political theory in which all sides of the state as an organized community are grasped under one structural point of view. He calls this theory "political" in the broad Aristotelian sense of the word. However, a mere glance at this system is enough to come to the conclusion, notwithstanding deep appreciation for the serious detailed investigations, that this political theory is not built on a structural thing-concept, but on an untenable metaphysical and naturalistic substance concept of the state. Kjellén writes:

> The state stands before us, not as an accidental or artificial form of human communal life, constricted in juridical concepts, but as a phenomenon that has grown up organically, with deep roots in history and factual reality, a phenomenon of the same basic type as a single human being – in other words, as a biological entity or living being.[1]

This is unvarnished humanist metaphysics, and not a cosmology aimed at a structural analysis. The concept of the state that Kjellén arrives at through what he believes is a strictly unbiased analysis of empirical political reality rather than an *a priori* one[2] is borrowed from the arsenal of the historicist, naturalistically turned idea of the power-state as found already in Droysen's "Lectures on Politics" which were edited and published by Hübner.[3] Droysen wrote:

---

1 Rudolf Kjellén, *Grundriß zu einem System der Politik* (1920), p. 27: "It strikes one immediately that the basis of any introduction here does not reside, as is the case in almost all older systems, in the concept of the state, but in the experience of concrete reality." But by now we are familiar enough with this sort of "realism"!

2 Rudolf Kjellén, *Der Staat als Lebensform*, 4th impr. (1924), p. 175. See also his very important and relevant work, *Die Großmächte vor und nach dem Weltkriege*, 22nd impr. (1930).

3 Rudolf Hübner, "Droysen's Vorlesungen über Politik. Ein Beitrag zur Entwicklungsgeschichte und Begriffsbestimmung der wissenschaftlichen Politik," *Zeitschrift für Politik* 10 (1917): 327–76. On Ranke's theory of the "Great Powers," see Walther Vogel, "Rudolf Kjellén und seine Bedeutung für die deutsche Staatslehre," *Zeitschrift für die gesamte Staatswissenschaft* 81 (1926): 213.

The Crisis in Humanist Political Theory 123

Politics does not teach us what the situation of the world, the state, a single nation ought to be, but *how it is* and how it can arise according to known power conditions. It does not present ideals – but concrete reality and driving forces that are altogether different from those nebulous ones.

Kjellén too teaches that "the state is power, shouldered with dominion." It is the principle of power that presumably determines the structure of the "state as a form of life," and power is here taken in a very naturalistic sense. In this way Kjellén arrives at his "system of politics" which looks at the state from five different angles (the state as a territorial unit, an economic entity, a folk or nation, a society, and a government), and which treats all these categories from the point of view of power.

A truly cosmological theory of the structure of the state will indeed have to analyze all meaning-sides of the state under the central viewpoint of the structural principle we discovered, and in this way go to work in a comprehensive manner. But Kjellén's metaphysics cannot clarify this structural principle for us.

In the present context we can permit ourselves only an introductory review of such a meaning-analysis.

As an example, let us begin with the problem of state territory, which has been made so one-sidedly into the hallmark for the state concept by the theory of the state as a "territorial body" (*Gebietskörperschaft*).

It is impossible to speak of *state* territory or domain apart from the state's meaning-individual guiding function in its coherence with its historical function of dominion. The *general* structure of the jural sphere contains the spatial analogy both as to its law-side and its subject-side, and hence in the general sense of a jural *area of validity*. But in the case of *state territory* a juridical meaning-individuality comes to expression, for there is not a single non-political organized community that has the right of governmental rule over a *territory*, even though the legal acts of every legal subject and the internal legal norms of every organized community obviously have an area or domain of validity.

In Kelsen's *Allgemeine Staatslehre* the logicistic postulate of a "pure method" leads to a complete erasing of this structural difference. He sees space merely as a general element contained in a legal proposition.[1] Viewed in this manner, obviously no fundamental difference can exist between the domain of the state and the domain of validity of the law of

---

1 About the antinomy in which the form-content scheme entangles itself in this connection, see my *De Beteekenis der Wetsidee voor Rechtswetenschap en Rechtsphilosophie* (1926), pp. 33 ff.

non-state communities: "For these, too, are orderings of human conduct, and thus, along with human conduct, space and time are included in the contents of these partial orderings of norms."[1] With that, all problems which the territory of the state poses for general political theory magically disappear. But they disappear only in the study room of the "norm-logician." In reality, of course, they continue to exist!

In our view of the state there is no reason whatsoever to deny that the state as an organized community does possess natural sides as meaning-functions, which make up a real element in the structural whole of the state. In this sense, the view that the state indeed has a natural function of space definitely does not belong, as Kelsen believes, to the "weirdest of misconceptions in modern political theory."

But it would be a serious error to view these sides of nature in a naturalistic fashion, detached from the normative structural principle of the state.

"Political geography" and "Geopolitics"[2] sinned greatly in this regard when they lost sight of this structural principle and began to talk of "geopolitical laws of nature."[3] Such laws are only possible on the basis of a cosmological structural theory of the state, and are on that basis indeed indispensable. For the territory of the state can never be understood *purely* in a functional manner. Its territory signifies a normative task for the state in order to maintain its own existence as a governmental jural community. The "integration theory" has quite properly shed light on this, although the concept of "integration" is, as we saw, quite inadequate for grasping the structural principle of the territory of the state. Here also, the "leading function" retains its meaning-individual governmental legal character, normed by meaning-individual public legal principles.

A state's territory is an integral component of the reality of the state and as such cannot be placed in opposition to the state where the latter is seen as a self-contained organized communal subjectivity. This is the kernel of truth in the resistance which has been waged by both the organic and the phenomenological theories against the mechanistic view

---

1 Kelsen, *Allgemeine Staatslehre*, p. 143.
2 Regarding the modern distinction between political geography en geopolitics, see R. Hennig, *Geopolitik. Die Lehre vom Staat als Lebewesen* (Leipzig, 1928), p. 9. The four editors of the *Zeitschrift für Geopolitik* (1924–), in their standard work *Bausteine zur Geopolitik* (Berlin, 1928), describe this distinction as follows: "Geopolitics is the theory of the earth-bound nature of political processes. It has as its foundation the broad basis of geography, in particular political geography as the theory of political spatial organisms and their structure. . . . Geopolitics wants to be a tool for political action and a guidepost for political life."
3 See Hennig, *Geopolitik*, pp. 13 ff.

of state territory as a pure *object* of *dominion*.[1] On the other hand, a functional understanding of constitutional law does require a juridical *objectification* if the spatial subject-function of the state is to be understood in a *juridical* sense. Abandoning an insignificant colony, for example, can hardly be considered a *real alteration* of an existing state, as a one-sided subjectivistic view of state territory is forced to assume. The meaning-individual existence of a state is determined structurally by its leading and founding meaning-functions, *not* by its spatial subject-function.

Juridically the territory of a state can only be grasped in terms of a public legal subject-object relation, but in this relationship the spatial function in a structural sense itself appeals to the spatial subject-function of a state as a systatic unity. For the (public-legal) legal personality of the state is but one of its functional subject-sides. Ceding or cutting up central portions of its territory undoubtedly strikes the state *qualitatively* as a real organized community, since this affects its *position as a historical power* in connection with its *juridical position as a government*. Being a small or a large, a weak or a strong power is decisive for the *material legal position* which a state occupies in the order of international law. Just think of the content of treaties between states, of the *leading role* that the Great Powers play in the integration of customary law into international law, and so on.

In their *subjective theory* Fricker, Jellinek and others consider national territory juridically to be an organic part of the state as a legal personality. But this is untenable in a structural sense, witness the internally antinomic consequence drawn by Jellinek regarding the *impenetrability* of the national domain. One need only consider the problem of *extra-territoriality* in international law, such as the joint administration of a territory by more than one state, as was the case between 1864 and 1866 with Austria and Prussia in Schleswig-Holstein, or in 1918 with Germany, Austria-Hungary, Turkey and Bulgaria in Dobrudja.

Our view does not merely do justice to the meaning-structural side of the *national territory*, but to all other meaning-functions of the state, including one of the most controversial functions, the *psychic* meaning-function of the state – though not, of course, in the sense of a metaphysical "common soul," the analog of the equally metaphysical "individual soul" as a reification of the temporal psychic function! By a

---

[1] This object theory had a purely Romanistic *private law* orientation. Karl Fricker was the first to challenge this view in his book on the state's territory, *Vom Staatsgebiet* (1867). In the Netherlands the object theory was opposed, among others, by A. A. H. Struycken, *Het Staatsrecht van het Koninkrijk der Nederlanden*, 2nd impr. (Arnhem, 1928), pp. 206 ff.), without, however, presenting a clear alternative.

state's psychic function we mean that it is the task of government to foster the feeling of solidarity, the psychic awareness of statehood among its citizens, under the guidance of the internal jural function of the state. The greater or lesser degree to which the state has achieved this is an important factor in its structural reality, just as the objective reality of a work of art, which is aesthetically qualified, varies with the degree to which the artist has succeeded in realizing the process of aesthetic unfolding of the material.

We need hardly point out what significant role is played in all of this by geographical, ethnic, social and economic factors. As for the geographical factors, we would just mention the fact that a state's psychic function is based on a substrate of spatial, physical and biotic factors. The feeling of "belonging" (what the Germans call *"Heimatsgefühl"*)[1] plays an important role in the sense of solidarity among the citizenry. In this psychic meaning-side of the state we find an interweaving of land and people which can only be clarified from the full meaning-structure of the state as an organized community. In this we can never ignore the connection with the leading jural function. If we do this along the lines of the "sociological theory of the state" we would immediately have to concede to Kelsen that among a certain segment of the citizenry the feeling of solidarity may be more strongly focused on ethnic relatives outside the national territory than on ethnic strangers inside it, and hence that one can find no point of connection in the "national psyche" for the concept of the state. This argument loses its force, however, if, following our structural theory, we always hold on to the meaning-sides of the state in terms of its structural principle. The psychic meaning-side of the state is guided by the normative jural side, but within this structural context it undoubtedly forms a part of the real state. The psychic function in its general meaning-structure already shows anticipations of the jural meaning. In people's *sense* of justice the psychical meaning is deepened by approximating the guiding jural function.[2] But such a deepening of meaning must be realized under the normative *guidance* of

---

1   See Waldecker, *Allgemeine Staatslehre*, p. 482.
2   *General Editor's note*: Dooyeweerd clearly has the intention of highlighting an anticipation within the structure of the sensory (psychic) aspect. Yet he actually mentions here a retrocipation: *"rechtsgevoel."* A similar ambiguity is found in his work *Roots of Western Culture* (1979; repr. 2003), p. 46 n. 1, where he writes about the sensitive-psychic function: "It also unfolds itself within its own aspect in the aspects that follow, so that we can speak of logical feeling, historical and cultural feeling, lingual feeling, feeling for social convention, feeling for economic value, aesthetic feeling, moral feeling, and the feeling of faith certainty." Clearly, *historical feeling* (sensitivity) represents a retrocipation from the historical aspect to the sensitive aspect, whereas it is *emotional control* that illustrates an anticipation from the sensi-

the jural function itself. Trying to derive the meaning of the jural from the *sense of what is just* therefore amounts to a *hysteron proteron*, a reversion of the proper order. Similarly, and even more strongly, it is a reversion of the correct order if one tries to derive the reality of the political community from the lawful psychic interactions between citizens. A state's psychic meaning-function, too, can only be understood in terms of its meaning-individual structural principle.

In the nature of the case, a state's people can also be looked at according to its numerical side. But as soon as this view detaches itself from the principle of the state in a mathematical logicism we end up again in the functionalist metaphysics of the humanist science ideal. We have already shown the political tendencies of state absolutism inherent in this metaphysics. As noted above, the entire absolutistic natural-law theory from Hobbes to Rousseau arrived at the construction of the state's people along pseudo-mathematical lines from the individual to the mathematical totality, a construction served by the rationalist contract principle.

In modern times we meet this mathematical logicism once more, in a crude form, with the founder of the Marburg School of Neokantianism, Hermann Cohen. Cohen applies the mathematical categories of unity, multiplicity and totality to the field of law and ethics, in order to construct the relation between individual, society (embracing all non-state organized communities), and the state. Thus the state ends up as a moral totality in the Platonic sense. One ought to read Cohen's expositions on the state and its "self-consciousness" in his *Ethik des reinen Willens* in order to realize what are the incredible political consequences of this mathematicism.[1]

As we see it, mathematical science does not yet possess an idea of number in which also the meaning-individual anticipations of constitutional law within number come to expression. The concept of an integral totality, oriented to natural-scientific infinitesimal calculus, is useless for political theory. The numerical anticipations alluded to are so intricately complicated by their coherence with the intervening meaning-structures that a straightforward application of the mathematical concept of "integral" to a state's people simple leads to a naturalistic metaphysics. For political theory, that is not just useless but highly confusing and dangerous.

tive aspect to the historical aspect. Further on in the text of *Roots*, however, Dooyeweerd correctly speaks about *emotional trust* and *emotional certainty* – phrases capturing true sensory anticipations to the certitudinal function.

1 See his *Ethik des reinen Willens*, 4th ed. (Berlin, 1923), pp. 243 ff., 519 ff. (the principle of the state is the principle of moral self-consciousness), and also his work *Logik der reinen Erkenntnis* (Berlin, 1922), pp. 202 ff.

In connection with our exposition of the political problem of sovereignty in what follows, the *economic* meaning-side of the state in its people is obviously of great interest. Under the guidance of its meaning-individual jural function the state must bring about the unity of its people, also in an economic sense. It ought not to do this by presenting itself as the *economic* integrator of free enterprise, but by maintaining the *political* solidarity of all branches of economic life within its territory. For we have already seen that also free enterprise communities fulfill a function within the state, although in their internal structure they are not political communities.

The state may not allow its people to tear itself apart economically without moving a finger for countering such a process of dissolution. Nor can it tolerate a situation in time of war when firms within its territory rupture the political solidarity of its people by supplying the enemy. Obviously this, too, is an essential duty for the state in international affairs.

When the state itself takes on the role of a monopolistic corporation, this must be viewed just as much from the same angle. In such cases the state acts in an economic function, but always under the "guidance" of its public-legal meaning-function.

***

Finally, from the standpoint I have developed, I wish to shed light on the juridical consequences of the constitutional problem of sovereignty, which nowadays is so fiercely attacked.[1] In the present context I am first of all interested in the material boundaries of competence of the state vis-à-vis organized non-political communities.

From the beginning the Calvinist theory of law and politics had protested against Bodin's concept of sovereignty which in principle denied the sphere-sovereignty of non-state organized communities and elevated the will of the personal bearer of political sovereignty to the level of being the only source of validity of positive law.[2] Althusius had already strongly raised the Calvinist standpoint in this matter against this absolutist humanist theory of sovereignty when he posited that "every type

---

1 I pass over the problem of sovereignty in *international* law. For now, see my essay on "norms and facts" that will be published in a forthcoming issue of *Themis*. [H. Dooyeweerd, "Norm en Feit; een kritische beschouwing naar aanleiding van het geschrift van Mr. S. Rozemond over Kant en de Volkenbond," *Rechtsgeleerd Magazijn Themis* 93 (1932): 155–214.
2 See my extensive analysis of Bodin's concept of sovereignty in the series "In den Strijd om een Christelijke Staatkunde, XIII," *Antirevolutionaire Staatkunde* 2 (1926): 247–61; Eng. trans. *The Struggle for a Christian Politics*, pp. 195–212.

of organized community has its own proper laws whereby it is governed; and the laws in each differ as required by its kind."[1]

Remark: Deserving of attention is Waldecker's comment[2] that especially since the second edition of the *Politica* the Aristotelian teleological viewpoint was increasingly replaced by functions of organized communities. "Functio" and "ministerium" appear in indissoluble coherence. Waldecker calls it an astonishing fact for this time, and in keeping with the known humanist tendency of historiography he does not hesitate to see a connection between the symbiotic function concept of Althusius and modern natural-scientific thought. Of course this is a reading of dubious value, similar to Gierke's reading of a direct connection between the contract theory of Althusius and Rousseau's theory of popular sovereignty. Nonetheless the function concept of Althusius, in the context of his concept of an organized community, remains a highly remarkable improvement over the still prevailing teleological theory of the time.

On the other hand, Waldecker is absolutely correct when he emphasizes the fact that in his symbiotic theory Althusius succeeded in transcending the Aristotelian substance concept. Waldecker inherited his deep appreciation for Althusius from his teacher Gierke, whom he also follows in the untenable construction of a continuous development from Althusius to Rousseau and Kant.

Gierke already noticed and appreciated this insight into the internal structure of communal law that Bodin's great antipode had developed. On the other hand, in a historically inadmissible fashion Gierke linked Althusius' theory of sovereignty to Rousseau's humanist theory of sovereignty, which sanctioned state absolutism on the basis of natural law.[3]

As mentioned earlier, the absolutistic theory of sovereignty cannot possibly provide a *juridical foundation* for its theory regarding state omnipotence, regardless of whether or not it assumes a personal subject for this sovereignty. In typically dogmatic fashion Bodin postulates his concept of sovereignty without justifying it. Hobbes gives at least an *account* of how he constructs his *Leviathan state*, and he places his cards on the table that reveal the naturalistic and individualistic metaphysics underlying his view of the state. The theory of state sovereignty informed by the idealist-historical concept of the power-state gives a simi-

---

1 "Propriae leges sunt cujusque consociationis peculiares, quibus illa regitur. Atque hae in singulis speciebus consociationis alea atque diversae sunt, prout natura cujusque *postulat*." Johannes Althusius, *Politica* (1610) 1.19.
2 Ludwig Waldecker, *Allgemeine Staatslehre* (1927), p. 398.
3 See my criticism of Gierke's reading of Althusius in my article on "the sources of positive law" in *Antirevolutionaire Staatkunde* (quarterly) 4 (1930): 253–56 and in my oration on "the significance of the law-idea for the science and philosophy of law" (1926), pp. 110–12. I am pleased to note that Carl Schmitt, too, has offered a similar critique in his work *Verfassungslehre* (1928), p. 77: "In the thought of Althusius the people already had a *potestas constituta*. The secularization of the concept of constitutive power did not occur till later. It is altogether incorrect, as Gierke has done in his famous work on Althusius, to see a connection between the concepts of a believing Calvinist such as Althusius and a romantic deist such as Rousseau."

lar account of its universalist metaphysical theory of organized communities, which account, as we have seen, is rooted in the personality ideal informed by transpersonalism. And it is along a pseudo-logical avenue that Kelsen's criticistic positivism arrives at an absolutistic theory of the sovereignty of a state's legal order, behind which we once more discern the specter of an individualist theory of organized communities.

However, no theory regarding the state's juridical omnipotence can ever be founded on *positive law*. If empirical positivism were naive enough to attempt this it would necessarily become guilty of a *petitio principii*, an instance of circular reasoning without parallel, claiming that the will of the state is the fountain of all positive law, or that the law itself states this.

Calvinist political theory posits its theory of *sphere-sovereignty* in opposition to the theory of absolutist state sovereignty in all its forms: sovereignty of the individual, popular sovereignty, logicistic theory of the sovereignty of law. And it has always emphasized that its theory of sphere-sovereignty indeed differs from the *revolutionary* character of the opposing views.

In order to make this theory indeed *juridically* fruitful, the universal cosmological significance of the principle of sphere-sovereignty had first to be illuminated. Next, a cosmological theory of structure had to be erected, which could offer a sharply delineated criterion for sphere-sovereignty within the juridical domain. As long as this was not done, "sphere-sovereignty" remained a vague political slogan which no jurist could use. The image of "the closed front door," before which the sovereignty of the state stops, is of course useless for science.

I believe I have accomplished the task of making my structural theory useful juridically, on the one hand, by demonstrating the theory of sphere-sovereignty in its universal cosmological sense and its worldview significance, and on the other, by formulating a sharp material criterion for the competency of organized communities. This criterion for juridical sphere-sovereignty can be formulated as follows:

> *Every organized community is juridically sovereign in its own sphere with respect to its internal law. The internal law of an organized community must be seen as its internal structural law, the meaning of which cannot be detached from the individual leading function of that organized community in unbreakable connection with its meaning-individual founding function.*

In closing this section, we wish to demonstrate the usefulness of the criterion with some concrete examples. In the process, some questions will automatically arise about the structure of the state as an organized community. In preparation for this, however, we have to enter into a prior discussion of the internal authority structure of the state and those of other organized communities.

In light of the considerations discussed earlier, it is utterly inadmissible to transfer specific historically founded organizational principles that hold for the structure of the state, to the authority structure of organized communities designed in a totally different way. The authority structure of an organized community is determined by its meaning-individual structural principle in indissoluble meaning-coherence with its founding and leading functions.

The internal authority of the nuclear family, according to its structural principle, has its meaning-individual foundation in the biotic sexual union and lineage. In coherence with this biotic substrate it is qualified by its guiding or leading function.

This also provides the juridical side of parental authority with its structural meaning-individuality. Hobbes' radical rationalistic individualism could of course not leave untouched the cosmic structure of parental authority. In a functionalist fashion he sought an abstract juridical foundation for family authority, and failed to find it anywhere but in the same legal ground which he also specified for the authority of the state, namely, a contract![1]

Modern revolutionary democracy basically operates in the same manner when it wants to transfer the *political* principle of co-determination to the non-state communities, and blithely speaks of "industrial democracy," "family democracy," "school democracy," and so on.

In his famous book *La démocratie de l'après guerre* (1922), Georges Guy-Grand, has given a sharply outlined picture of these tendencies of modern democracy to level all structural differences.

Kelsen calls himself an adherent of the modern democratic idea and has shed a sharp light on the relativistic worldview of which it is the political expression. He quotes with approval Max Weber's notion[2] that the modern state, sociologically speaking, can simply be viewed as a large "enterprise" and that there is no essential difference between a private economic enterprise, such as a large factory, and the contemporary state:

---

[1] See my "In den Strijd om een Christelijke Staatkunde, XV" *Antirevolutionaire Staatkunde* (quarterly) 1 (1927): 184–85. [Eng. trans. *The Struggle for a Christian Politics*, pp. 275–76.]
[2] Max Weber, *Parlament und Regierung im neugeordneten Deutschland* (Munich and Leipzig: Dunkler & Humblot, 1918), p. 15.

> For this reason [writes Kelsen] the problem of organization is in both cases basically the same. And democracy is not just a question for the state, but also for the economic enterprise.[1]

This is typical for modern democratic thinking! To bring up Kelsen's own nightmare: this view embodies the same political postulate that grounds his entire logicistic political theory, behind which we detected everywhere the naturalistic and individualistic metaphysics of the humanist science ideal. The cosmological structural principle of the state and the firm is completely eliminated here.

In a modern enterprise the position of authority is clearly based on the historical position of power of the entrepreneur, a position that could only disappear along with the disappearance of the whole form in which modern economic life is organized. The fact that in the course of historical development this position of power in the world of enterprise more and more loses its *individualistic* character – that the modern forms of enterprise in trusts, cartels, concerns and pools more and more push the figure of the individual entrepreneur into the background – this fact in no way alters, in principle, the meaning-individual foundation for authority in the modern enterprise.

The leading function of the enterprise as an organized community is that of the economic sphere and, together with its founding function, it imprints on the authority of the enterprise, also in its juridical function, a type of structure that has no equal in any other type of organized community.

The structure of authority in the state is totally different from that of the family as well the enterprise and the church. State authority is based in a meaning-individual way upon a *political position of power*, which develops into the office of government, that is, into rule of the nation under the guidance of the jural right of a government.

In a parliamentary democracy, political power certainly does not lie with the so-called "sovereign people," which in the absence of a government is not yet a true, unified community. In such a democracy political power resides in a distinctive balance, a historical relation of power between a government and the political parties that are capable of gaining a majority through elections.[2] The more a party system begins to crumble as a result of conflicting interests, the more a government's political power will rise, obliging the head of government to assess the po-

---

1 Kelsen, *Vom Wesen und Wert der Demokratie*, p. 17. Harold J. Laski, *A Grammar of Politics* (London, 1925), p. 73, talks of the state as "a body on the same footing as the Miner's Federation."
2 As soon as *one* political party acquires governmental power and (as in a modern dictatorship) absorbs the party system within the structure of the state, the modern con-

litical situation when forming the cabinet. Conversely, the scales tip decidedly in favor of majority parties which under normal conditions will exercise their influence in parliament. The fundamental principle of the parliamentary system is that the overall direction of the government's program and policy is set at the time of the formation of the cabinet.[1] This is a political principle in the widest sense of the word, a historically founded organizational principle for the structure of authority in the state *as a whole*. It is determinative of the entire organization of the state's authority structure and for this very reason it is impermissible, when interpreting constitutional law, to leave it out of consideration and deny it any juridical significance by treating it as a mere "political convention."[2] For constitutional law is not some abstract, juridical arrangement, positivized once and for all in a written constitution. Rather, it receives its juridical meaning from the living structural unity of the state as an organized community. It is involved in a continuous process of positivization, which must ever be discharged in close contact with historical developments.

It must be embarrassing for a "purely juridical method," which stems essentially from logicistic positivism, that when consistently applied it has to lead to the most preposterous consequences. According to it, the magic wand of the constitutional legislator would be able to elevate the norms of the parliamentary system from "pure conventions"[3] to *juridical, constitutional* rules by means of a few simple articles in the consti-

figuration of a dictatorial party-state emerges, which is the very opposite of the parliamentary form of government.

1   *Translator's note*: Dooyeweerd is describing the function of a multi-party system necessitating coalition governments, not a two-party system where elections produce a clear majority.
2   Such treatment occurs in the juridical method of Gerber and Laband, represented in our country by J. Th. Buys. In Britain, as we know, A. V. Dicey is the prominent representative of this standpoint, which has found fairly general acceptance in connection with the English theory of "common law" as customary law that is exclusively positivized by the courts. In the Netherlands the need to treat "political conventions" as part of constitutional law has been defended, next to Hugo Krabbe, in particular by A. A. H. Struycken in his *Staatsrecht*, pp. 193 ff., and Jacques Oppenheim in his two inaugural addresses at the University of Groningen in 1885 and 1893, entitled *De Volksregeering in het constitutioneel stelsel*, pp. 23 ff., and *De Theorie van den organischen staat en hare waarde voor onzen tijd*, pp. 9 ff. The same position is held by W. van der Vlugt, H. Romeyn and R. Kranenburg. The conventions in question are taken by Struycken and Kranenburg to be customary law that is part and parcel of constitutional law. See also my dissertation, *De Ministerraad in het Nederlandsche Staatsrecht* (Amsterdam, 1917), pp. 27 ff.
3   Orig.: "bloot-politieke stelregels"; the term was introduced into our language [Dutch] by B. A. Kahn in his important dissertation, *Conventions, of politieke stelregels* (1919).

tution. After all, in a number of modern constitutions adopted since the World War such norms appear in all kinds of shapes, even though practice in various states of Central and Eastern Europe revealed immediately that one can never detach an organizing principle for a state's authority structure from its historico-political foundation, and that where this foundation is lacking a simple set of constitutional articles cannot possibly create a truly parliamentary regime. In Britain on the other hand, where it originated and has worked exemplary under the regime of a two-party system, the parliamentary system presumably cannot be accorded any legal significance because its norms cannot be subsumed under positivism's formalistic scheme regarding the sources of law, which acknowledges only two such sources: *law* and *custom*.[1]

Although the parliamentary system is not exhausted by its juridical function, it is in fact of fundamental constitutional significance by virtue of the entire structural principle of the state, whose leading function, after all, lies in the jural domain. But its flexible character, which is so closely tied to the historical position of power of the party system, makes it impossible to assign a rigid, static character to these jural norms. And when the individual historical substrate for it is absent, the parliamentary principles cannot be made into effectual constitutional law, no matter if they appear a hundred times in a written constitution.

The parliamentary democratic form of government, which is indissolubly connected with the *representative system* and which can never be taken in the sense of private law, is clearly a *political* form of the authority structure of the state. Only on the basis of the authority structure of the state is it possible to construct a sound theory of forms of government.[2]

To transfer the principles of political democracy to the structure of authority in a firm or enterprise betrays a misinterpretation of their real meaning, and at the same time a misinterpretation of the meaning-indi-

---

1 For a critique of this formalistic theory, see my "De Bronnen van het stellig recht in het licht der wetsidee," *Antirevolutionaire Staatkunde* (quarterly) 4 (1930): 32 ff., where I work out a new theory of the sources of law on the basis of my own standpoint.

2 Not on the basis of the "methods of legal generation," as Kelsen believes in his logicistic theory of the state. Nor on the basis of the vague concept of "integration" of the Berlin School. In essence, Schmitt's classification of forms of government according to the principle of *identity* and *representation* is no different than the old distinction between *democracy* and *autocracy* and thus again comes down to the organizational principles governing a state's authority structure. Meanwhile the terms "identity"and "representation" are highly misleading! Cf. the correct criticism of this point in M. Kraft-Fuchs, "Prinzipielle Bemerkungen zur Carl Schmitts Verfassungslehre," *Zeitschrift für öffentliches Recht* 9 (1930): 515 ff.

vidual structure of the enterprise. There is no economic system in which authority in the enterprise can be detached from ownership of the means of production. And in the modern economic system it is the entrepreneurial economic function, in its coherence with the historical power of capital, which determines the organizational form of the authority structure within the enterprise. As we shall see below, this certainly does not mean that authority in the enterprise is therefore of an absolutist nature. Quite the contrary! It only means that the leading or guiding of the enterprise does not rest on a historico-political basis, but on an economic-historical position of power in the production process.

With the above exposition we have at the same time taken a stand, on principle, against modern syndicalist theories (Cole, Taylor, Webb, Hobson, Laski, Duguit, Sorel, etc.), who want to confront what they call a "monistic" conception of the state, which has *sovereignty* at its core, with a more "pluralist" conception.[1] Political pluralism, in essence, is *political nihilism*, to the extent, at least in principle, that it completely thrusts aside the meaning-structure of the state.

No matter how much the "political pluralists" may vary in their viewpoints, they do agree on one point: the unity of the state has to be dissolved into a federalism of mutually independent syndicates or corporations, each of which is mandated to administer a specific branch of public service and to champion the special interest of this branch. They sharply attack the concept of sovereignty,[2] the idea of popular representation in the traditional sense of the word, and Rousseau's theory of the "general will," which they regard as pure fiction. Instead they desire a type of "functional representation" – a representation of the professional classes, which they call "organic" representation. One implication of this pluralist idea for the franchise is the plural vote. Pluralists like Laski and Cole (in his earlier period[3]) ultimately reduce all "functions," which are to find their representation in parliament, to those of economic production and consumption, each of which they would like to see represented in two independent parliaments: one social and one po-

---

1 An excellent overview of the different theories is given by Kung Chuan Hsiao, *Political Pluralism: A Study in Contemporary Political Thought* (1927). The term "political pluralism" is probably derived by Laski from the philosophy of William James.
2 See Harold J. Laski, *The Problem of Sovereignty* (1917), *Authority in the Modern State* (1919), and his *Grammar of Politics* (1925), pp. 44 ff. and 241 ff. His train of thought in many respects resembles the ideas of Duguit.
3 In his work of 1920, *Social Theory*, G. D. H. Cole revised his view of the state as presented in his work on *Self-Government and Industry* (1917). He no longer viewed the state as simply representing consumer interests.

litical.¹ When Marxist-Socialist thinking dominates it reduces all meaning-functions to the historical-economic ones and when carried out consistently must reject the very idea of the state.

Engels' well-known statement that the future socialist society would "replace the government of persons by the administration of things," is the honest conclusion of a historicist-economistic worldview that has no room for the structural principle of an organized community known as the state.

Now undoubtedly not all pluralist theories are so inclined. Among the circles of "guild socialism" we find pluralists like Samuel George Hobson, who distinguishes sharply between states and guilds. His idealist view of the state is that it represents the highest moral and cultural interests of society and that in the final analysis "the state, as representing the community at large, must be the final arbiter" of all social relationships.² Thus he factually breaks with the pluralist view of the state.

Aside from such inconsistencies, the core of political pluralism is always that the state must be erected as a federalist system of autonomous, non-state syndicates, whose functions are to be coordinated with the real political "function,"³ while completely erasing the structural differences between the organized communities.⁴

Immediately a dilemma looms here. Either a political organization has to be imposed upon what are essentially non-political communities, a type of organization that has to be all the more tyrannical as the false political structure asserts itself more intensively in the trade syndicates. Or else, conversely, an organization is forced upon the state that is incompatible with its structural principle and would be a first step on the road to anarchy. As Hsiao has put it: this is a dilemma between "political" and "economic" monism.⁵

If the first road is taken, a kind of "pluralism" that is by definition *individualistic* will immediately be converted into a *universalistic meta-*

---

1   In his *Grammar of Politics* Laski has been converted to a system with just a single house of parliament.
2   S. G. Hobson, *National Guilds* (London, 1919), p. 133.
3   See e.g. Laski, *A Grammar of Politics*, pp. 71–72: "We may seek so to organise the various functions other than the State that they may join with it in a coordinate body for the making of final decisions. This, broadly speaking, is the view that has been urged by guild socialist theory."
4   Cf. ibid., pp. 69 ff., where the state is defined as "the body which seeks to so organise the interests of consumers that they obtain the commodities of which they have need." The only difference between the state and the other "associations" is found in the compulsory character of state membership and in the territorial nature of the state. Laski's argumentation for the last criterion is typical: "The interests of men as consumers are largely neighbourhood interests; they require satisfaction, for the most part in a given place."
5   K. C. Hsiao, *Political Pluralism*, pp. 122 ff.

physical view of the state such as we encounter in Othmar Spann's curious book on "the true state" (1923), in which the state, composed organically of commercial and other professional communities, has grafted its governing structure upon human society in its entirety.[1]

Should the second road be taken, all that remains is to *cancel outright the concept of the state*, such as we find openly formulated in the writings of Lenin.

What distinguishes the Calvinist view of the state fundamentally from all "political pluralism" is its maintenance of the structural laws for organized communities as they are grounded in God's sovereignty and serve as the foundation of their "sphere-sovereignty." In this sense already Althusius, *Politica* (1610), chap. IX, p. 115 (emph. added): "I call 'members of the State' or of the *universal symbiotic community* not individual human beings, or families, or even colleges constituted in a particular private and public association, but a number of provinces and districts that agree to form a single whole by mutual conjunction and communication."

From all this it follows that we must fundamentally reject the idea of converting, in whole or in part, the democratic system of a house of representatives into a system of representation along corporately organized professional communities.

In his important book on "the essence of representation,"[2] which is oriented to the phenomenological theory of the Berlin School, Leibholz, as we saw earlier, presents a very valuable discussion about the fundamental incompatibility of the political system of representation with the idea of a "representation by trades or professions." He observes correctly that in practice no political unity has ever – no matter how much theorists have asserted the contrary – been built on an organization of vocational or professional interests. On the representation of professional classes in the *corporate state* of fascism Leibholz writes:

> Corporative syndicalism, which already in pre-fascist times was demanded by the most diverse political parties, today also belongs definitely to the actual foundation for legitimating the fascist state, but is in its contemporary form purely decorative. Only if the sovereign dictatorship, which functionally integrates the state, were to collapse and no other representative authority took its place for activating the will to unify – we must not think now of a new dictator or monarch, but before everything else of [Italy's] Grand Council – only then would the new

---

1 Cf. esp. what Spann says in the latest edition of his *Der wahre Staat* (1931), pp. 276 ff., about "the governmental operations of the social orders as organized in communities," where not even tax service and military service are forgotten!
2 Gerhard Leibholz, *Das Wesen der Repräsentation* (1929), pp. 182 ff., which also contains an extensive bibliography.

chamber, after changing its founding principles, be able once more to become a representation and so play a politically decisive role.[1]

In a similar vein the French constitutional lawyer Hauriou observes, when referring to the fascist organization of the state, that "a political syndicalistic organization is only possible in an extremely authoritarian regime, and its assemblies will have merely a consulting role, and every decision will be in the hands of a very strong executive."[2] Indeed, for a state's structure of authority cannot rest on the same basis as the authority structure of the economic enterprise.[3]

Concerning Germany's National Economic Council, in which the trade and professional classes are to be represented, Leibholz rightly remarks that this council, even if its very limited authority is expanded, can never take the place of a real parliament. And he points out that Article 5 of the Provisional Economic Council Act of 4 May 1920, which designates members of the Council as "representatives of the economic interests of the whole nation" is in conflict with Article 165 part 3 of the Weimar Constitution, which expressly stipulates that the various trade and professional groups shall be represented "in accordance with their economic and social position."

This already shows that the National Economic Council cannot be a true representative body in the political sense of the word; further, that by virtue of sec. 11 of the Act the organizations which have appointed a member possess the right of recall, a provision which conflicts with the independent position that a true popular representative ought to have vis-à-vis his voters for the duration of the session. Furthermore, the fact that the Council conducts all of its activities in committees, without

---

[1] Ibid., p. 191. On the essentially authoritarian coercive character of dictatorial representation, see also Leibholz, *Zu den Probleme des fascistischen Verfassungsrecht* (Berlin and Leipzig, 1928), pp. 22 ff. See further the extensive explanation of the fascist corporate state in Erwin von Beckerat, *Wesen und Werden des fascistischen Staates* (Berlin, 1927), pp. 87–139, and Hermann Heller, *Europa und der Fascismus*, 2nd ed. (Berlin, 1931), pp. 66–135.

[2] Maurice Hauriou, *Précis de droit constitutionnel* (Paris, 1929), p. 559.

[3] The following comment is very good, keeping in mind that as an adherent of the "integration theory" Leibholz in the final analysis remains stuck in a power-state conception: "Representation of the trade and professional classes that champions their interests does not allow the identity principle to operate in a functionally integrating manner since these classes are not political organizations, like parties. In theory it would be conceivable to fall back on the unifying effect of this structural principle only if political life, as in the Marxist ideology, were a superstructure of economic life, that is to say, if politics were economized. Then, and only then, would there not be any difference between a political constitution and an economic constitution." Leibholz, *Das Wesen der Repräsentation*, p. 184 n. 2.

having the plenary meeting participate in these practical activities, points in the same direction.¹

Most interesting in the present context is the political practice of representation of the working classes in Russia's soviet republics. Bolshevist theory defines soviet representation as class representation on the basis of economic production. Mirkine-Guetzévitch in particular has demonstrated with ample documentation that soviet representation is in fact purely political representation and not a representation of the factors of production. Beginning and end of the Soviet system, like that of the fascist system, is the *governing political party* – which could hardly be otherwise in a state based on the dictatorship of the proletariat.² In practical politics, "theories" cannot be allowed to thrust aside the cosmic structural principle of state authority if one desires order, not chaos, to prevail in the state.

* * *

Having examined the meaning-individual authority structure in the state more closely, I must now briefly deal with the special integrating function of the modern state with regard to non-state law. For that I have to start out with the social analogies of the jural meaning.

1 Carl Schmitt, too, commenting in the *Archiv des öffentlichen Rechts*, n.s. 16 (1929): 233 on Art. 5 of the Act of 1920 which seeks to unite the pluralism of socio-economic life with the political unity of the whole, calls it an "empty fiction." The extent to which the notions of pluralism have penetrated a number of radical designs for the organization of the Economic Council appears from a (too generalizing) remark made by Friedrich Glum, *Der deutsche und der französische Reichswirtschaftsrat. Ein Beitrag zu dem Problem der Repräsentation der Wirtschaft im Staat* (Berlin and Leipzig, 1929), p. 49, namely that according to the "professional classes projects" the professional organizations will always supplant the political parties! Regarding subsequent legislative proposals, see Leibholz, *Das Wesen der Repräsentation*, and Marinus van der Goes van Naters, *Het Staatsbeeld der sociaal-democratie* (Amsterdam, 1930), which also provides an overview of how other countries have worked out the idea of economic representation.
2 Boris Mirkine-Guetzévitch, *Die rechtstheoretischen Grundlagen des Sowjetstaates* (Vienna, 1929), p. 50: "Based on the texts and commentaries, soviet representation is purely political and not a representation of production at all, so that appointments can easily be harmonized with the political rule of the Communist Party. Class and production, as well as social criteria, play no role in it. Only considerations of opportunity and usefulness for the revolutionary goal are taken into account, not production. It is a question of nominating members of the Communist Party, not delegating members of one or other branch of production. It is a question of appointing functionaries, not members of the working class, to the electoral colleges. That is precisely the chief contradiction in Soviet law, that there is no representation of the 'principle of production.' Rather, it is a purely political instrument in the service of an equally political (not economic) end."

Above we found that the distinction between grouping in an coordinated and a communal sense has its foundation in the social law-sphere with its core meaning of *sociation*. We also pointed out that on a primitive cultural level the social interindividual and intercommunal relations are initially limited to the members of the natural organized tribal communities (sib or organized family communities, municipal or tribal organized communities, and so on and so forth). There is no peaceful interaction with strangers. A stranger is *hostis* and *exlex* (enemy and outlaw). On a higher level of civilization these narrow walls of coordinate relations are broken through. Typically, the norms of fashion effectuate a differentiation between classes and ranks of people, as already noted by Jehring. Modern norms of fashion are observed throughout the civilized world. Fashion crosses the borders of national communities; it operates, to quote Tönnies, in a "socializing manner." In sharp distinction from "native dress," fashion widens the narrow focus that is oriented solely to the national community. In an external sense it brings the idea of world citizenship to expression, though it can in no way organize the great international relations into a single function of social community.

In contrast to this is the *integrating tendency* of social communal functions which at a primitive level of culture, as we saw, is entirely restricted to the *natural communities* (that is, to those particular communities that are founded on natural functions such as the biotic, the spatial, and so on). These communities exhibit structures of authority and solidarity already in their social function. The parental social function of authority over their children is not at all identical with the juridical or moral function, even though by virtue of the structural principle of the family it is only to be grasped in coherence with the moral function of authority.

In a general sense the social function of authority reveals itself in the demand for *respect* from the socially inferior to the socially superior. In the nuclear family this normative social demand of respect generally reveals itself in unbreakable connection with the demand for love, which is implied on the law-side of its "leading function."

The psychic anticipation, which underlies the social function of authority, is the "urge to submit," an impulse in the sensory function of human consciousness, which in modern times has been emphasized by MacDougall, Ross and Vierkandt. It is a general tendency in the human psychic function, which points forward to the communal connection in the social and later modal law-spheres, anticipating them.

However, the tendencies to differentiate and to integrate in the social function of sociation cannot be divorced from each other. For we know

The Crisis in Humanist Political Theory

that the cosmic coordinate structures can occur only in conjunction with organized communities as spiritual entities.

Social norms take on a particular differentiation in the cosmic structure of organized communities. Already in the natural tribe, for example, the norms for courtesy have an integrating as well as a differentiating – a communal as well as a coordinational – character. On close examination we note that the most intimate correlation exists between these two sides of the function of sociation. When it appears in a coordinational context, the social function evinces a general character. For instance, on the street one greets acquaintances without distinction. But between members of the same natural community this form of courtesy becomes individualized. The norm for decent behavior requiring that one ought to appear in public only when properly dressed is valid in *horizontal* fashion for the entire coordinational function where "individuals" are of equal rank. But between members of the same organized community this norm is specialized vertically: on a more primitive cultural level this occurs especially in a tribal community; when estates flourished in medieval times this specialization reflected a person's social position; in modern times this norm occurs especially along the lines of *social classes* and the extremely differentiated life of free associations (think of sports clubs and the like).

Now it is a remarkable phenomenon in modern society that for the norms of sociation and interaction to become individualized, the natural communities have to yield more and more territory to the organized communities with a historical foundation. The individualizing operation of this organized communal life is not of a vertical but of a horizontal character, directed towards a common destination of similarly structured organized communities. In other words, communal life itself displays a powerful tendency for organized human communities with similar structures to integrate. This is a typical phenomenon of the rationalization of sociation, closely related to the cultural dominants of the modern age.

The natural communities presented a restrictive and primitive picture, as if they were separated by walls of their particular mores. In modern times this has made way for a gigantic unfolding of an international interaction, a kind of commerce that not only outstrips the boundaries of family, municipality and tribe, but also the much wider boundaries of the historically founded national community. In the cosmic order of the law-spheres this shift is displayed first in the sphere of sociation.

In modern civilized society, national character determines less and less the specific forms of social interaction that each person has to observe in associating with the next person. What has arisen in its place is a kind of international code governing human interaction, courtesy, decency, tact, sports and play, amusement and fashion. With these manners one can be at home anywhere in the civilized world, and compared to this, national and local peculiarities gradually lose their significance. Whatever of national or folk practices are still alive are gradually being viewed as antiquated peculiarities that are dying out. Only when a Westerner engages in social interaction with nations that have preserved their historic culture, or with primitive tribal communities, does the vertical contrast between natural communities resurface in full force.

On the basis of the common Western civilization, however, the growth in specific social norms is increasingly dominated by "artificial" organized communities in countless numbers of associations, leagues and organizations that stretch over modern society like a multifarious grid. And as we already noted, this process of specification does not primarily rest on the "individual organized community" but especially on the common objective or destination of similarly structured communities. An integrating tendency is operative here which transcends the boundaries of the individual organized communities.

In the post-social law-spheres we find an analogical reflection of this horizontal integration within the social law-sphere. One has only to note the forms of integration in which economic enterprises with similar objectives have joined forces in large commercial and industrial groups. This horizontal tendency towards integration also penetrates coordinate societal relationships. In the field of law we note the integrating significance of collective bargaining agreements, by means of which large, powerful trade unions restricted the liberty of individuals to enter a labor contract long before collective contracts were declared legally binding in civil law. We have standing clauses in rental and sales agreements, in insurance policies, and so on, all of which are are positivized by large organizations in the various branches of commerce and industry. Particularly in collective bargaining agreements we have a clear example of a transition from societal regulation to state law. *It is remarkable that this horizontal integration of non-political coordinate law is accomplished by organized communities which as such have no juridical competence for this form of creating law. It is only because of their "leading position" as "dominant groups" on the basis of their historical position of power that they succeed in having this non-political integrating law accepted.*

However, we must strongly emphasize the nature of this jural integration. On the basis of their meaning-individual structure, economically qualified organized communities such as trusts and cartels do not allow their integrating activity in the area of communal and coordinational law to be governed by the jural law-idea. They aim primarily for *eco-*

nomic integration, and precisely for that reason there is no guarantee that this process of integration will be guided by the jural law-idea.

After the decline of natural organized communities there is no other organized community besides the state that can guide the horizontal process of integrating non-political coordinational law in a properly jural sense. For the state is the only organized community which in a universal sense finds its leading function in the jural domain.

Given its conception of the state, the *theory of the power-state* is unable to offer a harmonious explanation of this relation of the state to non-state law, and so it ends up with a fundamental dualism that is self-destructive. On the other hand, the abstract *humanist theory of the just state*, which levels all structural differences within the jural sphere, likewise destroys the concept of the state, either by conceiving of the state itself in its original classic shape, which construes the state in a private-legal sense; or, in its second, formalist conception, by viewing only *private law* as genuine *material law*, thus denaturing the state's internal communal law into *purely formal law* which serves only power or extra-jural "cultural aims"; or, finally, in its third, logicistic form, by simply identifying law and state.

The truth of the matter is that the state must primarily positivize its own internal public law and for a considerable time leave the integration of non-political law to the natural organized communities (as occurred in the old folk-law of the Germanic tribal communities!).[1]

Historical development, however, necessarily carries the state to a position where it gradually has to take the process of horizontal integration into its own hands. This process does not cause the state to replace or set aside the integrating formation of law guided by extra-jural individual meaning-functions. Furthermore, the state can bring about this horizontal integration of non-political law only in a way that is determined by its own meaning-individual communal structure. In other words, when integrating non-political law the state can give its norms for integration binding force only by means of the organization of its governmental structure.

Yet there remains a fundamental difference between this law which is integrated by the state and the internal law of the state as an organized community. The former remains *state private law*, that is, private law integrated by the state. The latter remains *public-legal law* internal to the state. This structural difference is already apparent in the process of positivization. Law integrated by the state primarily calls on *civil juris-*

---

1 See also Eugen Ehrlich, *Beiträge zur Theorie der Rechtsquellen*, vol. 1 (1902), p. 238, as well as his *Grundlegung der Soziologie des Rechts* (Munich and Leipzig, 1913).

prudence for its implementation, whereas law internal to the state primarily calls on the state's administrative organs. Borrowing a distinction from Ehrlich's *Soziologie des Rechts*, we may say that the laws for integration essentially provide *Entscheidungsnormen* (norms for decision-making), and the internal law of the state consists of *Organisationsnormen* (norms for its organization).

Still one may not reason, in the line of Smend, that in the state the *judiciary power* is really not at all important. For on the one hand the organization of civil jurisprudence belongs in principle to the public-legal internal law of the modern state, and on the other the modern state has long known an administrative jurisprudence that deals with internal disputes between a government's organs and its subjects.

Looked at from this angle, we must reject both the humanist theory of the power-state and the abstract humanist theory of the just state, and we should distinguish sharply between a private-legal and a public-legal conception of the just state. Both are based on the meaning-substrate of typical historically dominant factors, which were not evident in Roman antiquity or the Middle Ages, nor in the individualistic era at the beginning of the 19th century.

The Roman concept of *imperium* knew of no legal appeal against acts of its administrative organs. The empire was autocratic throughout, and it had as its antipode the individualistic private-legal idea of the sphere of the *pater familias* with his absolute will. The Golden Age of Rome was founded on the balanced delimitation of the two spheres, the *jus privatum* and the *jus publicum* (private and public law). The Imperial Age with its increasingly absolutistic character was accompanied by a great expansion of public law, and yet it could not alter the fundamentally individualistic tenor underlying private law. In this way two spheres of law directly faced each other: that of public law and that of private law. In the technical sense of internal state law, public law had practically no point of connection with private law. In complete independence it developed the institutes of public property, public lands, state finances, and the like. The private-legal concepts of commercial law and contract law remained without any influence on these institutions; the latter were imbued with the spirit of the autocratic imperium.[1] That is the reason why the state did not provide any legal protection against its internal acts as an organized community.

Now it so happens that under the influence of Gierke's theory of the Germanic system of corporations the opinion arose (not at all shared by Gierke himself) that the distinction between public and private law was

---
1 See Gustav Adolf Walz, *Vom Wesen des öffentlichen Rechts* (inaug. oration, Univ. of Marburg, 1928).

unique to Roman law and had been derived from the Roman idea of the *imperium*. It became fashionable to contrast this Romanistic view of law (which for that matter had been elaborated in Roman times more in a practical than a theoretical manner) with the Germanic idea of law to which a dualism between two distinct legal spheres was presumably fundamentally foreign.

The Germanic idea of law was supposed to have been based completely on the corporation concept and from the start was devoid of both the individualistic view of private law and the public-legal idea of the state rooted in the spirit of the Roman *imperium*.[1]

All legal relations, from those between neighbors, mark and court associations all the way to the supreme bond of allegiance between king and people, are supposed to have woven themselves into one Germanic "legal system" rooted in a single, shared social conception of law. As Walz puts it:

> The Germanic concept of the state is completely different from that of the Romans. It is built upon the bonds of personal relationships of fidelity, of leaders and their retinue. There is no room here for the authoritative *imperium* of the *res Romana*. For that reason also the legal relations between king and people were not unilateral rights of authority, but rested on mutuality. Rights and duties were proportionate throughout. And legal protection was basically entailed in all legal relations.[2]

Remark: Walz attempts to provide a "socio-morphological" foundation for the distinction between public and private law. A more detailed elaboration of this "morphological sociology" is found in his extensive work *Die Staatsidee des Rationalismus und der Romantik und die Staatsphilosophie Fichtes* (Berlin-Grunewald, 1928), pp. 1–157. By *Sozialmorphologie* (the term is strongly reminiscent of Spengler!) Walz understands a general theory of "the shapes and forms prevailing in the relationships between human beings." It is a sociological discipline that is meant to serve as the foundation for the "sociological sciences" (law, social ethics, politics (!), economics, and ethnology). The elementary primal phenomenon of such a sociology is supposed to be the relationship between a multiplicity of human beings. Once again we can see the *formalistic* delineation of sociology's field of investigation – a delineation that lacks all clarity of meaning. The original elementary social phenomenon is supposed to reveal itself in three basic forms: in the form of the individualistic relationship of hostility, in the organic "relationship of subordination," and finally, in the power relationship of domination. In connection with this threefold articulation Walz introduces a distinction between three kinds of law: *coordinational law*, *inordinational law* and *subordinational law*. Where the organic relationship of "inordination" dominates social reality, as was the case in medieval law,

---

1 In addition to Krabbe, see also J. W. H. M. van Idsinga in his remarkable book *De Administratieve rechtspraak en de constitutioneele monarchie* (The Hague, 1893), 1:12 ff.
2 Walz, *Vom Wesen des öffentlichen Rechts*, p. 15.

no room is supposed to be available for the distinction between public and private law (as "subordinational law" and "coordinational law").

In the present context I cannot elaborate further on my principled objection to this view. Although it is clearly oriented to Gierke's romantic theory of organized communities, it fails to do justice to Gierke's historical perspective regarding the fundamental change of public law in the modern state. I make only two critical comments concerning the untenability of his theory: (i) on the one hand it does not acknowledge the structure of authority present within the non-political organized communities, and (ii) it continues in principle to orientate the idea of public law to the Roman *imperium* idea!

Meanwhile the entire view which traces the distinction between public and private law back to the typical Roman conception is unacceptable. As I see it, the contrast between a fairly primitive Germanic conception of the state and that of the state as it was developed to a high cultural level by the Romans must be rejected as lacking a sound historical foundation.

On the one hand, it is not intrinsic to the structure of public law that the subject, when confronted with the state, would have to be without rights. That is nothing but a particular, autocratic twist in the concept of public law. The issue is simply whether public law possesses a structure of its own as against private law, and whether this also comes out in typical legal principles.

On the other hand, the question whether juridical life of the Germanic Middle Ages knew no distinction between public and private law cannot be posed in such a general sense. Nor can it be answered (as was once thought, in particular under the influence of Haller's private-law theory) in terms of the "patrimonial state." Studies by Below on the political situation in the Middle Ages[1] have made a strong argument for the view that even in the so-called feudal period the fundamental difference between public and private law was never lost sight of, even though at the time the domain of public law, in keeping with the extremely weak position of the state, had dwindled to a minimum.

In this connection we must note that it is a fundamental error in methodology, when investigating legal history on this point, for instance to deduce the structure of the medieval "state" from the structure of the juridical relations of the Germanic royal court, which were essentially founded on an economic basis. This was tried by means of the theory

---

1 Cf. esp. G. von Below, *Der deutsche Staat des Mittelalters*, 2nd ed. (Leipzig, 1925). In the Netherlands, writers like Struycken supported Below's interpretation; see his *Het staatsrecht van het Koninkrijk der Nederlanden*, 2nd impr. (1928), pp. 207 ff.

concerning the rights of the Crown, a theory that was strongly influenced by Haller.[1]

What can be said is that constitutional theory, which began to flourish from the sixteenth century onward especially in France and which was in keeping with the rise of absolutist tendencies in the national monarchies, was inspired by the Roman *imperium* idea. This is especially true of Jean Bodin, who was the first to develop the absolutist concept of sovereignty in a systematic fashion. Yet already in the 14th century the *legists* (the secular jurists who were versed in Roman law) defended the independence of public law in harmony with the Roman conception of law. In the Low Countries Philip of Leyden, in his *De cura republicae et sorte principantis*, defended the inalienable sovereign rights of the Crown, typically based on Roman law. The practical basis for these theories lay in the transformation of the feudal state into the absolutist, bureaucratic state.

The creation of the Norman bureaucratic states in Sicily, England and Burgundy, and the victory of absolute monarchy in France at the end of the Hundred Years' War, ushered in a new view of the state. Frederick Barbarossa had already attempted to introduce a bureaucratic regime of government employees in Italy. The reception of Roman law provided these theories with a certain basis in positive law, and the theory of *raison d'état* reinforced the further penetration of the Roman *imperium* idea. The absolutist, humanist doctrine of natural law (Hobbes, Rousseau) strictly maintained the public-legal view of the state in the sense of Roman law. At the same time it accentuated the individualist character of its absolutist political theory by means of its construction of the contract and its view of the state as a *societas inaequalis*.

---

[1] Even in the thought of Stahl we find rudiments of the Hallerian theory, for example where he teaches that next to being a commander the true title of royal power is constituted by wealth in landed property (see F. J. Stahl, *Staatslehre* (Berlin, 1910), p. 249). See also G. Groen van Prinsterer, *Ongeloof en Revolutie* (Leyden, 1847), pp. 70–85, where he still relies completely on Haller's private-legal "patrimonial theory" (under the influence of Stahl, as we know, Groen later abandoned this theory). A critical case can be brought in against the methodological orientation of the court-law theory that was defended by Nitzsch and Inama-Sternegg under the influence of the historical school in economics. The case was already brought forward by the well-known representative of the Historical School, Heinrich Leo, in his *Studien und Skizzen zu einer Naturlehre des Staates* (Halle, 1833). In Sparta land labor was exclusively done by the *helots* or serfs. Yet the landlords of Sparta did not divide governmental authority among themselves. As subjects they belonged to the public-legal state as an organized community. The *helots* were *douloi tou koinou*, slaves of the community. Particularly in Sparta, where land ownership played such a fundamental role in societal life, *public law* manifested itself with an intensity and scope unparalleled anywhere else.

The distinction between public law and private law is a structural matter which can only be clarified on the basis of the cosmological structural principle of organized communities. But by virtue of the meaning-individual structure of the state this distinction can never be understood when it is detached from historical developments. For that very reason all *formalistic criteria* are in essence untenable. And the criterion of a power theory, such as was defended in our country by Loeff,[1] is equally untenable. In essence this merely aimed at reviving the autocratic idea of the Roman *imperium* in modern public law when the historical basis for this idea had disappeared long ago.

Modern historical development demands from the cultural dominants that they recognize the value of each individual human being for the unfolding of civilization in bonding the cultural community. For that reason it is as incompatible with the sharp dualistic separation of the individual sphere and the sphere of state power in the Age of Rome as with the absorption of the individual in the life of private organized communities during the medieval era and the individualistic structure of the coordinational society at the beginning of the nineteenth century.

The modern public-legal idea of the just state was carried through on the basis of this culturally dominant factor in modern history. It found its expression in a more or less developed organization of administrative jurisprudence. At the same time we see, along the lines of the integration process as discussed earlier, the rapidly increasing interweaving of public and private law. In modern times, private and public law interact constantly, invoking each other without forfeiting their own structure.

In its external private-legal relationships the state, on the one hand, in line with the private-legal conception of the just state, increasingly conforms to the horizontal norms for integration which are essentially of the nature of private law; think of the modern jurisprudence with respect to Article 1401 of the *Civil Code* concerning torts committed by the government (see Appendix E). On the other hand, there is a growing recognition of the public-legal side to private-legal relationships (think of the far-reaching regulation by public law of private property rights and contractual rights).

But the internal meaning-structural distinction between public and private law reveals itself in the meaning-individual structural difference in the legal principles which hold for the internal governmental law, for the integrational law of the state, and for the internal non-state communal and coordinational law – a difference that is also upheld in modern

---

1 Cf. J. A. Loeff, *Publiekrecht tegenover privaatrecht* (diss. Leyden, 1887).

judisprudence.¹ Since I have already elaborated this point extensively in my study on "the structure of legal principles and the method of legal science in light of the law-idea"² I may confine myself to referring to this treatise.

Let me just note in the present context that in its second phase the theory of the just state, which culminates in the demand for administrative jurisprudence, does not do justice to the public-legal idea of the just state in the sense as we described it earlier. This holds to the extent that it wishes to limit administrative legislation to a formal question of law. The issue surfaced in the familiar distinction between questions of right and questions of utility (or of special interests) such as it has been adopted in our country by Buys and others.

Terminologically already, this distinction is not very felicitous, as it conforms to the formal theory of the law-state, for which the *jural*, in the form of statutory *law*, is merely the *formal boundary* for the operation of the state, which by itself can pursue all possible goals.³

Ever since the famous decision of the *Supreme Court* of 20 November 1924, Dutch civil courts, on the basis of Article 1401, have reviewed the *formal* legitimacy (in the sense of formally conforming to the law) of the actions of the government without, however, in line with the decision of 1919,⁴ looking at the *material* question of law that was at issue. Recalling this, one senses immediately that the idea of a purely formal administrative jurisprudence could at most be consistent with the private-legal idea of the just state but could never meet the requirements for a public-legal idea of the just state and so lose *the essential difference between civil law and administrative law*.⁵

Of course, when judging a dispute of material administrative law the courts are not to take the side of the administration and as such judge the government's conduct in a favorable sense. The difference between administrative jurisprudence and political administration remains quite real. As Tezner already remarked:

> The administrative judge does not need to decide whether it is necessary or expedient from the standpoint of *good government* that a government

---

1 See e.g. Paul Duez, *La Responsibilité de la puissance publique* (*en dehors du contrat*) (Paris, 1927) regarding the jurisprudence of the French *Conseil d'Etat*.
2 H. Dooyeweerd, "De structuur der rechtsbeginselen en de methode der rechtswetenschap in het licht der wetsidee," in *Wetenschappelijke Bijdragen aangeboden door Hoogleeraren der Vrije Universiteit*, pp. 225–66.
3 See e.g. J. Th. Buys, *De Grondwet* (Arnhem, 1887), 2:327 ff.
4 See the decisions of 25 May 1928, 29 June 1928 (the "Strooppotarrest") and 8 February 1929.
5 This structural difference is of course entirely eliminated by Kelsen and his school; see e.g. Adolf Merkl, *Allgemeines Verwaltungsrecht* (Berlin, 1927), pp. 21 ff., 77 ff.: "The intended features of the public-legal character of administrative law," according to him, are naturally "a-typical and un-juridical."

official may impose a stipulation or measure on an individual. What the judge must decide is whether under certain circumstances it was necessary or expedient that a stipulation or measure was imposed on an individual, or waived as the case may be, such that *justice was done to the individual*.[1]

It is without a doubt consistent with the historically founded idea of a public-legal just state that the administrative judge assesses the internal, material legal questions according to the principles of public law.[2]

In this vein, furthermore, the competence of the administrative judge has been expanded, as for instance in the law on crisis jurisprudence of 26 July 1918, no. 494, and in Article 58 of the Civil Service Act of 1929 regulating the legal position of civil servants (albeit in the limited sense of judging a so-called "abuse of power").[3] Similarly, the same principle has been laid down in Articles 11 of the *Hinderwet*[4] and in Article 77 of the *Ongevallenwet*,[5] though in a sense which may be too broad from the point of view of jurisprudence.[6]

In conclusion I make bold to state here that to deny this structural distinction in juridical principles, as is done in modern theories on juridical sovereignty, would be a slap in the face for the very idea of law and, to be consistent, would entail the elimination of, for example, the structural difference between criminal law and the civil right to compensa-

---

1 Friedrich Tezner, *Zur Lehre von dem freien Ermessen der Verwaltungsbehörden als Grund der Unzuständigkeit der Verwaltungsgerichte* (Vienna, 1888), p. 93. See also idem, *Die deutschen Theorien der Verwaltungsrechtspflege* (Berlin, 1901).
2 See also Struycken, *Handelingen van de Nederlandsche Juristenvereeniging* 30/2 (1908): 132–42, who, however, completely blurs the boundaries between "administration" and "jurisprudence." See also J. A. Levy, *Administratieve rechtspraak* (The Hague, 1886). Van Idsinga, in his *De administratieve rechtspraak*, 1:18 ff. as well as in his committee report *Het Verslag van de Staatscommissie voor de administratieve rechtspraak beoordeeld* (Rotterdam, 1899) sharply opposes the distinction between legal questions and questions of utility as made by Buys, Roëll,Vos and Ruyll, in accordance with the recommendation of the state commission. But Van Idsinga completely loses sight of the boundaries when in his *De administratieve rechtspraak*, 1: 39, he fails to observe any material limits to the competency also of the civil judge with respect to the internal law of an organized community; citing the decision of the Court of The Hague of 21 January 1899, which of course was related only to the merits of a particular case, he exploits it for the sake of obliterating any material boundaries of a civil judge's competence!
3 By itself the assessment of a *détournement de pouvoir* may still be considered, if need be, a *formal* question of law.
4 *Hinderwet*: law protecting people against danger, harm or nuisance when an industry or commercial enterprise settles in their neighborhood.
5 *Ongevallenwet*: law compensating workmen for injuries sustained in the workplace.
6 See in connection with this the work of L. van Praag, *Rechtspraak en voornaamste litteratuur op de Rechterlijke Organisatie*, 3rd ed. (The Hague, 1916), 1:580 ff.

tion for damages – the very thing that was done by Kelsen in his book on constitutional law.[1]

If, after erasing the fundamental structural distinction between public and private law, one were to try and restore the difference between criminal law and the private-legal right to compensation for damages on the basis of the "sense" of justice of one's fellow citizens as the only material source of law, one would be guilty of a *hysteron proteron* such as we noted already earlier in connection with the psychologistic theory of law.

The state's criminal law remains a *governmental law*, similar to non-state penal law which always displays, as the law of an organized community, an authority structure. Within coordinational relationships, by constrast, no genuine penal law is possible because punishment essentially manifests a relation of authority and subordination between members of an organized community.

* * *

As one considers our views concerning the internal structure of the state as an organized community and its modern integrating function regarding non-state law, one may well wonder how the meaning of the state's internal law and the state's integrational law can possibly be deepened under the impact of the idea of law. After all, against this possibility one might, on our standpoint, raise the argument that a *disclosure*, a *deepening* of the meaning of law can only occur under the guidance of *later* meaning-functions, while we have argued explicitly that the state as such is qualified by a meaning-individual *jural* function. If we are right in maintaining that a meaning-individual jural function does indeed lead or guide the internal structure of the state, how then can this "leading function" itself be *led* in turn without losing its place in the structure of the state?

In order to reduce this seemingly obvious argument to its proper dimension, we need only recall that not a single "thing-structure" may be absolutized (as is done in metaphysics) into a *thing in itself* which as such would be detached from the religious root of our entire temporal cosmos. As a community the state can only become real through human

---

1 H. Kelsen, *Hauptprobleme der Staatsrechtslehre, entwickelt aus der Lehre vom Rechtssatze*, 2nd ed. (Tübingen, 1923), p. 139, where he reduces the typical meaning-individual concept of *guilt* in criminal law to the abstract concept of unlawful conduct or *tort* in what is essentially coordinational law. Against this see my "Beroepsmidsdaad en strafvergelding in het licht der wetsidee," *Antirevolutionaire Staatkunde* (quarterly) 2 (1928): 291, 308.

activity, and as we saw earlier, the human being as such has no "leading function" in time.

In this manner all temporal things, natural as well as spiritual ones, depend on human activity for a deepening of their meaning. As such they do not lose their thing-structure, unless they are being transformed into another entity with a new thing-structure that has a different leading function. That also holds for the state as an organized community. But this particular organized community has, *as such*, its "leading function" in the jural aspect. And all deepening of its meaning, which the state's structure exhibits in the area of law, remains essentially determined by its meaning-individual structural principle. Both the private-legal and the public-legal idea of the just state contain a juridical deepening of meaning in the authority structure of the state as against the autocratic types of organized governmental authority. Yet throughout this deepening of meaning the state remains qualified by its jural function. As soon as one were to put this structural principle aside, the state would cease to exist. One cannot seek the "leading function" of the state in any other law-sphere without disrupting the very concept of state. *Nevertheless, the idea of right, which points beyond the meaning of the jural towards the meaning of the cosmically later spheres, and which as the idea of the consummation of right points beyond time towards the religious fullness of meaning of divine justice, retains its sway over the meaning-individual jural domain of the state.*

* * *

Finally, then, I should like to give in conclusion a few practical examples to illustrate our new-found criterion for applying the cosmological principle of sphere-sovereignty to the area of law. Based on my previous comments on the integrating role that the modern state plays in relation to non-state law, I shall also use the opportunity to clear up some misunderstandings that have already arisen in certain quarters about my view of sphere-sovereignty in the juridical field.[1] I shall choose my examples mainly from internal church law and internal corporate law. I must emphasize that I shall not be speaking of what is desirable from a

---

1   Cf. articles in *De Nederlander; dagblad tot verbreiding van christelijk-nationale beginselen* (17 September 1930), *De Gids; orgaan van het Christelijk Nationaal Vakverbond in Nederland* (9 October 1930), and *Patrimonium; orgaan van het Nederlandsch Werkliedenverbond 'Patrimonium'* (25 September 1930), occasioned by my presentation to the Annual Meeting of the Association of Christian Employers at Groningen. [Cf. also H. Dooyeweerd, "De grenzen van de staatsinmenging in het bedrijfsleven in het licht der Calvinistische wetsidee" (unpublished), which defends the idea that arbitrary government interference in business lacks authority and can never achieve binding force.]

political point of view, but only of the strictly material legal limits to internal state-sovereignty.

As we know, the civil judge, who essentially has to concretize governmental integrating law, when applying Article 1401 of the Civil Code to disputes arising within the state as well as within non-state organized communities, refrains from entering into an assessment of the *material* legal issue and applies only a *formal* criterion of unlawfulness, whereas since the famous decision of the Supreme Court of 31 January 1919 the courts for the rest apply a *material* criterion.

Remark: That judges are not competent to assess matters of a church member's "faith and confession, and conduct of life" was explicitly stated by, among others, the Court of The Hague on 28 February 1888 in regard to Article 3 of the General Regulations of the Dutch Reformed Church of 1 May 1852. Recent examples in Dutch jurisprudence are found in the decision of the District Court of Utrecht (18 April 1928) regarding the property of the Reformed parsonage of Tienhoven. Here the court explicitly established that it did not have to provide a *spiritual evaluation* but only a *civil legal* one. Therefore it refused to review the material lawfulness of the decisions of the Synod of Assen (1926). A similar position was taken in the verdict of the District Court of Maastricht (30 May 1930) regarding the ecclesiastical termination of a Jesuit's membership in his religious order.

See also the important material collected on this point by Van Praag, *Rechtspraak en voornaamste litteratuur op de Rechterlijke Organisatie*, vol. 1 (1916), sec. 17.5a-5b, pp. 647 ff. In respect of the *pre-judicial* nature of ecclesiastical decisions regarding questions of faith, confession and conduct of life for the civil judge, the author remarks correctly that it is completely in harmony with the prevailing relationship between church and state in our country, and that it is also in the interest of an unshaken trust in the impartiality of the judge (ibid., p. 651). He is justified in confronting the opposite view with the rhetorical question whether the judge then has to obtain expert advice about confessional issues or whether the judge has to decide these on the basis of his own knowledge. For a more extensive discussion, with extracts from court decisions, see Van Praag, *Rechtspraak*, vol. 2 (1925), pp. 134 ff.: "The nature of a church precludes the decision of the normal judge regarding internal ecclesiastical laws."

Regarding the internal law of organized communities of *non-ecclesiastical* corporations the author formulates, on the basis of existing jurisprudence, the following principle: *The civil court is deprived of assessing the material lawfulness of decisions of rescinding someone's membership*. Once again, the material legal question is related to the "leading function" of the corporation.

The explanation for this difference is to be found in the material criterion for sphere-sovereignty in the field of law as we have indicated earlier. Judging the material legal question among the internal differences of organized communities would force the civil judge to take sides in an area of internal law that falls under the meaning-individual guidance of the destination function of such an organized community.

Suppose, for instance, that someone would file an action in a civil court based on Article 1401 of the *Civil Code*, in order to establish the unlawfulness of an ecclesiastical decision to suspend or defrock a minister. Imagine further that the judge would want to go behind the formal juridical question (whether a rule of internal church law had formally been violated) and initiate an investigation into the material question of law (whether the minister, for example, had in fact deviated from official doctrine). One senses immediately that this would land the judge within the area of internal ecclesiastical law. But that would be impossible without taking sides in a question of faith and doctrine, in which a *civil judge* is not competent. And a *state legislator* is even less qualified to get involved in such internal questions of church law. If he does so anyway, the resulting legislation will merely have the subjective *form* of law but cannot be recognized as binding positive law.

On the other hand, by virtue of its juridical sphere-sovereignty the state is fully competent to guard against the church if she were to assume rights in the *public domain* the exercise of which would endanger the internal order of the state. This would hold even if such ecclesiastical activities possessed a pistically qualified structure. The church cannot claim sphere-sovereignty in the internal order of the state.

Far more controversial than the juridical sphere-sovereignty of the ecclesiastical community is that of the enterprise as an economically qualified organized community. How can the criterion as we have defined it be applied in this case? The problem is indeed extremely complicated here because the "leading function" of the enterprise itself can never guide the process of making positive law. Another reason is that a large modern enterprise with its immense, and often international, concentration of economic power has a massive impact on the internal life of the state, indeed on the whole of human society.

On the other hand, since the previous century the modern state has begun to intervene in the world of economic enterprise with mounting intensity by means of social legislation. Moreover, the state, either by itself or via its subdivisions (provinces and municipalities), exploits various enterprises in monopolistic fashion; the state has become a shareholder in large private firms; and so on, and so forth.[1]

Remark: The direct exploitation of firms by the state or its public-legal subdivisions is, as is fairly widely acknowledged, tied to characteristic limitations, a condition that is fully comprehensible in terms of the structural principle of organized com-

---

1 A case in point is the post-war city-state of Vienna under a socialist government: it acquired a controlling interest in no fewer than sixty-six important free economic enterprises, in addition to those already owned and operated by Vienna itself!

munities as explained here. Direct exploitation will always be tied to the typical state structure with its leading jural function. Therefore it is not warranted unless there are public-legal jural grounds for it. Even though state exploitation is always *economically* bound to *economic norms*, the economic management remains dependent upon the guidance of the public-legal function of the state and not upon the meaning-individual entrepreneurial function. For that reason not many firms lend themselves to exploitation of this kind. Vladimir Zhelezhnov, in his work on political economy, writes:

> By its very nature it is more appropriate for a public firm to operate with simple and regularly occurring challenges of big scope, where management can proceed bureaucratically according to a fixed scheme, without constantly having to face solutions to newly emerging questions. A firm of this sort is not so much built on the economic interests of the entrepreneur as it is on its technological readiness, its reliability, and its awareness of its public obligation. In modern industrial life the range of challenges to be reckoned with are limited. Operating a big business enterprise is in the majority of cases dependent to a large degree upon market fluctuations, such that it is ever necessary to adapt to new conditions and make quick decisions that involve considerable risk. Under theses circumstances a public corporation, with its inherent sluggishness and inertia, is not a serious option. For this reason public corporations are only suitable for a relatively small number of economic tasks, ones that serve the common interest. Among them are canals and railways, postal and telegraph services, utilities, and the like. [1]

Writing in a similar vein, Robert Liefmann, *Die Unternehmungsformen mit Einschluss der Genossenschaften und der Sozialisierung*, 4th ed. (Stuttgart, 1928), pp. 241 ff., believes that the idea of a "general *state corporation* is indeed the simplest – one may also say the most thoughtless – solution" for the problem of reforming the production system.

Among many others see also Carl von Tyszka, *Die Sozialisierung des Wirtschaftslebens* (Jena, 1919), pp. 35–43, and Bruno Heinemann, *Sozialisierung, ihre Möglichkeiten und Grenzen* 2nd ed. (Berlin, 1919), pp. 28 f.).

In short, the life of the state and the life of the economic enterprise have in modern times been intertwined by a thousand fibers.

Taking all this into account, how are we to give practical application to the meaning-criterion for juridical sphere-sovereignty in the area of economic enterprise? Once more we begin by emphasizing that internal corporate law differs fundamentally from internal church law, internal family law, and the like, in that it is firmly linked to the "leading function" of the enterprise but that this "leading function" can be applied here only as a meaning-individual substrate of organized communal law. Internal corporate law itself can only receive genuine guidance, a

---

[1] Vladimir Zhelezhnov, *Grundzüge der Volkswirtschaftslehre*, trans. into German by E. Altschul, 2nd ed. (Leipzig and Berlin, 1928), p. 182.

deepening of its meaning, from later meaning-functions (the moral and the pistical) while always fully maintaining its meaning-individual foundation.

As the organized political community and the universal integrator of non-state law, the state can in this case do nothing but see to it, as best it can, that the citizen as a legal subject is not materially absorbed by an absolutized economic function, that the political solidarity of the nation is preserved also in an economic sense, and that the economic vitality of the people is not compromised.

Thus the state through its social legislation at one time put an end to the legal defenselessness of the economically weaker party which, under the pernicious slogans of the Manchester school, had de facto been reduced to wage-slavery. Similarly, once the ban on "combinations" was lifted, the trade unions, using their increasing historical and economic power, de facto terminated the fiction of individualistic freedom of contract and launched the battle for just working conditions.

On the other hand, it belongs equally to the competence of the state legislator, with his right to govern, to guard against potential excesses of modern trusts and cartels by which consumers unjustly become victims of restricted production, inflated prices, and so on, aimed at making exorbitant profits. Yet we must also realize that we should not exaggerate the danger of such excesses because, thanks to the cosmic coherence of the law-spheres, they could backfire on the entrepreneurs.

However, it can never be part of the competence of the state to interfere in the *internal structure* of corporate law. The internal authority of an enterprise does not derive from the authority of the state. Suppose government legislation would make it mandatory for all economic enterprises of a certain size to install employee councils which would share authority in the internal guidance of the enterprise with the employer. Such a law, which would interfere with the internal structure of the enterprise, could not be accepted as binding positive law.[1] By the same token, the state would overstep the bounds of its competence if it were to prescribe, in a positive spirit, as a kind of super-manager, that corporations introduce certain work procedures to boost productivity, or cut back their production, or levy economic tariffs, and so on and so forth.

Let us once more draw a parallel with the boundaries of competence for the civil judge confronted within the internal law of the business enterprise. We can note that our courts have repeatedly given evidence of

---

1 Cf. e.g. Article 65 of the Weimar Constitution which merely declares, however, the principle of "equal rights," a principle that, as we know, is worked out only very briefly in the Company Councils Act of 4 Feb. 1920.

the insight that any material legal question that is typically related to the economic destination of an enterprise is withdrawn from the judgment of the civil judge in the case of disputes.

In its formal standpoint on this matter the jurisprudence goes even further. For instance, in its decision of 4 February 1901 the Court of The Hague upheld the verdict of a lower court which stated that the civil judge may not presume to give an opinion as to whether the general meeting of a limited liability company, acting on its bylaws when annually establishing its profit, has properly estimated the company's assets.[1] In such cases the state would overstep the juridical boundaries of its position as government and indeed usurp an economic guiding function, which it cannot possess by virtue of its cosmic structure.

Wherever the state functions as a governing community, it must never allow its actions to be guided by the meaning-individual leading function of the economic enterprise as a free organized community. Ultimately, maintaining the sphere-sovereignty of the internal law of organized communities can only lie with the highest authoritative organs of those organized communities themselves. And as we have seen, the criterion for this is not open to their subjective choice but resides in the divine laws for the structure of these communities themselves.

Seen in this light, no subterfuge is acceptable that would once again submit the assessment of the material boundaries for the state's competence versus other communities exclusively to an administrative court of the state itself, in whose decisions the non-state communities would then have to acquiesce (see Appendix F). The Leviathan state may for a time factually violate the juridical sphere-sovereignty of non-state communities through brute force. But *juridically* the state lacks any overrid-

---

[1] See also Struycken in *Rechtsgeleerd Magazijn* 28 (1909): 324–25 on the question whether or not the civil judge may test the legal validity of a certain action by an organ of a limited liability company against that company's stated goal as laid down in its by-laws. However, Van Praag, *Rechtspraak*, 1:655 n.1, disagrees with Struycken's interpretation of the 6 March 1908 decision cited below.

Of course the civil judge does not bid farewell to the framework of *formal* questions of law when he determines, on the basis of a company's goal as formally described in its by-laws, whether or not certain decisions by the meeting of shareholders are formally at variance with it (cf. e.g. the verdict of 6 March 1908 by the Court of Amsterdam which upheld a decision by a lower court of 20 Jan. 1905). After all, in cases like this the judge is not to pronounce an independent material legal verdict but can confine himself on a formal level to the bylaws. See also Van Praag, *Rechtspraak*, 2:133.

ing competence[1] whatsoever vis-à-vis the sphere-sovereignty of non-state communities.

Never can the state coerce non-political communities into compliance in their internal meaning-structures as though they were its subjects, which it can do in their *external* position as *subjects* of the government (for instance, in the execution of taxation debts and so on and so forth). The directors of a firm, for example, can never be prevented by the state from closing their enterprise as a consequence of their unwillingness to comply with rules given by the state which interfere unlawfully with the internal structure of the enterprise and which they cannot square with their own independent sphere of responsibility. When this occurs in mutual solidarity, a power struggle is unleashed.

Nor should we overlook the fact that every positive legal order, if it has kept to its divine foundation, by itself offers remedies, one way or another, against such transgressions from the side of the state. This it does by suggesting ways and means to render the enforcement of the substance of such arbitrary decrees impossible.

By way of example I would just mention here the practical implementation of the Company Councils Act of 1920 in Germany and the fiasco of the Sherman Anti-Trust Act of 1890 in the United States of America. The thorny road of the latter offers an excellent illustration of the material boundaries of state-sovereignty. After the larger trusts in the United States (first of all Standard Oil Company) had revealed their monopolistic character, the pressure of public opinion produced the Sherman Act, which prohibited trusts in their current form. Dissolved in name, these trusts then dodged the law by forming "holding companies." By itself this was perfectly permissible in positive law. However in 1904 it was determined that this form of organization, too, was in contravention of the Sherman Act. This caused the trusts to adopt a new form which exists to this very day – the amalgamation of the individual enterprises into one giant enterprise. The state turned out to be powerless with its legislation directed against this form of legitimate resistance!

By decision of the federal court, Standard Oil Company was formally dissolved in 1912. The verdict ruled that the shares of the separate corporations which belonged to the trust were to be distributed among the shareholders. What turned out to be the case? Nine wealthy industrialists held the majority of the new shares. As long as these individuals retained their solidarity in management, the trust could keep on developing the same economic activities.

The well-known millionaire Vanderbilt used these words to characterize the leaders of the trusts as they faced a state that overstepped its

---
1 Orig. "*Kompetenz-Kompetenz.*" (Trans.)

bounds: "I have never yet seen such smart men. I do not believe it possible to suppress trusts by whatever laws or edicts. They will keep surfacing forever."[1]

So long as organized communities are a necessary factor in the inner vitality of a nation, the state has indeed the meaning-individual juridical task, by virtue of the leading function of its structure as an organized community, to take measures that support, restore and stimulate the life of non-political communities. Primarily this applies to the natural organized communal life of the nuclear family, insofar as this is threatened in its normal structure by the devastating effect of sin. But in the widest sense of the word, too, this competence of the state is valid for the world of the enterprise and for cultural communities.

One must not think, however, that when the state takes measures such as depriving parental rights, appointing a guardian for the children, and so on, it materially interferes with the internal structure of the family bond. For such measures are adopted only when the internal structure of the family community has itself already been disrupted. Nor does the state interfere because it legally possesses absolute sovereignty over non-state communities in their internal structure, but rather because as state it has to ensure the preservation of the nation, in the life of which the family performs such a basic role. In this emergency situation the state uses its governing authority to provide artificial supports to these communities that threaten to disintegrate, as an emergency substitute for a natural structure that factually no longer exists.

What is valid for the juridical boundaries of state competence in the case of the internal law of non-state organized communities is essentially just as valid for internal coordinational law. In that case the meaning-structure can only be determined teleologically since, as we know, coordinational relationships do not themselves exhibit a thing-structure. Despite the state's integrating task with regard to this type of law, as discussed earlier, the state can never have the competence to interfere in the internal meaning-structure of coordinational relationships by determining on its own the legal contents of private contracts entered into for specific purposes. In this sense the human person as a legal subject also has a fundamental individual freedom vis-à-vis the state, both as to its governing and its integrating function.

---

1 Quoted in Alfred Marshall, *Industry and Trade: A Study of Industrial Technique and Business Organization* (London, 1919), pp. 511–14 and 533–34).

Remark: It is again possible to draw a parallel here with the principle of contractual freedom, as illustrated, notwithstanding Articles 1374 and 1375 of the *Civil Code*, by the civil judge's acknowledgment of material limits to his competence.[1] I fully concur with Van Praag's observation that this may lead to abuse because contractual *freedom* is often little more than a semblance, since not just those who are economically weak but also others frequently have to enter into contracts (for example, with transport and insurance companies) where they simply have to accept the conditions of the other party even when these are unreasonable. I also agree fully with his remark that

> neither the autonomy of corporations and institutions nor the right of contract appears to me to be an impediment to providing legal protection for interested parties against arbitrary or one-sided treatment by those who factually wield the power. It is a demand of justice that this be done wherever it can be done without undue injury to those interests which have an equal right to exist.[2]

Indeed; but so long as the stipulations of the legislator are inspired purely by considerations of justice, there is no question of either infringing the internal right of contract or breaching the internal law of an organized community. This is totally different, however, from conditions under state absolutism, where the right of contract is based merely on a *delegation* by the legislator to the coordinational relationships. The political absolutism defended in positivism and idealism has no juridical defense against the absorption of private law into public law. This holds for Kelsen and essentially also for Burckhardt.[3]

On our standpoint this is also evident in the fact that a contract, as an explicit source of coordinational law, cannot be viewed as a *derivative* of statutory law.[4] All kinds of arguments have been brought against the view that the contract is an independent source of law. These arguments are based on a misunderstanding of the truth that a contract, just like statutory law, when formally viewed, is simply a subjective form in which legal principles are positivized into positive law through organs that are competent to form law within an organized community or a coordinational relationship. The whole argument, first raised in the Historical School, that the formation of law can only be done through a su-

---

1 More on this in Van Praag, *Rechtspraak*, 1:656 ff.
2 Ibid., 661.
3 Cf. Walther Burckhardt, *Die Organisation der Rechtsgemeinschaft* (Basel, 1927), p. 26.
4 The specifics of the relation between the state sources and the non-state sources of coordinational law cannot be understood in the logical-functional way of Kelsen, but only in a meaning-structural way. I shall elaborate this point extensively in my not yet completed study on "the sources of positive law." [Cf. H. Dooyeweerd, "De bronnen van het stellig recht in het licht der wetsidee," *Antirevolutionaire Staatkunde* (quarterly) 8 (1934): 57–94. (General Editor.)]

The Crisis in Humanist Political Theory

pra-individual will is based on a *petitio principii*. Especially in international law this has to lead to the most tortuous constructs, since international law cannot point to a single form of organized communal will (not even in the form of "customary law") that stands above individual states and positivizes it.

Every objection against the view that contracts are an independent source of law arises essentially from either positivist or universalist, transpersonalist quarters. Positivism absolutizes the formative will of the subject in the element of *positivity* present in law. And so it thinks it possesses a secure point of support solely in the will of the state as a *supra-individual* will for the normative validity of positive law. This idea has lost sight of the fact that the will of the state cannot by itself be the ground for this validity, as little as the concurrence of wills between coordinational subjects can accomplish this in a contract.

Transpersonalist universalism on the other hand has to eliminate the contract as an independent source of law because on principle it dissolves human legal subjectivity into the jural totality of the state as an organized community with its *general will*.

In our view of law, in which the jural principle and the formative human will are indissolubly connected, and in which the structural difference between organized communal law and coordinational law is taken into account from the start, all these arguments lose their force. Neither the arbitrariness of a government nor an arbitrary contract is in itself a source of law.[1] In all its individual forms, positive law is always the positivizing of divine jural principles, whose structure is determined by the divine world order.

* * *

And so we have attempted to sketch the basic outlines of a Calvinist view of the state on the basis of a Christian cosmology and epistemology. We believe the conclusion is warranted that such a view of the state can overcome the crisis in which contemporary political theory finds itself. And for that reason the adherents of the various humanist political theories, too, will have to take notice of it and not be deterred from doing so as a result of a bias about the "neutrality" of scientific thought. Calvinist thought has been reinvigorated in modern times and once more demands a leading role in culture.

---

1 For me, a "source of law" is every form in which organs that are competent to form law positivize material jural principles into the positive law of an organized community or a coordinational relationship. See my study on the sources of law cited above.

Christianity is incompatible with the thought of humanism or paganism. Let those who still have not seen this, and who still do not believe in the possibility of Christian scholarship, be warned. Woe to him who does not discern the signs of the times! The spiritual awakening that is more and more opening people's eyes to the intimate connection between scholarship and worldview has already been at work for quite some time and will not be stopped by the ancient neutrality slogan which naively ignores its own presuppositions.

Christian scholars today face a choice. Either they acknowledge that nothing in this temporal world can be withdrawn from the claim of the Christian religion and that this religion will not be content with the role of a decorative superstructure atop a scholarship that is at bottom and in essence idolatrous. Or they should withdraw from a field where they are deeply convinced the banner of Christ's kingship cannot be boldly planted. No other choice exists.

Tertium ultra non datur
(There is no alternative)

Appendix A

(see page 110)

That the analogical meaning-moments mentioned on page 110 are indeed present within the general meaning-structure of history explains the appearance of naturalistic and psychologistic conceptions of history, for in these conceptions the relevant anticipatory substrates of the meaning of the historical are identified with the historical meaning itself. In point of fact, the analogical elements in question refer back to the spheres of number and space. The concept of space with which the discipline of history operates is obviously not mathematical, physical or biological in nature, since it is a concept of *historical* space. In other words, the meaning of space occurs only analogically within the general meaning-structure of cultural development. But it is also true that this analogy can never be understood in a "purely historical" way. It can be conceived only in its cosmological meaning-coherence with spatial meaning and those meaning-structures intermediate between the spatial and historical spheres.

Likewise the functional concept of historical *time*, as we saw earlier, is qualified by *cultural development* and has, as we explained, a *subjective* and an *objective* direction. For example, a work of art like Goethe's *Faust* has an objective meaning-function within the development of civilization which as such lies in history's *objective* direction of time. But, as we have argued, the objective direction of time is always dependent upon the *subjective*, through which it has to be *objectified* and *actualized*. This state of affairs enables us to understand at once why objective aesthetic value is founded in historical development, a truth that is immediately apparent when we recall, for instance, that for the ancient Greeks, given their historically founded norms for the evaluation of beauty, the objective aesthetic value of a "Hermes" of Praxiteles must have differed in a *meaning-individual* way from its value for us today.

Litt's conception of meaning, which we analyzed earlier, harbors an insoluble antinomy, for on the one hand he acknowledges that within objective meaning-structures – such as scientific theories, works of art, and so on – an immanent factual *development* takes place, but on the other hand he calls the meaning-structure as such *timeless*.[1]

The distinction between a subjective and an objective direction within the historical time order, which is routinely lost sight of, has an important value for the problem of *historical periodization*. When strong individual "shapers" of history are few, the objective direction in the historical time order will predominate in periodization. In fact, for prehistory it is customary to divide the periods exclusively according to objective points of view – for example the Stone Age, the Bronze Age, and so on – since the sources that we have do not suggest any subjective viewpoints.

The concept of historical causality, too, ought to be understood in the light of the concept of historical time. Historical causality is a functional analogy of physical causality within the normative meaning of cultural development. It is a causality that is implicit in the element of *historical power*. To reduce historical causality either to physical or to psychical causality is completely inadmissible, just as it is inadmissible to ban the concept of causality (along with the concept of space) from the perspective of history.[2]

Spengler's radical, irrationalist historicism claims that a dead mechanical causality reigns in nature (this is the only law-like regularity he accepts), whereas history is ruled by a living fate or destiny (*Schicksal*). History for him is the "*physiognomy* of all becoming," and *nature* (as the product of thought no less) is the "system of whatever came to be." History, as the "true reality," is not subject to laws. Here we see once again the irrational pole of humanism which, as we know, absolutizes the individual subject-side of temporal reality at the cost of the law-side.

---

1 Theodor Litt, *Individuum und Gemeinschaft*, p. 342.
2 Thus Litt, as well as Ernst Troeltsch, *Der Historismus und seine Probleme* (Tübingen, 1922), pp. 30 ff., and Oswald Spengler, *Der Untergang des Abendlandes* (Munich, 1920), 1:165–66.

Appendix B

(see page 112)

For an extensive cosmological analysis of the meaning of the jural, as well as for that of the other general meaning-structures, I have to refer to my book *De Wijsbegeerte der Wetsidee*. There I present this meaning-analysis in an extended chapter dealing with "the cosmological problem of time" that will take up almost half the book.[1]

In the present context I merely wish to present my view, namely that retribution is the irreducible *nucleus* of the general meaning-structure of the jural, and defend it against attempts to denature it to an abstract general concept which allegedly could be applied in many other domains. For that purpose writers have invoked everyday language where mention is made of a *retribution* in *nature*, a retribution in an *economic, social, historical* and *moral* sense. It should be clear by now, after all our preceding considerations, that when theoretical thought uses the naive testimony of everyday language in order to submerge the meaning of *retribution* in the logicism of an abstract general concept, the cosmic meaning of the naive attitude toward reality is thoroughly distorted.

When someone, as the result of a bad life-style, acquires a serious disease and we say that that it is *what that person deserves*, then surely no one will think that retribution here is understood in a functional biotic sense or even in the meaning of any other functional natural meaning. Rather, we remark upon the succession of facts as a religiously founded cosmic connection in a typical attitude lacking any *theorization*, and without any theoretical meaning-analysis we simply grasp the cosmic meaning of the jural in its religious foundation in the will of the divine Creator.

What happens in nature – and that is the consistent testimony of the naive attitude – is not unconnected to the meaning of retribution. Rather, in an organic way it is interwoven with it in cosmic time, and in a religious sense it forms a unity with it. In terms of our law-idea we

---

[1] See *De Wijsbegeerte der Wetsidee*, 2: 3–356; cf. *A New Critique of Theoretical Thought*, 2: 1–426. For a schematic analysis I must for now refer to my study "De structuur der rechtsbeginselen en de methode der rechtswetenschap" in *Wetenschappelijke Bijdragen* (Amsterdam, 1930), pp. 231 ff.

can say that potentially all natural functions, within the cosmic meaning-coherence, anticipate the functional meaning of the jural, just as the latter in turn is founded in those anticipating natural meaning-functions.

The same perspective is relevant for the particular emphasis in the language of Jhering, Ehrlich and others on the connection between retribution and the meaning of economic equivalency. As such the meaning of the economical does not contain the retributive meaning at all, although by virtue of the cosmic meaning-coherence the meaning of value-balancing frugality (the general meaning-structure of the economic sphere) has important anticipations of the jural sphere, just as the jural meaning in turn displays an essential economic sphere of analogies.

Whatever the context may be in which naive self-consciousness speaks of retribution, it always intends to capture nothing else but *the merely systatically understood meaning of justice.*

When the legal order in its retributive sense compels the employer to pay the wages of the employee, then the contents of this retributive duty makes no sense apart from its meaning-coherence with economic *balancing of values*. Yet the retributive demand that each party fulfill his contractual obligation can never be reduced to a merely economic demand.

It is only in its indissoluble connection with its analogical and anticipatory meaning-elements as well as in its highly differentiated meaning-individuality that retribution as the meaning-kernel of the jural reveals its *sphere-universality.*

The denial of this sphere-universality in the meaning-individuality already caused Aristotle to oppose the conception of Pythagoras that the meaning of the jural ought to be understood as *tò antipeponthos*, as retribution. In *antipeponthos,* in fact, the meaning of retribution was understood in too narrow a sense. *Antipeponthos*, after all, simply expressed the individual meaning of *punitive retribution*, and that solely in the primitive form of *talio* (commensurate punishment). In the fifth book of his *Nicomachean Ethics* Aristotle praises justice with a verse quoted from Rhadamantos: "Should a man suffer what he did to others, right justice would be done to him."[1]

Naturally Aristotle had a strong position against the Pythagoreans where he argues that their concept of retribution, which indeed does not contain anything more than a balance between suffering and doing, neither fits *distributive* nor *restorative* justice. But when he tries to define

---

[1] *General Editor's note*: Translation from *The Basic Works of Aristotle*, Edited by Richard McKeon, *Introduction* by C.D.C. Reeve. New York: The Modern Library. Paperback ed., 2001 (Copyriht 1941, by Random House Inc.), p. 1010.

the meaning of the jural himself, and thinks he can do so without recourse to the meaning of retribution, offering no further grounds than the etymology of the Greek word for justice and colloquial speech in general, then his approach ends in dissolving the sovereign, essential meaning of the jural in an abstract general concept that is merely logical in nature. In Aristotle's conception, the meaning of the jural can be defined as creating or restoring *equality* in human relationships, an equality which, depending on whether justice reveals itself in a *distributive* or a *commutative* form, ought to be realized according to a geometrical or arithmetical proportionality. But in itself "equality" does not bring to expression a sovereign meaning-function, for it is a logical concept of relation which does not acquire a material synthetical qualification except in a meaning-synthesis with the meaning of a particular law-sphere. And yet, modern legal philosophy has reintroduced this abstract concept of equality in order to characterize the material meaning of the jural, which is then identified, as in Aristotle, with the *deepened* jural meaning of *justice*.

Leonard Nelson, for example, in his book on "a philosophical theory of law," believes he can summarize the basic principle of his "material theory of law" with the norm of "personal equality," which he defines as "the exclusion of every benefit that is conditioned by the numerical determination of the single person."[1] He states emphatically that with this "law of personal equality" he has discovered a "synthetic judgment a priori," a judgment that is to be distinguished from a merely analytical (!) "proposition of equality" that brings to expression only the norm of formal equality before the law and which as such is but an inference from his *formal* concept of law.[2] Yet, what is missing in Nelson's *material* concept of law is the meaning-synthesis. In his material definition everything depends on the *jural meaning* of personal equality. But since he does not clarify this in any way his *material* principle of equality *lacks* all jural meaning. Every attempt to rationalize the meaning-kernel of the jural by dissolving it in concepts that are not further qualified will remain utterly sterile.

An example of such an attempt to define the meaning of retribution is found in the definition of Leo Polak. It states that retribution concerns an "objective, trans-egoistic harmonization of interests."[3] Obviously Polak has penetrated to the *aesthetic* and *economic meaning-analogies* of retribution and now believes that the meaning of retribution can be

---

1 Leonard Nelson, *System der philosophischen Rechtslehre* (Leipzig, 1920), p. 80.
2 Ibid., p. 81.
3 See his book of 1922, *De fundering van het strafrecht*, and his article "Zur sittlichen Rechtfertigung der Strafe," *Kant-Studien* 35 (1930): 59.

explained by reducing it to the analogies in question. *But apart from the meaning-kernel these meaning-analogies are entirely lacking in any distinct meaning.*

The rationalization of the meaning of retribution that has taken place here dissolves the meaning-analogies themselves in abstract general concepts which as such lack all jural sense. The general meaning-kernel of the jural can be rationalized as little as it can be done to the meaning-kernel of the numerical, the spatial, the kinematic, the biotic, or to the meaning of sensitive consciousness, logical analysis, cultural development, symbolical signification (the meaning of language), social intercourse, the economic meaning of frugality, aesthetic harmony, and so on and so forth.

If this rationalization were possible the jural meaning would have no sphere-sovereignty, nor would any meaning-synthesis be possible.

Appendix C

(see page 116)

On this formalistic criterion of the state see the comment by Walther Burckhardt in his book on "the organization of the legal community":

> The public-legal organization of the state with its subdivisions is the legally constituted framework that is intended to create objective law by the legislative power of the state and to apply and enforce it by its executive and judicial powers. Private-legal organization, by virtue of private decision-making, is the existing contingent framework that is intended to decide legal action for the contingent goals of its private decision-makers and to execute the legal relationships flowing therefrom.[1]

In essence this whole distinction, in its formalistic, functionalist orientation, is a perfect tautology. This is even more strikingly apparent in the definitions he gives:

> Private organized communities are those that arise and exist without any objective (that is, public-legal) requirement, whereas organized communities that have public-legal status are those that have to exist according to objective law (to wit, the subdivisions of the state) or those that must exist according to *objective reason itself*.[2]

This entire pseudo-criterion is connected to Burckhardt's formalistic distinction between public law and private law as coercive law versus non-coercive law. Private law is then supposed to coincide with the domain of private-legal actions in the narrow sense of juridical acts aimed at establishing legal relationships, while public law coincides with the domain of coercive law that excludes the will of parties.

> *Coercive* law in its proper sense concerns those norms that prescribe behavior without any consideration of the deviating will of those subjected to them. *Non-coercive* law, by contrast, concerns those norms of conduct that are only applied in cases where subjects do not determine any-

---

[1] Walther Burckhardt, *Die Organisation der Rechtsgemeinschaft* (Basel, 1927), p. 350.
[2] Ibid., p. 342 (emph. added, H.D.).

thing different (thus lacking the competence to take legal action), as mentioned above, or in order to supplement incomplete legal acts.[1]

Through this formalistic criterion, which on the one hand leads to a denial of the existence of subjective public rights and on the other to a denial of the possibility of jural norms outside the context of the state (both equally indefensible), Burckhardt finds himself forced to reckon any state-law that is undeniably of a private-legal character (such as all of the Civil Code's *jus congens*), together with internal constitutional law, among public law. This conclusion, which in itself already shows how untenable this criterion is, leads to antinomies similar to those found in the theory of Thon, a theory that has long been discredited.

The very distinction between coercive and supplementary law requires a *specification of meaning* and certainly cannot serve as an essential criterion between public and private law without further clarification. The difference between public and private law cannot be maintained on the formalist standpoint, because legal formalism fails to penetrate to the cosmic meaning-structure of jural phenomena.

---

[1] Ibid., p. 27.

Appendix D

(see page 120)

The form-matter scheme was introduced into sociology by the founder of the formal school, Georg Simmel, in his work of 1908, *Soziologie*. Similar to Kelsen, who in his *Hauptprobleme* compares the discipline of law to geometry insofar as sociology deals only with the *form* of social phenomena, Simmel too employs the image of geometry in order to differentiate the point of view of formal sociology from the material social sciences. As geometry establishes the actual spatiality of spatial entities, so sociology, according to Simmel, ascertains the social *forms* of the real social structures. Proof, indeed, of the objective value of the form-matter scheme in the humanities!

However, Simmel does not use the form-matter scheme entirely in a Kantian sense. This becomes apparent where he contrasts the special nature of the transcendental question, "How is society (in the sense of *psychological interaction!*) possible?" with the transcendental question of the *Critique of Pure Reason*, "How is universally valid experience [of nature] possible?"[1] According to the criticistic standpoint shared by Simmel, the unity of nature arises exclusively from the subjective thought forms that supposedly transform the disconnected sensory impressions into a synthetic unity. By contrast, says Simmel, the social unity is realized by its elements (who are, after all, consciously and synthetically active) without the need for a perceiving (epistemological) subject. Given this fundamental difference, elaborated extensively by Simmel, the question, "How is society possible?" acquires for him a totally different meaning from the question, "How is nature possible?" The latter is answered by the *a priori* forms of knowledge, whereas the former is answered by the *a priori* conditions present in the elements, through which they are combined in reality to form the "synthesis" *society*. An inquiry into the social "forms," as undertaken in Simmel's book, investigates those processes that ultimately take place within the individuals and make it possible for them "to be social" to begin with. These processes are not seen as temporally prior causes of this result, but as "partial processes of synthesis that we collectively designate as society."

---
1 See Simmel, *Soziologie*, pp. 28 ff.

Simmel's conception of the problem of form is best known from his article on "the fragmentary character of life."[1] In deviation from Kant he assumes a series of *a-theoretical* forms that are not subordinated *under* theoretical thought-forms but correlated *with* them. All these forms (of *art*, *religion*, and so on) accrue upon *life* as experienced empirically, constituting a parallelism of distinct form-worlds. Simmel views these *worlds* as *categorical forms* that extend themselves over a "world-material" that is unknown to us. All these formal worlds individualize themselves in "psychic-historical reality" (the historicism in Simmel's *philosophy of life* is palpable here). It is natural to view these "social forms" as conceived by Simmel also as a form-world that is individualized by "psychic-historical reality." But then it becomes even more evident how much his form-matter scheme is without foundation. Are these "forms" of his still subjective categories of a transcendental consciousness, as they were for Kant? Where do they find their unity, and how are they related to one another? In vain one looks for an unequivocal answer to these questions in the thought of Simmel. Sometimes his view of the forms seems to approximate Plato's world of ideas. His form-world also echoes motifs from Leibniz's monadology. He writes: "A genuine overlapping and interweaving of one world in another is impossible, since each one already expresses the totality of world contents in its own particular language."[2]

Vagueness in the concept of form in Simmel's sociology is apparent from what he writes about whether or not the "social forms" have an *epistemological* nature. For him this is but a terminological issue. The social structures that are normed by their forms are not *cognitions* but practical processes and real states of affairs. Yet the inquiry (on his *a priori* conditions) into the general concept of "sociation" (*Vergesellschaftung*) does have "something similar to knowledge." Inquiry into the question which specific categories man needs to bring along, as it were, in order to arouse in him *awareness* of being in society could be designated as "the epistemological theory of society" ("society as a fact of knowledge"). It is clear how much Simmel remains stuck in the absolutization of the meaning-synthetical standpoint at the cost of the given meaning-systasis.

The formalistic standpoint is carried through in a strictly systematic fashion in the "general sociology" of Von Wiese.[3] Simmel's thought may be unclear in its overall argument but everywhere it is sprinkled with profound intuitions, which are absent in Von Wiese. The fact that the latter rejects the label "formal sociology" is not significant, nor does

---

1 Simmel, "Der Fragmentcharacter des Lebens," *Logos* 6.1 (1917): 29–40.
2 Ibid., p. 35.
3 Leopold von Wiese, *Allgemeine Soziologie*, 2 vols. (Leipzig, 1924–29).

he himself consider it very important.[1] Yet at bottom his standpoint is formalistic in the extreme. He actually applies the form-matter scheme, which he claims to reject, in a more dogmatic way than does his mentor Simmel. According to Von Wiese, sociology's field of investigation is delimited by a fundamental social category which he traces back to the general logical category of *relation*. It receives its *"specificum sociologicum"* (his term) from the peculiar feature of "meeting" and "parting." This is a purely subjective mode of understanding.

> Ethics, psychology, aesthetics, politics etc. view human relationships from different angles and in terms of different categories. Sociology, however, looks at them solely in terms of the manner and degree of meeting and parting and their mixed forms. The theory of relations only knows relationships that attract or repel. Sociologically speaking, no other relationship is possible.[2]

The bifurcation of all human relationships in coming together and splitting up is supposed to provide sociology with its own independent set of problems and its own proper nature as an exact science.

The radical formalistic logicism that emerges in Von Wiese's view of sociology (in sharp contrast with Simmel's) has also stamped the phenomenologically oriented Freyer in his book on sociology as a "science of reality."[3] It is best characterized in the following statement:

> If one asks why only these two forms exist as the sole types of relationships, either one answers that empirically they are found always and everywhere; or one derives them from man's biological nature which in part urges him toward uniting with his fellow human beings and in part urges him toward affirming his I-ness over against his peers; or else one explains them – which at this initial stage I would prefer, as I try to do above – *in terms of the only two possibilities for the direction of movement as such (in their relations to one another)*. This is the most formal, general mathematical mode of viewing. To use an image: human beings are like figures on the chessboard of life who with every move (relation, social process) alternate between moving closer to or further away from each other.[4]

The ends for which people enter formal social relationships are said to be the organizational principles of division for the other "sciences of social man" (economics, politics, law, aesthetics, morality, pistology, and so on).

---

1 Ibid., 2:27.
2 Ibid., pp. 10–11.
3 Hans Freyer, *Soziologie als Wirklichkeitswissenschaft* (Berlin, 1930), pp. 51 ff.
4 Ibid., pp. 51 ff. (italics mine, H.D.)

Curiously, Kelsen did the reverse by reducing the jural to a logical thought-form and relegating the contents of the jural – its *ends* – to the other "social sciences." This is how formalism passes the contents to and fro in a way that they ultimately cannot find shelter anywhere.

We are gradually getting tired of this scholasticism of modern humanism. It no longer has any future. It does injustice to the titanic, faustian thirst for knowledge of a Leibniz by making an appeal for its fruitless formalism to his great idea of a *mathesis universalis*. (Thus one of Kelsen's pupils, Fritz Schreier.)

To delineate the *basic category* of a *formal discipline* according to a "genus proximum" and a "differentia specifica" is a purely Aristotelian-Scholastic prescription for concept formation – which no longer has anything to do with the transcendental concept formation of Immanuel Kant.

Appendix E

(see page 148)

Rather odd is Van Idsinga's standpoint on the distinction between public and private law.[1] He points to England, where a distinction between a private and public matter is supposedly well known yet without honoring a conception of "public law" as a "different order of rights" based upon "a different kind of laws" governed by principles other than "private law."

The author then makes the following odd statement: "Failure to appreciate the difference between a public matter and a private affair is a medieval error. It must undoubtedly be the aim of modern constitutional law to rectify this mistake and eschew it, but the means to achieve this is to be found elsewhere than in an artificial division of Law." I leave aside the question whether or not British law knows the distinction between private and public law. It seems to me that the issue is handled in too simplistic a manner when attention is paid solely to formal procedures (such as the *ultra vires* procedure). But when Van Idsinga writes: "Between these two affairs there may be a world of difference, but law, governing both, is completely one and forms a whole with intertwined parts such that it is impossible to divide this tissue," he entangles himself in an internal contradiction which consistent individualism at least escapes. For if there is indeed a world of difference between a *public* and a *private* affair, how is it then possible that the law governing a *public affair* has the same character as the law regulating a *private* affair? A consistent *legal formalism* has at least a *consistent individualism* as its foundation.

But how are we to understand Van Idsinga's standpoint? No doubt an important role is played by his curious conception of the state, which is strongly influenced by Gneist. In a constitutional monarchy, he writes, the state is the King personally, whose position can be entirely identified with the jurisprudence.

What is thus equated, namely *chief magistrate* and *state*, is gradually distinguished by Van Idsinga from *society* ("maatschappij") as the indi-

---

1 J. W. H. M. van Idsinga, *De administratieve rechtspraak en de constitutioneele monarchie* (The Hague, 1893), 1:15.

vidualistic play of rival personal interests, and from the *national community* ("volksgemeenschap"). The state is

> the ethical power that emerges in the history of human civilization, granting the *person* the possibility of an *independent* development and also keeping him tied to the community by guaranteeing his independence only to the extent to which its fulfillment can be combined with that of the community, such that their inevitable differentiation avoids irreparable divisions and that man in this way of peace – i.e., in the way of Law – achieve a freedom that can be the foundation of a higher, spiritual community and a purely internal morality. And in no other form has this power revealed its true essence and function more, or fulfilled its task as a just state better, than in the form of the constitutional monarchy that was set up in England.[1]

Thus the state is justified as the promoter of personal morality by *means* of "the Law." This essentially personalist, humanist view of state and law unfortunately infected the Christian-historical political theory of Van Idsinga, even though it is clear that the Lutheran conception of the human personality present in the thought of Stahl also makes its influence felt here,[2] which has as little to do with the humanist view of *personhood* as the Christian idea of *freedom* has anything to do with the humanist idea of *autonomy* (in a *Kantian* sense).

What is totally absent in the thought of Van Idsinga, in spite of his sharp contrast between *society* and *community* derived from Gneist, is a proper analysis of the meaning-structure of organized communities and coordinational spheres. This explains his strange construction of the state. For how can the *state*, as Van Idsinga himself says, be identical to an *organ* endowed with authority and at the same time as such be set *opposite* the people of a state?

---

1 Ibid., 2:361.
2 Ibid., p. 340.

Appendix F

(see page 157)

Friedrich Darmstaedter does not know sphere-sovereignty in the sense we have expounded it, yet from a modern liberalist standpoint it is remarkable that in his work on "the limits of the operation of the just state" he launches a sharp attack against denaturing the idea of the just state as it is found in positivist political theory (in particular in Kelsen's identity theory).[1] Darmstaedter wants to breathe new life into the classic humanist idea of the just state by means of a modernized version of it. Behind mere *legal* freedom and equality he wants to penetrate once again to the *natural* freedom and equality of the citizens of the state and in advancing and maintaining these to find at the same time the essence of law and the criterion of circumscribing the task of government.

This natural freedom and equality is supposed to consist in this, that the state, regardless of where it operates, pursues no other aim but to make possible for people a free civil society as the well-spring of all culture and prosperity in their mutual dependence. The modern liberal idea of the just state supposedly distinguishes itself from the idea of the power-state and the welfare state, not in its *size*, but in the *aim* and *direction* of its task. The state does not itself have to generate prosperity and culture, but it should remove from a free society any obstacles to the production of these material goods and through its legal order encourage its citizens to devote themselves increasingly to a free communal life of giving and receiving.

This is the old rationalistic teleological theory of the state. It does not investigate the meaning-structure of organized communities but operates with the dualism of state and "society," where civil society is personified as the *Gesamtgesellschaft* (total society) in the sense of the totality of relationships between individuals. The just state is then viewed as the "form" of society – a form that must derive from the "unformed mass" of society not only its *material contents* but also its *worth* or value: "The just state is that form of state which ultimately presupposes, over against its people, community rules as its self-worth, original gov-

---

1 Fr. Darmstaedter, *Die Grenzen der Wirksamkeit des Rechtsstaates* (Heidelberg, 1930), pp. 248 ff.

erning authority as its mediating value."[1] In other words, the state has no worth or value in and of itself.

Here we encounter therefore the Kantian form-matter scheme, albeit in the turn given to it by Lask, as it is applied to the relation of state and society. We take note that according to Darmstaedter "society" itself does not have a law-conformative structure since it has to receive it from the state, even though the state in turn has to determine the form in accordance with the nature of the matter.[2] Darmstaedter now looks for a guarantee that natural freedom and equality are ensured in an administrative jurisprudence that would, independently of both the legislature and the executive, in the final analysis be able to decide whether or not the state in its legislative and administrative acts has infringed upon "the natural freedom and equality of its citizens." This jurisprudential organ itself continues to be, of course, a state organ and as such is subject to the constitution.[3] This is supposed to set limits to the "unlimited parliamentarianism" with its formalization of the concept of law.

But nowhere is it more apparent how little Darmstaedter has considered the *nature* of the problem in determining the material boundaries of the state's competence vis-à-vis the non-state organized communities and the coordinational spheres. He does not realize that an administrative judge would be confronted with an impossible task if he also had to decide the internal *material* legal issues present in the communal law of non-state communities. Conversely, from the perspective of the non-state communities, too, he assesses the situation far too simply.

To take one example: is it conceivable that a church would ever be willing to accept that the question whether or not the state has legitimately intervened in her internal ecclesiastical law would ultimately be decided by a state organ, which might for that purpose also have to presume to give an opinion regarding the church's internal questions of faith and confession?

It is a profound fallacy to insist that in this temporal world order there has to be an authority that is capable of overruling absolutely every other authority in a juridical sense, under the pretense that otherwise anarchy would reign. God did not ordain any "absolute" power in time. The truth is that it is precisely the theory of the state's totality of juridical power that rests on an anarchistic, revolutionary basis, because it ignores the divine structural laws of human society.

Everyone acquainted with life knows that there are material limits to the competence of the state. It is unworthy of legal science to ignore the

---

1 Ibid., p. 201.
2 See the characteristic exposition on pp. 143 ff.
3 Ibid., pp. 199, 248 ff.

The Crisis in Humanist Political Theory 179

connection between law and life through a sterile formalism. Rather it should base itself on a cosmology that is capable of meaningfully clarifying these limits and indicating an unambiguous criterion for them.

Naturally we also have to reject Cole's standpoint regarding a "supreme court of functional equity."[1] Hsiao correctly remarks in this regard that such a court of justice, in which all societal "functions" are supposed to be coordinated, would have even greater power than the American Supreme Court, for it would possess "the extraordinary power of enforcing its own decisions by physical coercion, should the contending parties fail to carry out its arbitration." Hsiao is justified in asking: "What can this mean but a legal monism of the most absolute sort?"[2]

---

1 G. D. H. Cole, *Social Theory* (London, 1920), pp. 135–37. For that matter, his project would end in the self-destruction of political pluralism.
2 Kung-Ch'uan Hsiao, *Political Pluralism: A Study in Contemporary Political Theory* (London, 1927), p. 138.

Works Cited

Althusius, Johannes. *Politica*. Groningen: Johannes Radaeus, 1610.
Aristotle. *Nicomachean Ethics*. In *The Basic Works of Aristotle*, ed. Richard McKeon. Introd. C.D.C. Reeve. New York: Modern Library, 2001.
Beckerath, Erwin von. *Wesen und Werden des fascistischen Staates*. Berlin: J. Springer, 1927.
Below, Georg von. *Der deutsche Staat des Mittelalters*. Vol. 1, *Die allgemeine Fragen*. 2nd ed. Leipzig: Quelle und Meyer, 1925.
Bergson Henri. "Introduction la métaphysique. *Revue de métaphysique et de morale* 11 (1903)
Berthélemy, Henry. *Traité élémentaire de droit administratif*, 5th ed. Paris: A. Rousseau, 1908.
Barthélemy, Joseph. *La Crise de la démocratie contemporaine*. Paris: Librairie du Recueil Sirey, 1931.
Berthélemy, Joseph, and Paul Duez. *Traité élémentaire de droit constitionel*. Paris: Dallos, 1926.
Binder, Julius. *Philosophie des Rechts*. Berlin: G. Stilke, 1925.
Bluntschli, Johann Kaspar. *Allgemeines Staatsrecht*. 3rd ed. Munich: Literarisch-Artistische Buchhandlung, 1863.
Buijs, Johan Theodoor. *De grondwet; toelichting en kritiek*. Vol. 2. Arnhem: Gouda Quint, 1885.
Burckhardt, Walther. *Die Organisation der Rechtsgemeinschaf. Untersuchungen über die Eigenart des Privatrechts, des Staatsrechts und des Völkerrechts*. Basel: Helbig und Lichtenhahn, 1927.
Calvin, John. *Institutio christianae religionis*. 1559.
Carré de Malberg, Raymond. *Contribution à la théorie générale de l État: spécialement d apr s les données fournies par le droit constitutionnel fran ais*. Paris: Librairie du Recueil Sirey, 1920.
Cassirer, Ernst. "Kant und das Problem der Metaphysik: Bemerkungen zu Martin Heideggers Kant-Interpretation." *Kant-Studien* 36, no. 1-2 (1931): 1-16.
———. *Philosophie der symbolischen Formen*. Vol. 1, *Die Sprache*. Berlin: B. Cassirer, 1923.
Cohen, Hermann. *Ethik des reinen Willens*. 4th ed. Berlin: B. Cassirer, 1923.
———. *Logik der reinen Erkenntnis*. 3rd ed. Berlin: B. Cassirer, 1922.
Cole, G. D. H. *Self-Government in Industry*. London: G. Bell and Sons, 1917.
———. *Social Theory*. London: Methuen, 1920.

Darmstaedter, Friedrich. *Die Grenzen der Wirksamkeit des Rechtsstaates. Eine Untersuchung zur gegenwärtigen Krise des liberalen Staatsgedenkens*. Heidelberg: C. Winter, 1930.

Descartes, René. *Principles of Philosophy*. Trans. John Veitch. Edinburgh: Sutherland and Knox, 1853.

Dimitch, Velimir N. *La Courtoisie internationale et le droit des gens*. Paris: Librairie du Recueil Sirey, 1930.

Dooyeweerd, Herman. *De beteekenis der wetsidee voor rechtswetenschap en rechtsphilosphie*; rede bij de aanvaarding van het hoogleeraarsambt aan de Vrije Universiteit te Amsterdam den 15en October 1926 uitgesproken [*The significance of the cosmonomic idea for the science of law and legal philosophy*: Inaugural lecture, Free University, Amsterdam, 15 October 1926]. Kampen: J. H. Kok, 1926. To be published in translation in Series B of *The Collected Works of Herman Dooyeweerd*.

———. "De Bronnen van het stellig recht in het licht der wetsidee; een bijdrage tot opklaring van het probleem inzake de verhouding van rechtsbeginsel en positief recht." *Antirevolutionaire Staatkunde* 4 (1930): 1–67, 224–63, 325–62; 8 (1934): 57–94.

———. "In den strijd om een christelijke staatkunde; proeve van een fundeering der calvinistische levens- en wereldbeschouwing in hare wetsidee" [Episodes in the struggle for a Christian politics: An essay in grounding the Calvinistic world and life view in its law-idea]. *Antirevolutionaire staatkunde* (monthly) 1 (1924–1925): 7–25; 62–79; 104–18; 161–73; 189–200; 228–44; 309–24; 433–60; 489–504; 528–42; 581–98; 617–34; 2 (1926): 244–65; 425–45. Continued in *Antirevolutionaire staatkunde* (quarterly) 1 (1927): 142–95. Eng. trans. *The Struggle for a Christian Politics: An Essay in Grounding the Calvinistic Worldview in Its Law-idea*. Lewiston, NY: Edwin Mellen Press, 2008. *The Collected Works of Herman Dooyeweerd*, Series B, Volume 5.

———. *De Ministerraad in het Nederlandsche staatsrecht*. Amsterdam: G. van Soest, 1917.

———. *A New Critique of Theoretical Thought*. 4 vols. Philadelphia: Presbyterian and Reformed Publishing Company, 1953–58. Republished as *A New Critique of Theoretical Thought*. 4 vols. Lewiston, NY: Edwin Mellen Press, 1997. *The Collected Works of Herman Dooyeweerd*, Series A, Volumes 1–4.

———. "De structuur der rechtsbeginselen en de methode der rechtswetenschap in het licht der wetsidee." In *Wetenschappelijk bijdragen: aangeboden door hoogleeraren der Vrije Universiteit ter gelegenheid van haar vijftigjarig bestaan, 20 October 1930*, 223–66. Amsterdam: Dagblad en Drukkerij De Standaard, 1930.

Duguit, Léon. *Le droit social, le droit individuel et la transformation de l'état; conférences faites à l'École des hautes études sociales*. Paris: F. Alcan, 1908.

———. *Traité de droit constitutionnel*. 3rd ed. Paris: E. de Boccard, 1927.

Ehrlich, Eugen. *Beiträge zur Theorie der Rechtsquellen*. Vol. 1. Berlin: Heymann, 1902.

———. *Grundlegung der Soziologie des Rechts*. Munich and Leipzig: Duncker und Humblot, 1913.

Freyer, Hans. *Soziologie als Wirklichkeitswissenschaft. Logische Grundlegung des Systems der Soziologie*. Berlin: Teubner, 1930.

Fricker, Karl Viktor. *Vom Staatsgebiet*. Tübingen: Füs, 1867.

Gierke, Otto Friedrich von. *Die Grundbegriffe des Staatsrechts und die neuesten Staatsrechtstheorien*. Tübingen: Mohr, 1915.

———. "Labands Staatsrecht und die deutsche Rechtswissenschaft." *Smollers Jahrbuch für Gesetzgebung, Verwaltung und Volkswirtschaft* 7 (1883): 1097–1196.

———. *Das Wesen der menschlichen Verbände*. Berlin: Buchdruckerei von G. Schade [O. Francke], 1902.

Glum, Friedrich. *Der deutsche und der französische Reichswirtschaftsrat. Ein Beitrag zu dem Problem der Repräsentation der Wirtschaft im Staat*. Berlin and Leipzig: W. de Gruyter, 1929.

Goes van Naters, Marinus van der. *Het Staatsbeeld der sociaal-democratie*. Amsterdam: De Arbeiderspers, 1930.

Groen van Prinsterer, Guillaume. *Ongeloof en Revolutie*. Leyden: Luchtmans, 1847.

Gurvitch, Georges. *Vvedenie v obscuju teoriju mezdunarodnogo prava*. Prague: Faculty of Law, 1923.

Guy-Grand, Georges. *La démocratie et l'aprés-guerre*. Paris: Garnier Frères, 1922.

Haering, Theodor L. *Über Individualität in Natur- und Geisteswelt, begriffliches und tätliches*. Leipzig: B. G. Teubner, 1926.

Hauriou, Maurice. *La Souveraineté nationale*. Paris: L. Larose et L. Tenin, 1912.

Hauriou, Maurice. *Précis de droit constitutionnel*. Paris, 1929.

Haushofer, Karl, et al., eds. *Bausteine zur Geopolitik*. Berlin-Grunewald: K. Vowinckel, 1928.

Heidegger, Martin. *Kant und das Problem der Metaphysik*. Bonn: F. Cohen, 1929.

———. *Vom Wesen des Grundes*. Offprint from the *Festschrift, Edmund Husserl zum 70. Geburtstag gewidmet*. Halle an der Saale: M. Niemeyer, 1929.

Heinemann, Bruno. *Sozialisierung, ihre Möglichkeiten und Grenzen*, 2nd ed. Berlin: Curtius, 1919.

Heller, Hermann. *Die Souveränität. Ein Beitrag zur Theorie des Staats- und Völkerrechts*. Berlin: W. de Gruyter, 1927.

———. *Europa und der Fascismus*. 2nd ed. Berlin: W. de Gruyter, 1931.

———. "Bemerkungen zur staats- und rechtstheoretische Problematik der Gegenwart." *Archiv des öffentlichen Rechts*, n.s. 16 (1929).

———. "Der Begriff des Gesetzes in der Reichsverfassung." *Veröffentlichungen der Vereinigung der Deutschen Staatsrechtslehrer* 4 (1928).

———. "Die Krisis der Staatslehre." *Archiv für Sozialwissenschaft und Sozialpolitik* 55 (1926): 289–316.

Hennig, Richard. *Geopolitik. Die Lehre vom Staat als Lebewesen.* Berlin and Leipzig: B. G. Teubner, 1928.

Hippel, Ernst von. *Untersuchungen zum Problem des fehlerhaften Staatsakts. Beitrag zur Methode einer teleologischen Rechtsauslegung.* Berlin: J. Springer, 1924.

———. *Über die Verbindlichkeit des Gesetzes.* Breslau: Hirt, 1928.

Hobbes, Thomas. "Of Power, Worth, Dignity, Honour and Worthiness." In *Leviathan, or, The Matter, Form and Power of a Commonwealth, Ecclesiastical and Civil.* Vol. 3 of *The English Works of Thomas Hobbes of Malmesbury,* ed. Sir William Molesworth. London: J. Bohn, 1839–1845.

Hobson, S. G. *National Guilds: An Inquiry into the Wage System and the Way Out.* London: H. Bell and Sons, 1919.

Hsiao, Kung-Ch'uan. *Political Pluralism: A Study in Contemporary Political Theory.* London: K. Paul, Trench, Trubner, 1927.

Hübner, Rudolf. "Joh. Gust. Droysens Vorlesungen über Politik. Ein Beitrag zur Entwicklungsgeschichte und Begriffsbestimmung der wissenschaftlichen Politik." *Zeitschrift für Politik* 10 (1917): 327–76.

Husserl, Edmund. *Ideen zu einer reinen Phänomenologie und phänomenologischen Philosophie.* Vol. 1. Halle an der Saale: M. Niemeyer, 1913.

———. *Logische Untersuchungen.* Vol. 1, *Prolegomena zur reinen Logik.* 2nd ed. Halle an der Saale: M. Niemeyer, 1913.

Idsinga, J. W. H. M. van. *De administratieve rechtspraak en de constitutioneele monarchie.* Vol. 1, *De administratieve rechtspraak.* The Hague: Van Stockum, 1893.

———. *Het Verslag van de Staatscommissie voor de administratieve rechtspraak beoordeeld.* Rotterdam: D. A. Daamen, 1899.

Jellinek, Georg. *Allgemeine Staatslehre.* 3rd ed. Berlin: Springer, 1919.

Jhering, Rudolf von. *Der Zweck im Recht.* Leipzig: Breitkopf und Härtel, 1923.

Kahn, Bernard Arnold. *Conventions, of politieke stelregels.* Amsterdam: J. H. Kruyt, 1919.

Kant, Immanuel. *Kritik der reinen Vernunft.* Vol. 3 of *Werke,* ed. Ernst Cassirer. Berlin: B. Cassirer, 1923.

———. *Prolegomena to any Future Metaphysics.* Rev. ed. Trans. Paul Carus. Chicago: Open Court, 1902.

———. *Prolegomena zu einer jeden künftigen Metaphysik die als Wissenschaft wird auftreten können.* In *Werke,* vol. 4, *Schriften von 1783–1788.* Ed. Artur Buchenau and Ernst Cassirer. Berlin: Cassirer, 1913.

Kaufmann, Erich. *Das Wesen des Völkerrechts und die Clausula Rebus sic stantibus.* Tübingen: J. C. B. Mohr, 1911.

Kelsen, Hans. *Allgemeine Staatslehre.* Berlin: J. Springer, 1925.

———. "Comment." *Veröffentlichungen der Vereinigung der deutschen Staatsrechtslehrer* 3 (1927).
———. *Hauptprobleme der Staatsrechtslehre entwickelt aus der Lehre vom Rechtssatze.* 2nd ed. Tübingen: J. C. B. Mohr, 1923.
———. *Der soziologische und der juristische Staatsbegriff. Kritische Untersuchung des Verhältnisses von Staat und Recht.* Tübingen: J. C. B. Mohr, 1922.
———. *Der Staat als Integration. Eine prinzipielle Auseinandersetzung.* Vienna: J. Springer, 1930.
———. *Vom Wesen und Wert der Demokratie.* Tübingen: J. C. B. Mohr, 1920.
———. "Zur Theorie der juristischen Fiktionen." *Annalen der Philosophie* 1 (1919).
Kjellén, Rudolf. *Der Staat als Lebensform.* 4th ed. Trans. J. Sandmeier. Berlin-Grunewald: K. Vowinckel, 1924.
Krabbe, Hugo. *Die Grossmächte vor und nach dem Weltkriege.* 22nd ed. Karl Haushofer, ed. Leipzig and Berlin: B. G. Teubner, 1930.
———. *Die Lehre der Rechtssouveränität. Beitrag zur Staatslehre.* Groningen: J. B. Wolters, 1906.
———. *De moderne Staatsidee.* The Hague: Martinus Nijhoff, 1915.
———. *Het rechtsgezag; verdediging en toelichting.* The Hague: Martinus Nijhoff, 1917.
———. "Het Wetsbegrip." In *Verspreide opstellen,* vol. 1 of *Staatsrechtelijke opstellen, uitgegeven ter gelegenheid van het aftreden van Prof. H. Krabbe als hoogleeraar aan de Rijks Universiteit te Leiden.* The Hague: Martinus Nijhoff, 1927.
Kroner, Richard. *Von der Vernunftkritik zur Naturphilosophie.* Vol. 1 of *Von Kant bis Hegel.* Tübingen: J. C. B. Mohr, 1921.
Kuypers, K. *Theorie der geschiedenis, voornamelijk met betrekking tot de cultuur.* Amsterdam: H. J. Paris, 1931.
Laband, Paul. *Das Staatsrecht des deutschen Reiches.* 4th ed. Vol. 2. Tübingen: J. C. B. Mohr, 1901.
Laband, Paul, et al., eds. *Handbuch der Politik.* Vol. 1, *Die Grundlagen der Politik.* Berlin: W. Rothschild, 1912.
Laski, Harold Joseph. *A Grammar of Politics.* London: Allen and Unwin, 1925.
———. *Studies in the Problem of Sovereignty.* New Haven: Yale University Press, 1917.
———. *Authority in the Modern State.* New Haven: Yale University Press, 1919.
Leibholz, Gerhard. *Das Wesen der Repräsentation unter besonderer Berücksichtigung des Repräsentativsystems.* Berlin: W. de Gruyter, 1929.
———. *Zu den Probleme des fascistischen Verfassungsrechts.* Akademische Antrittsvorlesung. Berlin and Leipzig: W. de Gruyter 1928.
Leibniz, Gottfried Wilhelm. "Meditationes de cognitione, veritate et ideis." In *Philosophische Schriften,* ed. C. I. Gerhardt, vol. 4. Berlin, 1890.

Lenin, Vladimir I. *Zur Frage der Diktatur.* Vienna: Arbeiterbuchhandlung, 1921.
Leo, Heinrich. *Studien und Skizzen zu einer Naturlehre des Staates.* Halle: Anton, 1833.
Levy, J. A. *Administratieve rechtspraak.* Vol. 2 of *Antirevolutionair staatsrecht.* The Hague: Belinfante, 1901.
Liefmann, Robert. *Die Unternehmungsformen mit Einschluss der Genossenschaften und der Sozialisierung.* 4th ed. Stuttgart: Ernst Heinrich Moritz, 1928.
Litt, Theodor. *Individuum und Gemeinschaft. Grundleging der Kulturphilosophie.* 3rd ed. Berlin: B. G. Teubner, 1926.
Loeff, Joannes Aloysius. *Publiekrecht tegenover privaatrecht; proeve van theoretisch-kritisch onderzoek naar het karakter van het publieke recht.* Diss. Leyden, 1887.
Marck, Siegfried. *Substanz- und Funktionsbegriff in der Rechtsphilosophie.* Tübingen: J. C. B. Mohr, 1925.
Marquardsen, Heinrich von, ed. *Handbuch des öffentlichen Rechts der Gegenwart.* 4 vols. Tübingen: J. C. B. Mohr, 1921.
Marshall, Alfred. *Industry and Trade: A Study of Industrial Technique and Business Organization.* London: Macmillan, 1919.
Meinecke, Friedrich. *Die Idee der Staatsräson in der neueren Geschichte.* Munich and Berlin: R. Oldenbourg, 1924.
Merkl, Adolf. *Allgemeines Verwaltungsrecht.* Berlin: J. Springer, 1927.
Mirkine-Guetzévitch, Boris. *Les nouvelles tendances du droit constitutionnel.* Paris: M. Giard, 1931.
———. "Die Rationalisierung der Macht im neuen Verfassungsrecht." *Zeitschrift für öffentliches Recht* 8, no. 2 (1929): 161 ff.
———. *Die rechtstheoretische Grundlagen des Sowjetstaates.* Foreword by Hans Kelsen. Vienna: F. Deuticke, 1929.
Mohl, Robert von. *Encyklopädie der Staatswissenschaften.* Tübingen: H. Laupp, 1859.
Montesquieu, Charles de Secondat, Baron de. *The Spirit of Laws.* Trans. Thomas Nugent. London: Printed for J. Nourse and P. Vaillant, 1750.
Natorp, Paul. *Die logischen Grundlagen der exakten Wissenschaften.* 2nd ed. Leipzig: Teubner, 1921.
Nelson, Leonard. *Die Rechtswissenschaft ohne Recht. Kritische Betrachtungen über die Grundlagen des Staats- und Volkerrechts, insbesondere über die Lehre von der Souveränität.* Leipzig: Veit, 1917.
———. *System der philosophischen Rechtslehre.* Leipzig: Verlag der Neue Geist, 1920.
Oppenheim, Jacques. *De volksregeering in het constitutioneel stelsel*; rede bij de aanvaarding van het hoogleeraarsambt aan de Rijksuniversiteit te Groningen. Groningen: J. B. Wolters, 1885.
———. *De theorie van den organischen staat en hare waarde voor onzen tijd.* Groningen: J. B. Wolters, 1893.

Oppenheimer, Franz. *System der Soziologie*. Vol. 1, *Allgemeine Soziologie*. Pt. 1, *Grundlegung*. Jena: G. Fischer, 1922.

Philip of Leyden. *De cura reipublicae et sorte principantis* (1355). Leyden, 1516.

Polak, Leonard. *De Fundeering van het strafrecht*. Amsterdam: Vereeniging voor Wijsbegeerte des Rechts, 1922.

———. "Zur sittlichen Rechtfertigung der Strafe." *Kant-Studien* 35, no. 1 (1930).

Praag, Leo van. *Rechtspraak en voornaamste literatuur op de Wet van 18 April 1827*. 3rd ed. 4 vols. The Hague: Belinfante, 1916–1930.

Preuss, Hugo. *Gemeinde, Staat, Reich als Gebietskörperschaften. Versuch einer deutschen Staatskonstruktion auf Grundlage der Genossenschaftstheorie*. Berlin: J. Springer, 1889.

Reinach, Adolf. "Die apriorischen Grundlagen des bürgerlichen Rechtes." *Jahrbuch für Philosophie und phänomenologische Forschung* 1 (1913): 685–847.

Rickert, Heinrich. *System der Philosophie*. Tübingen: J. C. B. Mohr, 1921.

Rohatyn, S. "Der verfassungsrechtliche Integrationslehre." *Zeitschrift für öffentliches Recht* 9 (1930).

Rosin, Heinrich. *Das Recht der öffentlichen Genossenschaft*. Freiburg im Breisgau, 1886.

Scheler, Max. *Die Stellung des Menschen im Kosmos*. Darmstadt: Reichl, 1928.

Schmidt, Richard. *Allgemeine Staatslehre*. Vol. 1, *Die gemeinsamen Grundlagen des politischen Lebens*. Leipzig: C. L. Hirschfeld, 1901.

Schmitt, Carl. *Der Begriff des Politischen*. Vol. 5 of *Probleme der Demokratie*. Berlin-Grunewald: Rothschild, 1928.

———. *Die Diktatur von dem Anfängen des modernen Souveränitätsgedankens bis zum proletarischen Klassenkampf*. Leipzig: Duncker und Humblot, 1921.

———. *Die geistesgeschichtliche Lage des heutigen Parlamentarismus*. 2nd ed. Munich: Duncker und Humblot, 1926.

———. *Politische Theologie. Vier Kapitel zur Lehre von der Souveränität*. Leipzig: Duncker und Humblot, 1922.

———. *Verfassungslehre*. Leipzig: Duncker und Humblot, 1928.

Schreier, Fritz. *Grundbegriffe und Grundformen des Rechts. Entwurf einer phänomenologisch begründeten formalen Rechts- und Staatslehre*. Leipzig: F. Deuticke, 1924.

———. *Die Interpretation der Gesetze und Rechtsgeschäfte*. Leipzig: F. Deuticke, 1927.

Simmel, Georg. "Der Fragmentcharakter des Lebens. Aus den Vorstudien einer Metaphysik." *Logos* 6, no. 1 (1917): 29–40.

———. *Soziologie. Untersuchungen über die Formen der Vergesellschaftung*. Leipzig: Duncker und Humblot, 1908.

Small, Albion W. *The Meaning of Social Science*. Chicago: University of Chicago Press, 1910.

Smend, Rudolf. "Die politische Gewalt im Verfassungsstaat und das Problem der Staatsform." In *Festgabe der Berliner Juristischen Fakultät für Wilhelm Kahl zum Doktorjubiläum am 19. April 1923.* Tübingen: J. C. B. Mohr, 1923.

———. *Verfassung und Verfassungsrecht.* Leipzig: Duncker und Humblot, 1928.

Somló, Bódog. *Juristische Grundlehre.* 2nd ed. Leipzig: F. Meiner, 1927.

Sorel, Georges. *Réflexions sur la violence.* 4th ed. Paris: M. RiviPre, 1919.

Spann, Othmar. *Gesellschaftslehre.* 3rd ed. Leipzig: Quelle und Meyer, 1930.

Spencer, Herbert. *Principles of Sociology.* Pt. 5, *Political Institutions.* London: Williams and Norgate, 1882.

Spengler, Oswald. *Der Untergang des Abendlandes. Umrisse einer Morphologie der Weltgeschichte.* Munich: Beck, 1920.

Stahl, Friedrich Julius. *Staatslehre; im Auszug neu herausgegeben.* Berlin: Reimar Hobbing, 1910.

Stein, Lorenz von. *Die Verwaltungslehre.* 2nd ed. Stuttgart: Cotta, 1869.

Strauss, D. F. M. "An Analysis of the Structure of Analysis: The *Gegenstand* Relation in Discussion." *Philosophia Reformata,* 49 (1984): 35–56.

Struycken, A. A. H. *Het staatsrecht van het koninkrijk der Nederlanden,* 2nd ed. Arnhem: Gouda Quint, 1928.

——— (ed.) *Handelingen der Nederlandsche Juristen-Vereeniging.* The Hague: Belinfante, 1870– .

Tezner, Friedrich. *Zur Lehre von dem freien Ermessen der Verwaltungsbehörden als Grund der Unzuständigkeit der Verwaltungsgerichte.* Vienna: Manz, 1888.

———. *Die deutschen Theorien der Verwaltungsrechtspflege. Eine kritisch orientierende Studie.* Berlin: Heymann, 1901.

Thoma, Richard. *Rechtsstaatsidee und Verwaltungsrechtswissenschaft.* Tübingen: J. C. B. Mohr, 1910.

Tönnies, Ferdinand. *Gemeinschaft und Gesellschaft. Grundbegriffe der reinen Soziologie.* 6th ed. Berlin: K. Curtius, 1926.

Triepel, Heinrich. *Staatsrecht und Politik. Rede beim Antritte des Rektorats der Friedrich Wilhelms Universität zu Berlin am 15. Oktober 1926.* Berlin: W. de Gruyter, 1927.

Troeltsch, Ernst. *Der Historismus und seine Probleme.* Vol. 3 of *Gesammelte Schriften.* Tübingen: J. C. B. Mohr, 1922.

Tyszka, Carl von, *Die Sozialisierung des Wirtschaftslebens. Grunsätzliches über Möglichkeiten und Notwendigkeiten.* Jena: Fischer, 1922.

Vogel, Walther. "Rudolf Kjellén und seine Bedeutung für die deutsche Staatslehre." *Zeitschrift für die gesamte Staatswissenschaft* 81 (1926).

Vollenhoven, D. H. T. "Problemen van de tijd in onze kring." Paper read to the Amsterdam chapter of the Association for Reformational Philosophy, 29 March 1968. Amsterdam: Filosofisch Instituut der Vrije Universiteit, 1968.

Waldecker, Ludwig. *Allgemeine Staatslehre.* Berlin-Grunewald: W. Rothschild, 1927.

Walz, Gustav Adolf. *Vom Wesen des öffentlichen Rechts.* Stuttgart: F. Enke, 1928.

——. *Die Staatsidee des Rationalismus und der Romantik und die Staatsphilosophie Fichtes, zugleich ein Versuch zur Grundlegung einer allgemeinen Sozialmorphologie.* Berlin-Grunewald: W. Rothschild, 1928.

Weber, Max. *Parlament und Regierung im neugeordneten Deutschland. Zur politischen Kritik des Beamtentums und Parteiwesens.* Leipzig: Duncker und Humblot, 1918.

——. "Über einige Kategorien der verstehenden Soziologie." In *Gesammelte Aufsätze zur Wissenschaftslehre,* pp. 403–50. Tübingen: J. C. B. Mohr, 1922.

——. "Methodische Grundlagen der Soziologie." In *Grundriss der Sozialökonomik,* Pt. 3, *Wirtschaft und Gesellschaft.* Tübingen: J. C. B. Mohr, 1922. Also contained in *Gesammelte Aufsätze zur Wissenschaftslehre,* pp. 503–23.

Wiese, Leopold von. *Allgemeine Soziologie als Lehre von den Beziehungen und Beziehungsgebilden der Menschen.* 2 vols. Leipzig: Duncker und Humblot, 1924–1929.

Windelband, Wilhelm. *Präludien. Aufsätze und Reden zur Einleitung in die Philosophie,* 3rd ed. Tübingen: J. C. B. Mohr (P. Siebeck), 1907.

Wittmayer, Leo. "Die Staatlichkeit des Reiches als logische und als nationale Integrationsform." *Fischers Zeitschrift für Verwaltungsrecht* 57 (1925).

Zhelezhnov, Vladimir. *Grundzüge der Volkswirtschaftslehre.* 2nd rev. ed. Translated from the Russian by Eugen Altschul. Leipzig and Berlin: B. G. Teubner, 1928.

Index of Names

A

Althusius, Johannes, 29, 128f, 137
Anschütz, Gerhard, 34
Aquinas, Thomas, 20, 78
Aristotle, vi, 20, 78, 166f
Assenmacher, Johannes, 92
Augustine, 115

B

Bähr, Otto, 32
Barthélemy, Henri, 24
Barthélemy, Joseph, 24, 31
Beckerat, Erwin von, 138
Below, Georg von, 146
Bergbohm, Karl, 33
Bergson, Henri, 20, 71, 72, 90, 91
Bernheim, Ernst, 109
Berth, Edouard, 23
Beseler, Georg, 99
Binder, Julius, 56, 58
Bluntschli, Johann Kasper, 7, 8
Bodin, Jean, 5, 22, 128f, 147
Burckhardt, Walther, 116, 160, 169f
Buys, J. Th., 133, 149, 150

C

Calvin, John, 78, 88
Carré de Malbert, Raymond, 34
Cassirer, Ernst, 74, 85
Christ, 77, 78, 81, 114f, 115, 162
Cohen, Hermann, 127
Cole, G. D. H., 135, 179
Comte, Auguste, 8, 22, 119

D

Darmstaedter, Friedrich, 32, 177f
Descartes, René, 14f, 82
Dicey, A. V., 133
Dilthey, Wilhelm, 39f, 62, 80, 109
Dimitch, Velimir N., 121

Droysen, Johann Gustav, 122
Duez, Paul, 24, 149
Duguit, Léon, 22-24, 28, 34, 36, 135
Duns Scotus, 92

E

Ehrlich, Eugen, 143f, 166
Einstein, Albert, 90, 91
Engels, Friedrich, 136

F

Fichte, J. G., 17, 45, 58, 85, 87, 145
Frederick Barbarossa, 147
Freyer, Hans, 39, 59, 173
Fricker, Karl, 125

G

Gerber, C. F. von, 3-6, 8, 22, 55
Gierke, Otto von, 3-6, 31, 47, 65,
  99-105, 116, 129, 144, 146
Glum, Friedrich, 139
Gneist, Rudolf von, 32, 175f
Goes van Naters, Marinus van der,
  139
Groen van Prinsterer, Guillaume, 147
Grotius, Hugo, 36
Gurvitch, Georges, 37
Guy-Grand, Georges, 131

H

Haering, Theodor L., 117
Haller, K. L. von, 146f
Hauriou, Maurice, 60, 138
Heidenhain, Martin, 117
Hegel, G. W. F., 32, 36, 45, 58
Heidegger, Martin, 39, 64, 84
Heimsoeth, Heinz, 92
Heinemann, Bruno, 155
Heller, Hermann, 25, 28, 34, 36, 38,
  41, 57, 59, 60, 63,

66, 69, 138
Hennig, Richard, 124
Hippel, Ernst von, 56
Hobbes, Thomas, 14, 21f, 33f, 69f, 110, 127, 129, 131, 147
Hobson, S. G., 135, 136
Hoffmann, Paul, 39
Hönigswald, Richard, 39
Hsiao, Kung-Chuan, 135, 136, 179
Hübner, Rudolf, 122
Humboldt, Alexander von, 32
Hume, David, 16, 17
Husserl, Edmund, 39, 52, 53, 70, 80

I

Idsinga, J. W. H. M., 145, 150, 175f
Inama von Sternegg, K. Th. von, 147

J

James, William, 135
Jellinek, Georg, 7, 9-13, 29, 34, 55, 56, 125
Jhering, Rudolf von, 119, 121, 140, 166

K

Kahn, Bernard Arnold, 133
Kant, Immanuel, 9, 17-19, 21, 27f, 30, 32, 35, 42, 53,
75f, 82-87, 91, 129, 172, 174
Kaufmann, Erich, 56, 68
Kelsen, Hans, 6, 12, 19, 24, 25-28, 31, 32, 33f, 36f, 48-51, 53, 55, 58, 64, 67, 87, 97, 111, 118, 121, 123, 124, 126, 130, 131f, 134, 149, 151, 160, 171, 174, 177
Kjellén, Rudolf, 122f
Krabbe, Hugo, 25, 28, 34, 36, 133, 145
Kraft-Fuchs, M., 134
Kranenburg, R., 133
Kroner, Richard, 83
Külpe, Oswald, 76
Kuypers, Karel, 109

L

Laband, Paul, 3-6, 8, 32, 34, 35, 53, 55
Lask, Emil, 178
Laski, Harold, 104, 132, 135f
Leibholz, Gerhard, 38, 39, 60, 69, 137f
Leibniz, G. W., 21, 74, 172, 174
Lenin, Vladimir, 37, 137
Leo, Heinrich, 147
Levy, J. A., 150
Liefmann, Robert, 155
Litt, Theodor, 39-47, 50, 51, 52, 53, 85, 87, 120, 106n, 163f
Locke, John, 16
Loeff, J. A., 148

M

MacDougall, William, 141
Marck, Siegfried, 39, 101, 102, 108, 116
Marquardsen, Heinrich von, 35
Marshall, Alfred, 159
Meinecke, Friedrich, 68
Merkl, Adolf, 149
Mirkine-Guetzévitch, Boris, 31, 37f, 139
Mohl, Robert von, 35
Montesquieu, Charles de Secondat, 35, 66

N

Natorp, Paul, 72
Nelson, Leonard, 1, 167
Newton, Isaac, 90
Nicolaus of Cusa, 21
Nitzsch, K. W., 147

O

Oppenheim, Jacques, 133
Oppenheimer, Franz, 119f

P

Philip of Leyden, 147
Planck, Max, 95
Plato, vi, 14, 74, 78, 172

Polak, Leonard, 167
Praag, Leo van, 150, 153, 157, 160
Preuss, Hugo, 4, 99, 104f, 108
Puchta, G. F., 99, 103
Pythagoras, 166

R

Ranke, Leopold von, 122
Ratzel, Friedrich, 62
Reinach, Adolf, 69
Rhadamantos, 166
Rickert, Heinrich, 65, 73, 80, 109
Riehl, Alois, 76
Roëll, Antonie baron, 150
Rohatyn, S., 38
Romeyn, H., 133
Rosin, Heinrich, 105
Ross, C. D., 140
Rozemond, S., 128
Rousseau, J.-J., 30, 34, 35, 127, 129, 135, 147
Ruyll, 150

S

Sander, Fritz, 6, 27
Savigny, F. C. von, 99
Scheler, Max, 39, 96
Schelling, F. W. J., 30, 32, 45, 58, 99
Schleiermacher, F. E. D., 58
Schmidt, Richard, 7
Schmitt, Carl, 31, 35, 36, 39, 55-60, 62, 68, 129, 134, 139
Schreier, Fritz, 28, 38, 68, 174
Sigwart, Christoph, 11
Simmel, Georg, 40, 46, 109, 120, 171-73
Small, Albion W., 39, 41, 120
Smend, Rudolf, 26, 38, 48-67, 106, 111, 121, 144
Somló, Bódog, 113
Sorel, Georges, 59, 60, 62, 135
Spann, Othmar, 47, 119, 137
Spencer, Herbert, 54
Spengler, Oswald, 20, 114, 145, 164
Spranger, Eduard, 39
Stahl, F. J., 32, 111, 147, 176

Stammler, Rudolf, 33, 87
Stein, H. F. K. baron von und zum, 35
Stein, Lorenz von, 36
Strauss, D. F. M., 86
Struycken, A. A. H., 125, 133, 146, 150, 157

T

Taylor, G. R. S., 135
Tezner, Friedrich, 149f
Thoma, Richard, 34
Thomas, *see* Aquinas
Thon, August, 170
Tisza, Count, 122
Tönnies, Ferdinand, 115, 140
Triepel, Heinrich, 56
Troeltsch, Ernst, 109, 119, 164
Tyszka, Carl von, 155

V

Vanderbilt, Cornelius, 158
Verbrugge, Magnus, vii
Verdross, Alfred, 38
Vierkandt, Alfred, 40, 46, 140
Vlugt, W. van der, 133
Vogel, Walther, 122
Volkelt, Johannes, 39, 92
Vollenhoven, Dirk, vi, vii, 109
Vos, Henri, 150

W

Waldecker, Ludwig, 5, 29, 102, 108, 126, 129
Walz, Gustav Adolf, 144, 145
Wartemburg, Paul Yorck von, 62
Webb, Sidney, 135
Weber, Max, 9, 46, 61, 131
Wegner, Arthur, 56
Wiese, Leopold von, 40, 46, 172f
Windelband, Wilhelm, 72, 109, 113
Wittmayer, Leo, 39, 54

Z

Zhelezhnov, Vladimir, 155

Index of Subjects

A

absolute
- power, sovereignty, 79, 113, 135, 144, 147, 159, 178, 179

absolutism, 4, 5, 17, 21f, 25, 33f, 57, 105, 127, 128-30, 144, 147, 160; Schmitt on, 36

absolutization, 8, 14, *et passim*

Abstract
- concept, idea, 63n, 68, 77, 107, 131, 133, 143, 144, 151n, 165-68

abstraction, 2, 15, 16, 27n, 28, 71, 72, 75, 76, 79

administration, 30, 57, 61, 144, 149, 150n
- Smend on, 57, 61, 67; Tezner on, 149f

adminstrative law, 67, 149
- Laband on, 3, 36
- in Henri Barthélemy, 24n; Darmstaedter, 178; Duguit, 24; Heller, 34

analogy, analogical, vi, 61, 80-82, 85f, 90, 93, 98, 108-13, 123, 139, 142, 163f, 166-68

analytical function, 16, 18, 82, 85, 88, 90

anarchy, 136, 178

anastatic, 115

Anti-Christ, 115

anticipation, anticipatory, 80f, 107, 110f, 113, 115, 126, 127, 140, 163, 166

antinomy, antinomic, 15, 16, 20, 23, 27n, 28, 29, 44f, 68, 70, 78, 83, 87, 109, 111, 123n, 125, 163, 170

Anti-Revolutionary
- theory of the state, 111n

antithesis (religious), 77f, 162

arbitrary, 75, 102n, 160, 161
- government, 38, 152n, 158, 161

Aristotelian(ism), vi, 7, 20, 77, 122, 129, 167, 174

art, 163

aspects, 10, 81n, 98, 114, 126n
- spatial, 94n
- physical, 10
- psychical, 10, 126n
- historical, 126n
- jural (juridical), 10, 11, 12, 104, 152
- modal, v, 81n
- normative, 98
  See also functions; law-spheres

associations (voluntary), 63, 105n, 116f, 136n, 141, 142

authoritarian(ism), 138, 145

authoritative
- acts of government, 24

authority, 31, 104, 131, 140, 178
- of the state, 5, 30f, 54, 115, 116, 131-39, 147n, 151, 152, 155, 159, 176, 178
- in the church, 114f
- in enterprise, 132-38, 156, 166
- in the family, 4, 107, 131, 140
- and coordinational relationships, 3n, 51, 116, 117

autocracy, autocratric, 134n, 144, 146, 148, 152

autonomy, 4n, 33, 35, 111, 136, 160
- Kantian, 27, 176

B

Baden School, 56n
Berlin School, 38-70, 103, 134n, 137; *see also* constitutional law; integration theory
Bolshevism, 37, 139
Britain, 121, 134
budget law, 35
business firm, company, corporation, enterprise, 116, 128, 131f, 134f, 138, 142, 150n, 151-59
- founding function of, 108, 116
- employee councils in, 156
- employers association of, 152n ; authority of, 156
- government interference in, 32, 152n, 156, 158f, 166
- leading function of, 116, 135, 153-55

C

cabinet government, 133
- Smend on, 59
calling (cultural), 110, 113; *see also* task
Calvinist
- cosmology, 78-82, 92-161
- epistemology, 72-79
- philosophy, 2, *et passim*
- political theory, ix, 5, 71-82, 130-37, 151-61
capital (economic), 110, 116, 135
cartels, 132, 142, 156
causality, 22, 27, 43, 90, 119, 120
- historical, 164
- physical and psychical, 164
Central Europe, *see* Europe
church
- interests of, in Gierke, 6
- internal law of, 152-55, 178
- structure of, 75, 114f, 116, 132
- Van Praag on, 153; Waldecker on, 30

civil
- jurisprudence, 143f, 149, 150n, 153, 154, 157, 160
- law, 4, 22, 67, 70, 99, 142, 143, 149, 150
- society, 177
Civil Code (Dutch), 148, 153, 154, 160, 170
civility
- norms for, 121
civilization, civilized society, 109, 140-42, 148, 163
- Smend on, 49; Van Idsinga on, 176
  See also culture
Civil Service Act (Dutch), 150
civitas Dei, 115
civitas terrena, 115
clubs, 116
class
- interests, 37
- representation of, 135-39
- social, 140, 141
- struggle, 58n
co-determination, 131; *see also* industrial democracy
coercion, coercive, 4, 33, 158, 170, 179
- acc. to Burckhardt, 169; Duguit, 24; Hsiao, 179; Kelsen, 33; Krabbe, 25
- in fascism, 138n
  See also force
coherence, v, 3, 11n, 13, 51, *et passim*
collective
- agreements, 142, 160
- entity, 24, 101
- "I", 47, 97, 101, 102n, 116n
- consciousness, 101
- selfhood, 101
colony, 125
commercial corporation, 142, 150n
- in Spann, 137; Waldecker, 30
  See also business firm

commercial law, 144
common law, 133n
common
- interest, 155
- soul, 125
- speech, 63
community
- cultural, 148
- national, 132, 140, 141
- natural, 117, 141
- tribal, 141
- acc. to Althusius, 137; Hobson, 136; Litt, 40-47; Marck, 102n; Smend, 50, 59, 63; Van Idsinga, 176
   See also organized community
community of wills, 48, 51, 59, 60, 61, 63
Company Councils (Germany), 156n, 158; *see also* employee councils
compensation
- for damages, 150f
- for injuries, 150n
competency, 130, 142
- of a civil court judge, 150, 160
- of non-state communities, 159; Burckhardt on, 170
- of the state, 5, 33–35, 37, 113, 116, 128, 156- 59, 178
- of an historical subject, 113
concept and idea, 81
constitution, 133f
- Darmstaedter on, 178; Smend on, 55, 57, 63, 66, 67
- written, 5, 31, 133
- of the Soviet Union, 37, 38n
- of the Weimar Republic, 34, 56, 138, 156n
constitutional law, 5, 27, 118, 147
- acc. to Burckhardt, 170; Gierke, 104; Schmitt, 68; Smend, 53, 62, 67; Van Idsinga, 175f
- Calvinist, 71-82, 118-37, 151-61

- Christian-historical, 175
- Hallerian, 146f
- humanist, *passim*
- and political conventions, 133; politics (statecraft), 7, 8, 9, 34, 55; written constitutions, 133f
constitutional theory
- Berlin School, *see* integration theory
- pure juridical method, 3-6, 8, 133
- two-sides theory, 9-13, 19, 25, 104
   See also identity theory; integration theory
constitutional
- monarchy, 175f
- state (*Rechtsstaat*), 25f, 32, 36, 54, 58; *see also* just state; rule of law
- system, 5
constraint, 27; *see also* coercion
continuity
- spatial, 81
- in the cosmic order, 88, 89, 93, 94, 112
continuity postulate (principle), 15, 17, 53, 87, 107, 120
contract, 142, 159, 160, 161
- collective, 142
- labor, 142
- social, 22
- freedom of, 156, 160
- obligations of, 166
- rights of, 148
- theory of, 129
- in Althusius, 129; Duguit, 24; Hobbes, 22, 131, 147; Kelsen, 26
- in rationalism, 127
- as a source of law, 160f
contract law, 144, 148
coordinational law, 4, 22, 27, 142f, 148, 151n, 159, 160, 161

- acc. to Gierke, 3; Walz, 145f
coordinational
- communities, 116n
- relationships, 3n, 5, 26, 116, 117f, 141f, 151, 159, 160, 161
- society, 148
- spheres, 176, 178
- subjects, 161
copy theory, 72-74
corporate law, 152, 155, 158
corporate theory
- in Beseler, 99; Gierke, 99f
- Gierke on, 102n, 144f; Liefmann on, 155; Van Praag on, 153
  See also business firm
corporatism, 60, 135-39
Corpus Christianum, 92
cosmic reality, 14, 52, 71, *et passim*
  See also time
cosmology, 75, 79
- Calvinist, 78-82, 92-161
- religious foundation of, 72n
cosmopolitanism, *see* world citizenship
criminal law, 150, 151
- Kelsen on, 151n
critical
- approach, 75
- ontology, 77
- realism, 76
- theory of knowledge, 83, 84
criticist(ic), 11n, 12, 82, 171
- epistemology, 17, 19, 87
- positivism, 22, 130
  See also critical
critique of knowledge
- by Hume, 16f; Kant, 17f, 30, 75n, 83-85, 171; the Marburg School, 87
  See also criticist(ic)
crown (monarchy), 147
cultural development, 80, 90, 108f, 163f, 168

cultural objects, 95f, 106n; *see also* things
culture
- dominant factors in, 113n, 114, 141, 144, 148; Jellinek on, 10
- level of, 109, 117, 140-42, 146, 163f
- unfolding of, 115, 142, 148
- philosophy of, in Litt, 40
- shapers of, 113n, 142, 161
- and the state, 62, 136, 143, 177
customary law, 4n, 125, 133n, 161

D

decisionism, 58, 69
deepening
- of intuition, 89
- of law-spheres, 81, 91, 126, 167
- of meaning, 81, 88, 89, 126, 151f, 156
- of thought, 15, 16, 75, 76, 88, 113
  See also disclosure; unfolding
democracy, 31, 60f, 131-37
- principle of, 131, 134
- social democracy, 139n
- Guy-Grand on, 131; Heller on, 63n; Kelsen on, 31, 131f
destination function, 94, 141, 142, 154, 157
détournement de pouvoir, 150n
dialectic(al), 19, 41, 51, 64, 65, 70, 87, 97, 101, 102, 109, 111
- in Fichte, 45, 53, 87; Litt, 41-47, 51n, 87, 120; Smend, 49-69, 111n
- Heller on, 41n
dictatorship, 37, 58, 132n, 139
- Leibholz on, 137f; Schmitt on, 56, 58n
- Bolshevist, 37f
  See also Bolshevism; Soviet law
dimensional(ity)

– and the spatial sphere, 80f, 93n
disclosure, 81, 107, 108, 151; *see also* culture, unfolding of; deepening
dogmatic, dogmatism, 17f, 76, 86f, 96, 102, 129, 173
dominion (ruling power), 4, 12, 108-14, 123, 125
– in Kelsen, 34, 61; Kjellén, 123; Smend, 57, 61; Weber, 61

E

Eastern Europe, *see* Europe
economic(s), economic life, 128, 132, 158
– entities, 94, 123
– interests, 6, 37, 188, 155
– norms for, 155
– science of, 40, 145, 147n, 173
– sphere of, 80, 108, 116, 132, 166
– time in, 91
– of the family, 107
– and ethics, 114
– and the state, 6, 23, 32, 126-28, 135-38, 154-56; acc. to Kelsen, 131f; Leibholz, 138n; Marxism, 136, 138n, 139; Schmitt, 139n; Stammler, 87; Weber, 131
– and the patrimonial state, 146
 See also business firm; corporatism; functions; law-spheres
empiricism, 16f, 19, 20
employees
– councils of, 156
– of government, 147
England, 121, 147
– law in, 133n, 175f
 See also Britain
enkapsis, enkaptic, vii, 117f
Enlightenment, 25
en-static, 73f
entelechy, 20; see also teleology
enterprise, *see* business firm

epistemology, 2, 10, 11n, 13, 16, 42, 49, 75, 76, 85f
– Calvinist, 73-79, 88-94, 161
– criticistic, 17, 75, 82, 87
– empiricist, 16, 20
– functionalist, 75, 98
– humanist, 13f, 19, 26, 38, 71ff; dogmatic bias of, 18, 76, 86f
– (neo)Kantian, 9-13, 18, 27-30, 42, 73-87, 171f
– phenomenological, 75
epochè, 80n, 88, 89, 93
equality
– in Aristotle, 167
– in coordinational relationships, 141
– in an economic enterprise, 156n
– in international relations, 121
– Nelson on, 167; Darmstaedter on, 177f
equality before the law, 35, 167
equivalency
– causal, 119
– economic, 166
estates, 35n, 141
ethical
– idealism, of Fichte, 17
– view of law, Heller on, 69
– view of the state, 3, 7; Kelsen on, 24f, 27, 32- 37, 53; Van Idsinga on, 176
Europe, Central and Eastern
– parliaments in, 134
European states
– and China, 121
– and dictatorship, 37
extraterritoriality, 125

F

faith, 78, 80, 81, 94, 107, 108, 110, 114, 115, 126n, 153f, 178
– rational, 17, 30f, 62, 70; Schmitt on, 36

- and the unfolding process, 115
- and values, 62, 63
    See also pistis; pistology
family, 106f, 111, 140f, 155, 159
- authority in, 4, 107, 131
- internal law of, 107
- Gierke on, 103; Preuss on, 105
fascism, 37n, 59f, 62, 137-39
fashion (dress), 121, 140, 142
faustian, 13, 14, 110, 174
federation, confederation
- acc. to pluralists, 135f
- acc. to Preuss, 104
- Smend on, 66
force
- brute (physical), 6, 25, 26, 37, 110, 157
- and the state: Duguit on, 24f; Lenin on, 37; Waldecker on, 30
    See also coercion
formalism, formalistic
- legal, 170, 175
- positivist, 3, 5, 134
- science of law, 6, 28, 37f, 174
- in constitutional law, 70, 116, 143, 149, 169, 179
- in sociology, 145, 172-74
    See also law, pure theory of
form-matter scheme, 19, 42, 82, 85-87 171-73, 178
France, 122, 147
French
- jurisprudence, 149n
- National Assembly (1789), 35n
- scholars, 22, 31n, 138
free enterprise, 32, 128, 154n, 157
freedom, 3n, 5, 116, 176
- acc. to humanism, 15, 17, 35, 45
- in Darmstaedter, 177f; Heidegger, 85n; Kelsen, 33; Laband, 36; Stein, 35n; Van Idsinga, 176
- of contract, 156, 160
- of the individual, 33, 159, 177f
- and coordinational relationships, 3n, 26, 116, 141
    See also autonomy; rights
freedom idealism, 52, 58, 64, 65
frugal, frugality, 80, 166, 168
function
- anticipatory, 81, 82, 166
- destination, 141, 54
- founding (foundation) 80, 98, 106-16, 122, 129, 130-62, 163, 166
- guiding, 110, 115, 123, 131, 155, 157
- leading, 94-96, 106f, 110f, 114, 115, 116, 121f, 124, 125, 130-62
- natural, 20, 25, 27, 74, 96, 98, 100n, 106f, 108, 110, 124, 140, 165, 166
- normative, 97, 112
- object-, 74, 93f, 95, 96, 163
- qualifying, 93-96, 112, 142, 152, 167
- retrocipatory, 80, 110
- spiritual, 14, 15, 20, 74, 90, 96, 98, 112
- subject-, 71, 74, 79, 93f, 95, 98, 112, 117, 125
- terminal, 81, 115
    See also law-sphere
functions, v, 51, 52, 73, 74
- numerical, 81, 90
- spatial, 81, 90, 124, 125
- kinematic, 14, 90
- physical, 81, 82, 86, 95
- biotic (organic), 81, 90, 93f, 106, 111, 165
- psychical (sensory), 12, 14, 16, 17, 18, 72, 76, 80, 85, 86-90, 91, 97, 125f, 127, 140
- logical (analytical), 17, 26f, 39, 76, 80, 82-92, 110
- rational (analytical), 14, 15, 16, 18, 30, 77

- historic(al), 64f, 90, 108-12, 114, 123
- social, 65, 116, 121f, 140f
- economic, 116, 128, 132, 135, 136, 156f
- aesthetic, 20, 80, 96, 109, 126, 156, 163, 167, 168
- jural (juridical), vii, 44, 66, 111-13, 118, 121, 125, 126f, 128, 134, 140, 151-62
- moral, 21, 87, 107, 140, 156
- pistical (faith), 81, 114f, 126n, 156
  See also law-spheres
functionalism (-istic), 2, 17-30, 38, 51, 64, 68, 70-84, 85n, 91, 92n, 96f, 101, 114, 120, 127, 131, 169
fundamental rights, 4, 5; see also freedom; rights
fundamentals of law, Heller on, 69

G

Geisteswissenschaften, geisteswissenschaftlich, 38, 40, 45, 49, 53, 54, 61, 68; *see also* humanities
Gegenstand, 18, 75-89, 98
gegenständlich, 66, 88-90; *see also* oppositional
general will (*volonté générale*)
- in Gierke, 103; Rousseau, 30, 34, 135; Smend, 60
- in universalism, 161
- Hauriou on, 60
geography, political, 124
geopolitics, 62, 124
Germanic
- conception of the state, 145, 146
- law, 100, 143, 145, 146
- legal science, 102, 144
- view of law, 99, 145
God
- law of, vi, vii
- mind of, vi note
- sovereignty of, 78, 137

- Word of, 78
government, ix, 108, 112, 121, 124-26, 132-34, 143f, t5148-61
- and torts, 148
- acc. to Bluntschli, 7; Duguit, 28; Engels, 136; Kant, 32; Kjellén, 123; Laband, 35f; Smend, 48, 54, 60, 63; Spann, 137n
- forms of, 54, 61, 63, 134; Kelsen on, 31n
- in ancient Sparta, 147n; medieval Italy, 147
  See also absolutism; constitutional law; state
grace, divine: in Thomas, 78
Great Powers, 122n, 125
Greek
- aesthetics, 163
- idealism, 77
- word for justice, 167
  See also philosophy, ancient
guilds, 136
guild socialism, 136

H

historical
- causality, 164
- conditioning, 117
- culture, 142
- development, 88, 94, 100, 113, 115, 132, 133, 143, 148, 163
- method, 119
- nature of the church, 30
- nature of states, 7, 9, 10, 64, 66, 108
- norms, 64n, 163
- periodization, 90, 113n, 164
- power, 68, 110, 114, 115, 116, 125, 129, 132, 134f, 142, 156, 164
- relativism, 113
- space, 163
- thinking, 109

- time, 85n, 90, 109, 163f
- values, 59, 62
- view of law, 32, 68, 99
- in Gierke, 100-04, 146; Preuss, 104f
- in phenomenology, 64, 85n, 90
  See also functions; law-spheres

Historical School
- in economics, 147n
- in law, 99, 147n, 160; Germanist wing of, 99, 102, 145f; Romanist wing of 99, 125n, 145

historicism, historicist, 31, 64-70, 99, 108
- in Dilthey, 40; Engels, 136; Gierke, 65, 104; Kjellén, 122; Preuss, 104; Schmitt, 69; Simmel, 172; Smend, 64f, 111; Spengler, 113, 164
- in the Berlin School, 69; Historical School, 99

history, 109, 114, 163f
- in Bluntschli, 7; Gierke, 101, 103; Kjellén, 122; Rickert, 65n, 109; Schmitt, 69; Smend, 62, 63, 64; Spengler, 164; Van Idsinga, 176
- dominant factors in, 113n, 148
- shapers of, 30, 113n, 164; acc. to Jellinek, 10
- as a battle-field, 115

history (science of), 2, 7, 163
- periodization in, 164
- in Simmel, 40

humanities, human sciences, 38n, 39-42, 45-68, 87, 89, 97, 98, 120
- Gierke on, 100; Simmel on, 171

humanity (humanness): Smend on, 52
Humanity (human race): Oppenheimer on, 120

I

idea
- and concept, 81, 127
- and sign 74
- in ancient idealism, 14, 20, 77, 172
- in Hume, 16, Kant, 18, 30

ideal, *see* personality; science

idealism, idealist, 14, 17, 18, 19, 31, 36, 68, 73, 97, 111, 129, 160
- freedom, 64, 65
- in Gierke, 102f; Hobson, 136; Schelling, 99

identity theory, of state and law: 6, 7, 24n, 28, 32-36, 143, 177

idolatry, idolatrous, 72n, 77, 78, 162
imagination, 94
- transcendental, in Kant, 84f

immanence (creaturely), 77, 79, 83, 88, 164
immanence philosophy, 13, 19, 45, *et passim*
- its dogmatic prejudice, 17f, 96, 102n

immanent(ism), 14, 16, 17, 19, 20, 26-28, 29, 31, 38, 44, 45, 51, 73, 76

individual, individuality, vi, vii, 2, 19-22, 26-38, 73, 95-97, 101, 104-18, 123-39, 142-66
- central problem of temporal reality, 19, 92
- Christian view of, 77, 91-96
- Heller on, 66n, 69
- in irrationalism, 58, 164

individual persons, 23f, 25, 32-34, 96, 97, 117, 121, 127, 130, 132, 141, 142, 148, 159, 164, 177
- in Althusius, 137; Gierke, 100-03; Kelsen, 49; Marck, 102n; Litt, 40-48; Preuss, 105; Simmel, 171; Smend, 48-50, 59f; Tezner, 150
- Christian view of, 88, 91, 97
  See also selfhood

individuality-structure, vii, 52, 57, 92-96, 99, 104; *see also* things

individualism, individualistic, 21, 22, 32, 38, 45, 49, 96f, 99f, 130, 132, 136, 144, 15, 175
- metaphysics, 3-5, 118, 129, 132
- in Henri Barthélemy, 24n; Duns Scotus, 92n; Hobbes, 129, 131; Jehring, 119; Kant, 21; Kelsen, 130, 132; Laband, 3-5; Litt, 43-45, 47f; Schmitt, 58f; Walz, 145
- in nominalism, 19; Early Renaissance, 20; Roman law, 99, 104, 144f, 147; pluralism, 136

industrial democracy, 131, 134
- Kelsen on, 132
  See also business firm; employee councils

integration, 54, 125, 144, 148
- by the state, 143-59
- in non-state relationships, 140-43

integration theory, of constitutional law: 38, 48-70, 106, 124, 134n
- Kelsen on, 26n, 48n, 51, 53, 64n, 67, 111n; Leibholz on, 137, 138n; Rohatyn on, 38n; Schmitt on, 68; Smend on, 48-70, 106, 111; Wittmayer on, 54

interests, 6, 35, 37, 132, 135, 136, 137, 138, 149, 155, 160, 167, 176

interfunctional synthesis, 16, 75, 82-86

inter-individual interaction, 97, 140
- in Simmel, 46
- Smend on, 48
  See also social interwovenness

international
- enterprise, 154
- law, 121, 125, 128n, 161
- relations, 121, 125, 128, 140, 141

interpersonal relations, 145; see also coordinational relationships; inter-individual interaction

intertwinement, vii, 1, 2, 118, 155, 175; see also enkapsis; interwovenness;

interwoven(ness)
- of communities and relationships, 117f
- of functions, 14, 71, 75, 79, 84, 88, 107, 165
- of land and people, 126
- of law-side and subject-side, 113
- of law-spheres, 79
- of public and private law, 148
- of self and world, 43
- in Leibniz, 172; Litt, 46f, 51n, 97; Marck, 102n
  See also enkapsis; intertwinement

intuition, intuitive(ly), 89
- in Bergson, 71; Heller, 41n; Leibniz, 74; Litt, 41n
- of naive experience, 73
- Kant on, 18, 75, 83-86; acc. to Heidegger, 85; Kroner, 83n

irrationalism, irrationalist(-ic), 20, 58, 59, 61, 62, 70, 71, 72, 93, 112, 164
- and individuality, 20, 21, 58
- and the law-side of reality, 20, 112
  See also philosophy of life

irreducible, 109, 112, 124, 165

J

judiciary power, Smend on, 66f, 144
jural (juridical)
- law-sphere, 5, 27, 107, 111-14, 118, 165-68; in Kelsen, 174
- norms, 9, 51, 113, 134; in Jellinek, 9; Kelsen, 6, 61; Schmitt, 69; Smend, 53; outside the state, 170
- principles, 161

jurisprudence
- administrative, 144, 148-50, 178
- civil, 143f

- in France, 149n; the Netherlands, 148-51, 153f, 157, 160
- acc. to Laband, 4, 6; Schmitt, 58, 67; Smend, 67; Van Idsinga, 175; Waldecker, 30

jus congens, 170

justice, 31, 152, 160, 166, 167
- commutative, 167
- distributive, 166
- restorative, 166
- acc. to Aristotle, 166f; Duguit, 24; Tezner, 149f; Van Praag, 160
- in Smend, 56, 66; Wagner 56

just state (*Rechtsstaat*), 32-36, 143, 144, 148-52
- acc. to Darmstaedter, 177; Heller, 34, 63n; Kelsen, 33f; Preuss, 104f; Schmitt, 36; Smend, 63; Van Idsinga, 176
  - liberal theory of, 63, 177
    See also constitutional state; general will

K

Kantian(ism), 6, 13, 28, 42, 171-74, 176, 178; see also Neokantianism

kernel, of a law-sphere, 166, 167, 168; see also nucleus

kinematic function (motion), 14, 80-82, 86, 90, 93, 95, 168

knowledge, ix, 13, 18, 19, 38, 74-88, 98
- faustian thirst for, 13, 174
- juridical, in Jellinek, 12f
- natural-scientific, 40, 85
- in Kant, 18, 28, 75n, 76, 83, 86; Kelsen, 27; Leibniz, 74, 174; Litt, 40-48; Simmel, 5, 171f
  See also critique of knowledge; epistemology; *Gegenstand*

L

labor contract, 142
language, 74, 94, 107, 108, 109, 168

- everyday, 165
- acc. to Jellinek, 12; Leibniz, 74; Plato, 74

law, vi, vii, 1, 2, 3, 6, 13, 25, 79n, 87n
- acc. to Gierke, 65, 104; Heller, 69, 34; Kant, 18, 21; Kelsen, 26f, 33, 36; Krabbe, 25; Preuss, 105; Sander, 27; Schmitt, 36, 69; Smend, 65- 67; Van Idsinga, 175f; Waldecker, 5n
- coercive, 169f
- meaning of, 2, 5, 37, 38, 151
- natural (law of nature), 8, 19, 21, 100, 112, 119, 124
- non-state, 26, 27, 57, 123f, 129, 139ff, 178
  positive, 4, 5, 22, 26, 33, 35, 66n, 69, 128, 147, 154, 156, 158, 161, 161n
- private, 3f, 134, 143-51, 160, 169f
- public, 4, 30, 67, 143-51, 160, 169f
- public and private, 4, 22f, 24, 25, 30, 144, 169f, 175
- sociology of, 10
- sources of, 4n, 22, 28, 134, 151, 160f, 161n
- sovereignty of, 25, 31
- statutory, 149, 160
- subject-side of, 22
- written, 5, 66, 133, 134
- and norms, 8, 10, 19
- and subject, *see* law-side of reality
  See also Historical School; Roman law

law and the state, 25, 33, 36, 65, 67
- acc. to Duguit, 23f; Jellinek, 10; Laband, 35f; Stein, 35n

law, theories (views) of
- Calvinist, 128
- formalist, 28, 32, 34, 35f, 149, 150n
- identity, 28, 36
- integration, 66

- natural-law, 6, 9, 21, 22, 25, 30-35
- philosophical, 1, 21, 167
- positivist, 118
- psychologistic, 151
- pure law, 27-29, 32-38, 67n, 82, 87, 118, 121, 130
  See also Historical School; legal science

law-side
- of law, 65
- of a law-sphere, 109, 110, 112ff
- of reality, vi, 13, 19, 27n, 71, 74, 79, 93n 109, 111, 112ff, 164

law-side and subject-side, 13, 19, 79, 110, 112, 113, 123, 164

law-sphere, 52, 79, 92
- boundary (terminal), 74
- natural, 112
- normative, 74, 106
- coherence of, 51, 79-82, 98, 156, 166
- nucleus of, 80, 108f, 112, 165
- order of time in, 90
- and the special sciences, 1f
  See also function

law-spheres
- number, 74
- physical, 82
- psychic, 74
- analytic (logical), 80, 92n 108
- historical, 108-10, 163f
- social, 117, 121, 140f
- jural (juridical), 5, 27, 107, 111-14, 118 165-68
  See also functions

legal
- freedom, 177
- order, 6, 14, 58, 68, 130, 158, 166, 177
- protection, 144f, 160
- security, 32, 35; in Smend, 66

legal philosophy, 167; *see also* law, theories of

legal science, vii, ix, 1, 2, 3, 5, 7, 40, 118, 127, 130, 171, 178
  acc. to Gierke, 31, 102; Freyer, 173; Walz, 145

legists, 147

Leviathan, 110, 129, 157

liberal(ism), 32n, 49, 63, 177

logicism, logicist(ic), 19, 31, 34, 36, 37, 127, 130, 143, 165
- in Kelsen, 25-27, 33, 123, 132f, 134n; Laband, 4; Von Wiese, 173
- Gierke on, 6

Low Countries, 147; *see also* jurisprudence, in the Netherlands

Lutheran, conception of man, 176

M

majority (political), 25, 60, 132, 133

man
- his place in the cosmos, 111
- Lutheran conception of, 176

Manchester School, 156

Marburg School, 6, 26, 87, 127; *see also* Neokantianism

Marxism, 63, 136
- in Marck, 39
- Leibholz on, 138n

mathesis universalis, 174

meaning (purpose), v-vii, 2-8, 20, 26, 29, 37f, 52, 68, 69, 73, 76-82, 85, 87-93, 99, 102, 104
- of constitutional law, 8
- of individuality, 20
- of law, 1, 2, 3, 5, 6, 37, 38, 68
- of legal norms, 26
- of the state, 3

meaning (sense)
- in Litt, 41-46; Smend, 51, 54, 61

medieval
- aesthetics, 114

- culture, 144
- doctrine of society, Gierke on, 100
- ethics, 114
- law, 145f; Van Idsinga on, 175
- nominalism, 20, 21
- scholasticism, 78n
- states, 141, 146; acc. to Below, 146; Preuss, 105; Smend, 66

Middle Ages, *see* medieval
monads, monadology, 21, 101, 172
monarchy, 21, 147
- acc. to Heller, 63n; Smend, 62; Van Idsinga, 175f
  See also crown; royal

monopoly (commercial), 158
- by the state, 128, 154

myth, 59-62, 70

N

naive
- experience, 2, 18, 20, 29, 72-76, 87-89, 92-94, 96-99
- realism, 29, 72-75, 88, 98n, 108f, 165; Rickert on, 73; Windelband on, 72n

nation(al), 5, 21, 125, 126, 132, 140-42, 147, 156, 159
- acc. to Droysen, 123; Jellinek, 10, 12, 125; Kelsen, 48, 126; Kjellén, 123; Oppenheimer, 120; Schmitt, 68; Smend, 48, 55, 59-63; Van Idsinga, 176
- and corporatism, 138

National Assembly (revolutionary France), 35n
National Economic Council (Weimar Republic), 138f, 139n, 158
natural communities, 117, 140-42
natural law, 6, 9, 21, 22, 25, 30, 32, 34f, 53, 70, 106n, 113, 127, 129, 147
- acc. to Gierke, 100; Kelsen, 33; Meinecke, 68; Schmitt, 36

- in Smend, 60

natural laws (laws of nature), 8, 9, 19, 119, 124
naturalism, naturalistic, 4, 7, 13, 19, 22, 28, 33, 36, 38, 39, 96, 97, 111, 124, 163
- in Cohen, 127; Hobbes, 129; Kelsen, 64n, 97, 118, 132; Kjellén, 122f
- Gierke on, 100; Smend on, 39, 50

natural science, 14, 17, 54, 97, 98
- acc. to Gierke, 100; Litt, 40; Oppenheimer, 119
- in Comte, 8, 119; Kelsen, 28

natural-scientific
- method, 127
- positivism, 27
- research, Ratzel on, 62
- sociology, 8f, 19

natural-scientific thought, 14, 27, 40-45, 86, 88, 90, 92, 96, 129
- in Kant, 27, 42, 85; Litt, 40-45

nature, 2, 15, 53, 74, 78n, 93, 97, 98, 106, 124, 165
- acc. to Descartes, 14, 15; Gierke, 100; Litt, 40-45; Rickert, 80
- in Kant, 17-19, 33, 65, 85; Litt on, 42
- in Hobbes, 15, 70; Simmel, 171; Spengler, 164

Neokantian(ism), 19, 28, 31, 41, 56n, 73, 109, 127
- dogmatism in, 86f, 173
  See also Baden School; Marburg School

neutral, neutrality, 64n, 72n, 77, 78, 161f
Nicomachean Ethics, 166
nominalism, vi, 20f
Norman states, 147
normative
- aspects, functions, law-spheres, 74, 97, 98, 106-13, 126; of the

state, Jellinek on, 11f; Schmitt on, 69
- principles, 112f, 124
- sciences, 53, 87, 98, 121
Norm-logical school, 6, 19, 26-31, 37-39, 48, 61, 70, 119
norms, 19, 32, 107, 112-15, 121, 124, 148, 169
- logical, 113
- historical, 64n
- social, 121, 140-42
- economic, 155
- aesthetic, 163
- jural (juridical), 6, 9, 51, 53, 61, 113, 134, 143f, 170
   See also function; law-sphere
norms
- legal, 121, 123
- parliamentary, 133f
- in the family, 107
- in Neokantians, 19
- in Soviet law, 38n
- acc. to Heller, 69; Jellinek, 10; Kelsen, 26f; Krabbe, 25; Litt, 42; Schmitt, 56, 58, 69; Smend, 51, 53
- and natural laws, 8, 19
noumenon, noumenal, 13f, 73, 77
- in Kant, 17-21; Litt, 52; Plato, 14

O

object-functions, 93-96
ontology, ontological, 28, 77, 102n
opposition(al) thinking, 15, 72, 75, 76, 86n, 88, 89, 98
- in Litt, 40-45
   See also *Gegenstand*
organic
- coherence, v, vi, 13, 71-76, 84, 177
- function, 93; *see also* function, biotic
- metaphysics, 7

- representation, 135; *see also* fascism
- theories (views), 49, 61, 99, 100, 102n, 103, 104f, 105n, 122, 124, 125, 137, 145
organological, *see* organic
organized community, 2, 4, 10, 11, 31, 52, 57, 68, 88, 96-99, 105-61, 176, 177f
- acc. to Althusius, 129; Burckhardt, 116, t5169; Duguit, 24; Gierke, 99-104, 146; Jehring, 119, 121; Jellinek, 11; Kelsen, 130; Kjellén, 122; Litt, 97; Marck, 116n; Preuss, 104f; Schmitt, 58, 68
- free, voluntary, 116
- natural, 58, 105n, 143, 159
- law of, 4, 22, 151, 153, 157
- and coordinational relationships, 117f; in Van Idsinga, 176f
- and source of law, 161n
   See also state
organized community: non-state, non-political, 4, 5, 27, 57, 105n, 107, 108, 114-18, 123, 128-61
- in Cohen, 127; Darmstaedter, 178; Gierke, 99- 104; Kelsen, 26; Preuss, 104; Smend, 57; Waldecker, 5n

P

pagan(ism), 14, 20, 77, 78, 162
parliamentary system, 31, 36, 132-38
- Smend on, 59-61; Darmstaedter on, 178
parties (political), 132f, 139
- Glum on, 139n; Leibholz on, 137, 138n
pater familias, 144
patrimonial state, 146f
penal law, 151; *see also* criminal law
personality, 96, 97, 176; Gierke on, 100

- legal, of the state, 22, 125; acc. to Jellinek, 125; Preuss, 105
personality, ideal of, 2, 13, 14, 15, 16, 30-36, 38, 45, 52f, 58, 62, 64, 65, 68, 70, 71, 78, 87, 97, 99, 102, 120, 130
- in Duguit, 24n; Heidegger, 85n; Kant, 17-21, 27, 53; Kelsen, 16, 24n, 26, 28, 33f, 36, 37, 53
phenomenology, 19, 80, 85n, 89, 90, 98, 124
- dialectical, 38-48, 51-54, 57, 64, 65, 69n, 87, 96, 97, 101, 102, 120, 137, 173
philosophy, philosophic thought, 2, 75, 77f, 79, 89
- ancient, 14, 20, 77, 78n
- medieval, 20, 78
  modern, 90
- humanist, *passim* ; see also immanence
- social, 119n, 120
- of culture, 40
- of law, 1, 21, 167
- of politics, 8; see also political theory
philosophy of life, 21, 40, 58, 59, 62, 70, 71, 172
pistis, pistic(al), 115, 154, 156; see also faith
pistology, 173
Platonism, Platonic, 21, 75, 77, 127
plebiscites, 59, 61
pluralism (political), 104, 135-37, 179n
- socio-economic, 139n
- and syndicalism, 135-38
police state, 30
political geography, 124
political theology, of Schmitt, 58, 62
political theory, ix, 1-19, 118-61, *et passim*
- *geisteswissenschaftliche*, 38-70
- naturalistic, 28

- social, 9-13
- and constitutional law, *passim* See also integration theory; organic
popular sovereignty, 30, 31, 129, 130, 132
positive law, 22, 128, 130, 147, 154, 158, 160, 161
- in Bodin, 128; Heller, 66n, 69; Hobbes, 70; Kelsen, 26, 33; Laband, 4n, 5, 35; Leibholz, 69n; Smend, 66
- in positivism, 161
- non-binding, 152n, 154, 156
- and source of law, 161n
positivism, positivistic, 3-5, 8, 27, 31, 34, 70, 113, 130, 160, 161
- criticistic, 22, 130
- formalistic, 3, 37, 134
- logicistic, 32, 33, 36, 37, 133
- and constitutional theory, 22; legal theory, 118; political theory, 177; sociology, 13, 107, 120
positivize, positivization, 112-15, 133, 142, 143, 160, 161
power, 36, 37, 38, 68, 110, 114, 178
- constitutive, 129n
- economic, 154, 156
- ethical, Van Idsinga on, 176
- governmental, see power, of the state
- historical, 110, 115, 116, 125, 132, 134, 135, 142, 156, 164
- royal, 147n
- spiritual, 64, 110, 114
power, of the state, 6, 33, 35, 58, 69, 113, 125, 132, 143, 148, 158, 178, 179
- acc. to Burckhardt, 169; Droysen, 123; Duguit, 23f; Gierke, 103f; Hobbes, 110; Jellinek, 11, 12; Kjellén, 123; Krabbe, 25; Laband, 4; Loeff, 148; Preuss, 103-05; Schmitt, 68f; Smend,

48f, 56-66, 111, 144; Van Praag, 160; Wagner, 56
- abuse of, 150
- of the sword, 110
  See also coercion; force
Powers (nation-states), 121, 122n, 125
power-state, 5n, 32, 36, 57, 58, 68, 104, 105, 108, 122, 129, 138n, 143, 144, 177; see also *raison d'état*
prehistory, 164
pre-theoretic(al) experience, 18, 19, 72-76; see also naive experience
principle
- majority, 25, 60
- monarchical, 63n
- parliamentary, 133, 134
- of autonomy, 27, 33; causality, 90, 119; co-determination, 131; continuity, 107; contract, 22, 127, 160; equality, 121, 156n, 167; equivalence, 119; identity, 134n, 138n; individuation, 20, 92; infinity, 21; non-contradiction, 109; sufficient reason, 90
  See also sphere-sovereignty
principles, 6, 106n, 134, 161
- in Heller, 69; Kant, 75n; Leibholz, 138; Litt, 42; Van Idsinga, 175
- normative, 112-14
- public-legal, 112, 124, 146, 148f, 150, 160
- and functional laws, 112f
principles, structural, 95, 131, 134n
- of the family, 106, 107, 131, 140
- of organized communities, 106, 107, 116, 148, 154
- of the state, 114, 116, 121-27, 132-39, 152
psychic(al) function, 14, 72, 73, 88, 90, 91, 93, 94, 97, 100, 108, 112, 126, 140, 172
- in Bergson, 71f; Gierke, 100f; Hume, 16f; Jellinek, 10-12; Kant, 17f, 75, 76, 83-86, 91;

Litt, 41- 44-48; Smend, 48, 51; Waldecker, 29
- in phenomenology, 80n
- of the state, 125-27
  See also functions; sensory (sensitive) function
psychologistic
- conception of history, 163
- empiricism, 17
- epistemology, 11n, 16
- theory of law, 25, 151
psychology, 173
- association, in Hume, 16
- humanist, of Dilthey, 39
- mass, Jellinek on, 12
- naturalistic, Smend on, 50
public firms, 155

Q

quantum theory, 95n

R

raison d'état, 68, 111, 147; see also power-state
rationalism, rationalistic, 6, 16, 17, 30f, 58, 62, 70, 72, 112, 127, 177
- in Hobbes, 131; Kant, 17, 21, 30f; Kelsen, 6, 26, 87; Rousseau, 30
- in liberalism, 63n
- acc. to Smend, 49
- and individuality, 19-21
- and laws, 35
- and law-side of reality, 20f, 112
- and natural law, 6, 22, 25, 113
  See also reason
reason, 14, 17, 77, 78
- absolutization of, 14; faith in, 31, 36, 62; sovereignty of, 13-15
- objective, 169
- truths of, 30, 31
- acc. to Kant, 30, 75n; Leibniz, 74; Puchta, 99
- acc. to the Renaissance, 13

– and natural law, 30, 36
recall, right of, 138
refraction, 78, 79, 80, 81, 88, 94, 98
Reich, Wittmayer on, 53
reify, reification, 4, 14, 16, 17, 21, 27, 45, 46, 48, 49, 58, 65, 71, 72, 75, 77, 80n, 82, 89, 98, 102, 111, 125
relativism, relativistic, 31, 34, 36, 113, 131
relativity, theory of, 86, 90
Renaissance, 13, 20
representative government, 3, 59n, 134-39
retribution
  – Aristotle on, 166f; Polak on, 167
  – meaning of, 165
  – nucleus (kernel) of the jural law-sphere, 80, 112, 165-68
retrocipations, retrocipatory, 80, 81n, 109, 126n
revolutionary, 130, 131, 139n, 178
rights, 148, 149, 154, 156n
  – crown, 35n, 145, 147
  – individual, 32, 34, 146
  – objective, 38
  – parental, 159
  – property, 148
  – public, 170
  – subjective, 22, 23, 32
  – in Burckhardt, 170; Comte, 22; Duguit, 23f; Gierke, 65; Hobbes, 34; Schmitt, 58; Van Idsinga, 175; Walz, 145
  – and the Soviet state, 37f
    See also fundamental
Roman law, 6, 21, 23n, 104, 144-47
  – Preuss on, 104; Puchta on, 99
  – reception of, 147
Roman state, empire, imperialism, 23, 105, 144-48
Romanticism, romantic, 111n
  – in Fichte, 145; Gierke, 102f, 146; Rousseau, 129n; Schelling, 99, 102f

root, religious
  – of the created cosmos, 20, 77, 91, 151
  – of the human race, 77, 80, 88, 92, 98, 115
  – of the personality, the selfhood, 79-91, 96, 97
royal
  – court, 146
  – power, 147n
    See also crown; monarchy
rule of law, 32n; *see also* constitutional state; just state

S

sacraments, 114
scholasticism, scholastic, 174
  – medieval, 78n, 92n
  – of modern humanism, 174
science ideal, 13-34, 53, 68, 70, 71, 85, 87, 107, 110, 119, 120, 127, 132
secularization, 129n
self-consciousness, 72n, 78n, 79, 82-91, 97, 111, 127, 166
selfhood, 72n, 79, 83, 85n, 88, 97, 101
  – the individual I, I-ness, 97n, 117; in Gierke, 101; Hume, 16; Husserl, 52n; Litt, 40-47, 97, 101; Smend, 50
  – Kroner on, 83n; Marck on, 102n
    See also individual
sense (sensory) impression, perception, 74, 80, 86, 91, 94, 98n, 100
  – in Bergson, 72, 90; Heller, 66n; Hume, 16; Kant, 18, 21, 75, 83, 84; Litt, 44, 46; Plato, 14; Rickert, 73; Simmel, 171
sensory (sensitive) function, aspect, side, 74, 80, 85, 86, 90n, 92, 103, 126n, 140, 168
  – in Descartes, 14; Kant, 86
    See also law-sphere, psychic
Sherman Anti-Trust Act, 158

The Crisis in Humanist Political Theory

social
- interaction, intercourse, 3n, 29, 46, 91, 94, 107- 109, 116, 121, 140-42, 168
- interwovenness, 46f, 51n, 97
- legislation, 32, 154, 156
- phenomena, 10, 145, 171
- philosophy, 119n, 120
- sciences, 40, 119, 120n, 174
    See also functions; law-spheres
social (societal) relationship, 136, 142, 173
- the state as, 11, 33, 48, 49, 52, 100, 102
socialism, socialist, 136, 154n
sociation, 91, 117, 121, 140f
- in Simmel, 172
society, 98, 101, 112, 117, 148, 154, *et passim*
- acc. to Cohen, 127; Darmstaedter, 177f; Engels, 136; Gierke, 100, 102, 104; Hobson, 136; Jellinek, 11; Kjellén, 123; Oppenheimer, 119; Simmel, 171; Spann, 137; Van Idsinga, 175f
- and sociology, 8, 45, 121
sociology, vii, 2, 8, 97, 107, 121
- in Freyer, 173; Kelsen, 49f, 82; Litt, 40-48, 87, 120; Oppenheimer, 119f; Simmel, 49, 171f; Von Wiese, 145; Weber, 9
- formalistic, 46, 120, 145, 171, 172
- historicist, 67f
- humanist (*geisteswissenschaftlich*), 15, 40-45, 49, 97, 158
- morphological, 145
- naturalistic, 7, 22
- natural-scientific, 8, 9, 19
- phenomenological, 39, 46, 48, 53, 97
- positivistic, 13, 107
- universalist, 8, 47, 54, 119f

- and law, 10
- and political theory, 119ff
- and state, 50
sovereign, sovereignty
- absolute, 14, 15, 17, 79, 129, 130, 159
- divine, 13, 77, 78, 79, 137
- popular, 30, 31, 129, 130, 132, 135
- royal, 35, 147
- in Althusius, 129; Bodin, 5, 22, 57, 128, 129, 147; Duguit, 22f; Heller, 63; Hobbes, 129, 157; Kelsen, 26, 130; Krabbe, 25; Laband, 5; Preuss, 104; Rousseau, 129; Schmitt, 58, 68; Smend, 60, 63
- of law, 25, 31, 130
- of reason, 13, 14, 15, 72
- of the state, 5, 35, 57, 68, 114, 128, 130, 135, 158
    See also law-spheres; sphere-sovereignty
Soviet: law, state, 37f, 139
Sparta, 147n
sphere-sovereignty, 1f, 5, 57, 79-84, 89, 93-95, 108f, 112, 128, 130, 137, 152-58, 168, 177
sphere-universality, 82, 88, 89, 166
Staatsräson, idea of, 68; *see also* power-state; *raison d'état*
state, *passim*
- aims, goals, purposes of, acc. to Darmstaedter, 177; Gierke, 65; Hegel, 33; Smend, 48, 56, 61
- authority of, 4, 31, 133, 159, 178f; acc. to Krabbe, 25
- competence of, 5, 33, 178
- historical foundation of, 108ff
- power of, 56, 103
- structure of, 64, *et passim*
state
- as a cosmic meaning-structure, 51, 64

- as a legal personality, 22, 125
- as an organized community, 54, *et passim*
- as a system of legal functions, 25; *see also* law, and the state
- as a thought-form (-category, -construction), 1, 2, 6, 11, 13, 14, 15, 19, 26, 28, 29, 30, 171f, 174
    See also constitutional law; political theory

state, sides of
- numerical, 127
- spatial, 123-25
- psychic, 125-27
- social, 7, 19, 121-34,
- economic, 128
- jural (juridical), 8, 10, 19, 61, 63, 104, 111n, 126
    See also functions; law-spheres

state, theory (view) of
- anti-revolutionary, 111n
- organic, 99-104, 122-25
- structural, 118ff; *see also* constitutional law; political theory
- two-sides, 9-13, 19, 25, 104
- and economic enterprise, *see* economics, and the state
- and law, *see* law, and the state

Stoicism, 23n, 77
- Calvin on, 78n

subject-functions, *see* functions, subject-

subject-object relation, vi, 93n, 125
- in Litt, 40

subject-side
- of cosmic reality, 13, 19, 63, 64, 65, 79, 97, 164
- of law, 22, 65
- of a law-sphere, 26, 94, 95, 109, 110, 112, 125
    See also law-spheres, subject-side of; law-side and subject-side

substance, 6, 12, 14-18, 43, 49, 54, 82, 86, 98, 103, 118, 122, 129

Supreme Court
- of the Netherlands, 149, 153
- of the United States, 179

symbiotic, 29, 129, 137

symbolic
- forms, in Litt, 44, 46; Smend, 62
- signification, 74, 80, 90, 168

syndicalism, syndicalist, 22, 23, 104, 135-38

syn-static, 108

syn-systatic, 88

synthesis, 8, 15, 39, 68, 75-89, 93, 104, 109, 111, 114, 119, 167, 168, 171
- in Comte, 8; Hume, 16; Jellinek, 11; Kant, 18, 83-86; Kelsen, 19, 28; Smend, 54, 59f; Waldecker, 29

synthetic thought, 11, 13, 15, 16, 28, 29, 38, 51, 64, 71-89, 91, 93, 98, 108, 109, 111, 119, 167, 171, 172

systasis, systatic, 11, 29, 51, 74-77, 88-93, 98, 112, t5125, 166; *see also* en-static

T

talio, 166

task
- cultural, 106, 108, 110, 113
- of the church, 115
- of academic disciplines, Smend on, 49
- of philosophy, 5, 75, 130; Kant on, 75n
- of public firms, acc. to Zhelezhnov, 155
- of the state, government, 124, 126, 159; acc. to Darmstaedter, 177; Gierke, 103f; Smend, 55, 62, 64n, 76n; Van Idsinga, 176; liberalism, 177

teleology, teleological

- structure of coordinational relationships, 159
- view of the state, 116n; acc. to Darmstaedter, 177; Jellinek, 11, 55n ; Smend, 48f, 60; in Althusius, 29, 129

territory, territorial: of the state, 5, 110, 114, 123, 128
- in Bluntschli, 7; Duguit, 23; Fricker, 125; Jellinek, 12, 125; Kelsen, 26, 123f, 126; Kjellén, 123; Laski, 136n; Preuss, 104f ; Smend, 48, 57, 62f; Waldecker, 29f

theoretical thought, 43, 72, 86n
- neutrality postulate of, 78
- and pre-theoretical (naive) experience, 19, 72, 73, 75f, 165

thing(s), entities, vii, 21, *et passim*
- naive concept of, 18, 20, 74, 88, 98n, 105, 118, 122
- naive experience of, 20, 29, 75, 87, 92
- normative properties of, 74, 112
- structure of, 2, 73-75, 88, 92ff, 114, 152
- as substances, in themselves, 14, 16, 18, 94, 151

thought
- -category, 1, 11, 19, 26
- -construction, creation, 2, 94
- -form, 13, 29, 79, 82; in Kant, 83, 85; Kelsen, 174; Simmel, 171f

time, 81, 90f, 97, 152, 178
- in Bergson, 71, 91; Heidegger, 85; Kant, 18, 84, 86, 91; Kelsen, 124; Litt, 41, 43-45; Rickert, 73; Smend, 50-52
- in phenomenology, 51, 90; physics, 95n
- absolute, 91
- Archimedean point within, 13, 64, 71, 77-79
- beyond, notion of, 2, 13f, 152

- cosmic order of, 1, 13, 14, 45, 64, 71, 73f, 79- 94, 97, 98, 106n, 107, 112, 165
- historical, 90, 109, 163f
- problem of, vi, 14, 84, 89, 165
- in the law-spheres, 90f, 107, 163f
- as a prism, 79; *see also* refractions
- and the special sciences, 90

tort, 148, 150f
- Kelsen on, 151n
- Strooppotarrest, 149n

trade unions, 136, 142, 156

transcendence
- of cosmic reality, 20
- of humanity, 120
- of man, 72, 79, 91, 96, 98, 117
- of time, 14, 83, 96

transcendent
- norms, Heller on, 69
- *noumenon*, 13, 18

transcendental
- categories, 42
- concept formation, 174
- conditions, 75f, 82
- consciousness, 172
- critique, 86n, 87
- form of intuition, 86
- idealism, 18, 73
- imagination, 84f
- logic, 6, 18, 83, 86n
- objectivity, 17, 18
- schema, 84
- self-consciousness, 83, 85n, 88
- synthesis, 75, 85
- unity of apperception, 18, 171

transpersonal(ism), 46f, 58, 97, 130, 161

trias politica, 35, 66

tribe, tribal, 103, 141-43

trusts (cartels), 132, 142, 156, 158f

two-sides theory, of the state, 9-13, 19, 25, 104

tyranny, tyrannical, 26, 136

U

ultra vires, 175
unfolding, 94, 115
- of aesthetic material, 126
- of anticipatory moments, 88, 115, 126n
- of civilization, 148
- of culture, cultural things, 96, 148
- of international interaction, 141
- of law, Gierke on, 6
- of political integration, Smend on, 57
- of state power, Smend on, 66, 68
  See also deepening

universalia, vi, 20
universalism, universalistic, 20, 49, 97, 102, 130, 136, 161
- sociology, 13, 40, 47, 54, 119, 120n

universality, vi, vii, 35, 51, 79n, 82, 89
- in Kelsen, 36; Laband, 35; Litt, 43-47
  See also sphere-universality

utility, vs. right, 149, 150n

V

values
- balancing of, 80, 166
- in judgments, 120
- law-conformity of, 57, 59, 63, 66, 97, 109
- in Neokantianism, 41f, 56-69, 80, 109, 111, 120

view of reality, ix, 50, 51f
- historicist, 64, 65, 111
- idealist, 103
- naturalistic, 4, 28, 38, 64n, 96, 100
- of Kant, 17, 18; Kelsen, 26, 64n; Laband, 4; Litt, 39-48; Smend, 48-68
- of humanism, 2, 13, 14, 19, 28, 38, 57, 64, 71, 98
- of immanence philosophy, 72
- of naive experience, 73
  See also cosmology

view of society, 45, 119
Volksgeist, 99
voluntary (free) associations, 115-17

W

Weimar Republic, constitution of, 34, 56, 138, 156n
welfare state, 32, 177; *see also* social legislation
world citizenship, 120, 140
worldview
- connection to scholarship, 130, 162, *et passim*
- Christian, 77, 130
- historicist, 136
- humanist, 2, 13, 30, 33, 38, 53, 71, 76, 120
- positivist, 120
- relativist, 131
- of Kant, 27; Oppenheimer, 120

Z

zin, v, vi note, 1, 2, 3, 4n, 12, 29n; *see also* meaning (purpose)